Maimonides and the Hermeneutics of Concealment

SUNY series in Jewish Philosophy
Kenneth Seeskin, editor

Maimonides and the Hermeneutics of Concealment

Deciphering Scripture and Midrash in
the *Guide of the Perplexed*

James Arthur Diamond

State University of New York Press

Published by
State University of New York Press

© 2002 State University of New York

For information address the State University of New York Press,
90 State Street, Suite 700, Albany, New York 12207

Marketing Michael Campochiaro
Production by Diane Ganeles

Library of Congress Cataloging-in-Publication Data

Diamond, James Arthur.
    Maimonides and the hermeneutics of concealment : deciphering scripture and midrash
in The guide of the perplexed / James Arthur Diamond.
        p. cm. — (SUNY series in Jewish philosophy)
    Includes bibliographical references and index.
    ISBN 0-7914-5247-6 (alk. paper) — ISBN 0-7914-5248-4 (pbk. : alk. paper)
    1. Maimonides, Moses, 1135–1204. Dalālat al-ha'irin. 2. Maimonides, Moses,
1135–1204—Contributions in biblical hermeneutics. 3. Bible. O.T.—Hermeneutics. 4.
Maimonides, Moses, 1135–1204—Contributions in interpretation of midrash. 5.
Midrash—History and criticism. I. Title. II. Series.

BM545.D35 D53 2002
181'.06—dc 21

                                                                    2001042638

10 9 8 7 6 5 4 3 2 1

To my parents,
Morris and Rose Diamond

Now this fortunate unity of speech and thought belongs in the highest measure to the medieval Jew, and indeed in a dearly bought exclusivity. Not only does he find an established form for his highest thoughts, but also every thought that generally wants to legitimate itself as thought seeks this form. Here the quotation is by no means an adorning pendant, but rather it is the label for the envelope of his speech.

—Franz Rosenzweig

Contents

Acknowledgments

The origins of this book lie in the years of weekly trialogue stimulated by a close reading of the *Guide* between myself, Ken Green, and R. Zev Friedman. I am also grateful for the guidance and encouragement of Michael Marmura and David Novak through the completion of this project. The attentive readings of Ken Seeskin, Ken Green, and Josef Stern and their accompanying insights and suggestions have all contributed immeasurably to a more refined final product. This book also draws on the years of spirited discussions and disciplined reading of the Rambam's writings with my *chavruta,* Albert Dov Friedberg. Thanks also to Elliot Wolfson, whose model of dedicated scholarship was no small factor in my choice to enter the world of the academy.

Finally, it is to my family that I owe my deepest gratitude. I have dedicated this book to my parents, Morris and Rose, who rebuilt their lives without succumbing to a despair warranted by the experience of the devastation that was the fate of European Jewry. This accomplishment offers them a bit of *naches* in return for their selfless devotion to the task of raising a family in a tradition that values ethics and learning beyond all else. The love and friendship of my brothers, Irwin and David, have never wavered throughout my life and were especially indispensable for the duration of this enterprise. My children, Shimon, Yonah, and Nina, have taught me to appreciate why children were chosen at Sinai over patriarchs and prophets as the most suitable guarantors of Torah. The abiding support, constant encouragement, and deft intelligence of my wife, Florence, were all instrumental in contributing to the final realization of this book. My *Torah* is hers.

I gratefully acknowledge the *AJS Review* for permission to incorporate my article "Maimonides' Use of Midrash in the *Guide of the Perplexed:* Decoding the Duality of the Text," *AJS Review* 21, no. 1 (1996): 39–60. I wish to also acknowledge with gratitude the *Journal of Jewish Thought and Philosophy* for their permission to reprint my articles "Trial as an Esoteric Preface in Maimonides' *Guide of the Perplexed:* A Case Study in the

Interplay of Text and Prooftext," in vol. 7, no. 1 (1997): 1–30 and "Jacob vs. The Married Harlot: Intertextual Foils in Maimonides' *Guide of the Perplexed,*" vol. 10, no. 1 (2000): 1–25. Thanks are also due to Judi Singleton, Dora Psiachos, Linda Daniel, and Susan King for their technical assistance in preparing my manuscript for publication.

The epigraph to the work is taken from a translation of Franz Rosenzweig that appears in Barbara Galli, *Franz Rosenzweig and Jehuda Halevi: Translating, Translations, and Translators* (Montreal: McGill-Queen's University Press, 1995), p. 178.

The Poetry of Midrash and Heterogeneity of Scripture

In the introduction to his philosophical magnum opus, the *Guide of the Perplexed*, Maimonides provides us with a rationale for the composition of this work as well as instructions for the targeted reader on how to decipher its elusive and enigmatic style. Devices such as contradiction, diffuse and seemingly discordant treatment of subject matter, and deliberate ruses, he says, will be employed to accommodate both halakhic legal constraints on the overt teaching of physics and metaphysics and the wide intellectual disparity of his potential readership. The sensitive nature of the topics to be explored demands an unorthodox pedagogy that both illuminates and conceals, allowing entrance to the qualified few while excluding those who cannot cope with the intellectual rigors involved. Rabbinic stricture prohibits revealing anything more of the Account of the Chariot (metaphysics) than chapter headings, and therefore Maimonides cautions, "[M]y purpose is that the truths be glimpsed and then again be concealed so as not to oppose that divine purpose which has concealed from the vulgar among the people those truths requisite for His apprehension."[1]

Maimonides' treatise is addressed to readers who find themselves in an existential quandary whose only resolution appears to be an either/or choice between religion and intellect. Those who have achieved philosophical sophistication "must have felt distressed by the externals of the Law," plunging them into a "state of perplexity and confusion as to whether [one] should follow his intellect, renounce what he knew concerning the terms in question and consequently consider that he has renounced the foundations of the Law or he should hold fast to his understanding of those terms and not let himself be drawn on together with his intellect . . . perceiving that he had brought loss to himself and harm to his religion" (*GP,* pp. 5–6). Maimonides' remedy, offered in the *Guide*, is to expose the heterogeneous

1

nature of Scripture, whose external layer is but a veil for deeper truths that, when discovered, will allow those who are faithful and philosophically inclined to remain true to both their intellect and religious tradition.

Maimonides relates that he had once tried to compose a commentary that would "explain all the difficult passages in the midrashim where the external sense manifestly contradicts the truth and departs from the intelligible" (*GP*, p. 9), but had aborted this undertaking because he had concluded that if "we should adhere to parables and to concealment of what ought to be concealed we would not be deviating from the primary purpose. We would, as it were, have replaced one individual by another of the same species."[2] Realizing that his endeavor would promote further confusion rather than the clarity he had hoped for, Maimonides abandoned the project, later to be replaced by the present treatise, the *Guide*. No less than the dignity and respect of the Jewish people was at stake for Maimonides, since a literal and naïve fundamentalism was no longer tenable in the face of the formidable challenges posed by medieval philosophy.[3] To maintain the divinely endorsed reputation of a "wise and understanding people" and yet preserve the dignity of the rabbinic hermeneutic of its foundational documents called for a radical new reception of that revered legacy. The gap between rabbinic authorship and contemporary readership had widened to the degree that the two could no longer meet in the pages of the literal text. The divorce granted much later in time by his seventeenth-century philosophical archnemesis, Spinoza, to philosophy and theology,[4] whereby the meaning of the text would no longer be synonymous with its truth,[5] was not a viable option for Maimonides and his twelfth-century contemporaries. Nor did his piety and fealty to both religious tradition and reason allow him to renounce one in favor of the other. The marriage between reason and Judaism is consummated in the new contours drawn by Maimonides of the sacred texts.

Maimonides adopts a creative strategy with respect to the use of midrash and the manner in which he incorporates it into his work. The question as to how Maimonides could feel comfortable about treating revered and esteemed rabbinic utterances with so much interpretive latitude can be answered by reflecting on what type of literature he considered midrash to be. In response to those who hold that midrash captures the true meaning of biblical texts or is equal in status to traditional legal rulings, Maimonides declares that it has "the character of poetical conceits whose meaning is not obscure for someone endowed with understanding. At that time this method was generally known and used by everybody just as the poets use poetical expression" (*GP,* p. 573). Midrash is poetry, a genre that by definition stretches the bounds of conventional language to embrace the poet's inner thoughts and emotive yearnings. According to Maimonides, this art was at one time generally recognized for what it was, and he is simply reintroducing its authentic roots to his readers. The rabbis themselves set the stage for Maimonides' methodology with their "poetical conceits," which were never intended to be static authoritative texts that manifested the correct meaning of scriptural texts. Midrash, as "witty" poetry, possesses malleability not available with doctrinaire teachings in the realm of Jewish law *(halakhah)*. For this reason it is a suitable candidate for the kind of liberal and ambiguous usage Maimonides employs in the labyrinthine undertaking that constitutes the *Guide of the Perplexed.*[6] Northrop Frye's observations regarding the contemporary appreciation of poetic imagery may well apply to Maimonides' midrashic hermeneutic: "[A]ll commentary is allegorical interpretation, an attaching of ideas to poetic imagery. The instant that any critic permits himself to make a genuine comment about a poem . . . he has begun to allegorize."[7] Maimonides' use of midrash can be described as the allegorization of allegory.

This study shall confine itself to Maimonides' use of midrashic and scriptural prooftexts in the *Guide* and demonstrate that his expositions of many topics and issues in the *Guide* are implicitly rooted in complex, multilayered readings of midrash and Scripture. As mentioned, upon the failure of his earlier attempt at a straightforward commentary on midrash, Maimonides opted for an approach that would leave the simple understanding of the masses undisturbed, while accommodating the sensibilities of the philosophically inclined. It will be seen that midrash and Scripture are subtly woven into the text of the *Guide* by way of direct quotation and indirect reference so as to perform this deliberate balancing act.

In his list of the seven causes of contradiction that are common to all literary compositions (*GP,* pp. 17–20), Maimonides designates contradictions in haggadah and midrash as the sixth and seventh. The sixth results when an author fails to detect a contradiction between two basic propositions that, after many premises, may lead to "contradictory or contrary" conclusions. More relevant to our study, however, is the seventh, which is not due to confused and sloppy writing but rather is a consciously planned literary device of concealment designed to exclude unsophisticated readers and prevent them from discovering its use in the text:

The seventh cause. In speaking about very obscure matters it is necessary to conceal some parts and to disclose others. Sometimes in the case of certain dicta this necessity requires that the discussion proceed on the basis of a certain premise, whereas in another place necessity requires that the discussion proceed on the basis of another premise contradicting the first one. In such cases the vulgar must in no way be aware of the contradiction; the author accordingly uses some device to conceal it by all means.

Midrash is the only genre that is explicitly acknowledged as sharing the seventh cause with the *Guide*. The only other works that might contain contradictions of the same type are the books of the prophets, but this possibility is left as a "matter for speculative study and investigation" (*GP,* introduction, pp. 18–19). Since the Bible also deals with "very obscure matters," there is no reason to assume that the same demands of esotericism do not apply. Maimonides prefers to be evasive on this issue rather than publicly declare the divine author a master of deceit via the skillful art of contradiction. Much of the Bible is viewed by Maimonides as theology wrapped in a narrative garb from which it must be stripped so that its truth can emerge.[8] He therefore considers biblical and several midrashic sources to be esoteric texts whose meaning suggests itself to the few but remains obscure to most. Since he adopts the same ploy in his own work, it would be reasonable to assume that those midrashim similarly crafted are of a more sophisticated type and address only the most attentive of readers. In addition, as the declared subject matter of the *Guide* is *ma'aseh bereshit* and *ma'aseh merkavah*—domains that stretch the Jewish tradition's outermost limits of obscurity and mystery—midrashim quoted in the context of such discussions should themselves be intentionally obscure in the sense that they deal with or are related to the same sublime material.

Those parts of the *Guide* that utilize midrash and Scripture to further an argument or strengthen a proposition can only be understood when several layers of camouflage are stripped away so as to reveal the ultimate core of meaning. The combination of the core text, deliberately adopting a method of contradiction, with a rabbinic or biblical text, also harboring contradiction, compels members of the intellectual class to devise a reading that provides access to the book's true meaning. At the same time, this complex strategy impedes access to the book by the masses. Texts in general are difficult enough to decipher, since the absence of direct discourse between the reader and the author produces what Paul Ricoeur has called "a double eclipse of the reader and the writer."[9] That difficulty is compounded when an esoteric text incorporates other esoteric texts to maneuver its reception by a selective audience. Written in the form of a private communication between a master and his disciple, the *Guide* secures for itself that privacy long after it has entered the public domain. Once the apt disciple is drawn in, exacting demands are made of him to reengage those traditional texts he has grown up with and liberate them from a stifling literalism that is rampant among his coreligionists. One of the key devices of that engagement, which will be demonstrated by this study, is the calculated use of prooftext as a constant reminder that the *Guide*'s primary concern is with reading the prophets and reading the rabbis. In the realm of pure philosophical speculation existing reference works are more than adequate, and any novel contribution to that field is not to be preferred simply because Maimonides is the contributor (*GP*, II:2, preface, p. 253). Everything in the *Guide* must be traced to "elucidating some difficulty of the Law" or providing "a key to the understanding of something to be found in the books of prophecy, I mean to say of some of their parables and secrets" (*GP*, p. 264). Prooftexts serve to anchor the reader in the *Guide*'s true quest for biblical relevance.

Tutoring his prized pupil Joseph fostered a resolve on Maimonides' part to commit his teaching to writing, a project that was to remain in abeyance until Joseph ventured off on his own. The pain of separation from his beloved disciple and, in all probability, increased awareness of his own mortality rallied the desire to secure his unique methodology for posterity. Maimonides' determination to perpetuate his teachings and not allow future Josephs to be caught in a vice of perplexity is passionately expressed to Joseph: "Your absence moved me to compose this Treatise, which I have composed for you and for those like you, however few they are" (*GP*, epistle dedicatory, p. 4) His exceeding concern for his students, both existing and potential, combined with an all-consuming dedication to the dissemination of the truth at the cost of personal derision (*GP*, introduction, p. 16) roused Maimonides to set pen to paper. What "moved" Maimonides to bemoan the loss of personal contact and commence his project was, I believe, that final reminiscence of their sessions together where biblical and rabbinic excerpts "in which there was a pointer to some strange notion" were explicated. The *Guide* presents the opportunity for continuing education in this enterprise and indeed is its raison d'être. The prooftext is vital to ensuring the success of this venture. The anguish of separation and the inability to engage in oral discourse is alleviated by the act of writing, but it is a kind of writing that encourages a continuing discourse in the absence of the writer.

At every strategic turn the reader encounters a prooftext intended to revive those sessions where baffling biblical or rabbinic passages threatened to undermine the religious fabric of the student's life.

Justification for the anthropomorphic portrait of God drawn by the Torah is provided by the talmudic maxim that "Torah speaketh in the language of the sons of man" (*GP,* I:26). That maxim devised by the talmudic rabbis was intended to deal with exceptional occurrences in Scripture such as redundant language and had the effect of curtailing excessive exegesis of those passages. Maimonides, on the other hand, renders it constitutive of the entire Bible. What is originally a normative rule limiting halakhic invention is transformed by Maimonides into a license for philosophical creativity rehabilitating primitive prophetic language.[10] Such language is addressed to the human imagination catering to its own confusion as a first step toward metaphysical sophistication. Man *imagines* corporeality as a sine qua non of existence, and therefore the Torah adopts corporeal imagery to reinforce that idea. Man *imagines* certain human traits and characteristics as connoting perfection, and therefore the Torah predicates them of God to convey divine perfection (*GP,* I:26, pp. 51–57). Since this language is inadequate at best and indeed, if accepted at face value, is tantamount to idolatry,[11] it cannot remain intact. Intellectual maturity brings with it a steady and methodical obliteration of the text on the road to surrendering its vernacular for one that is entirely reconstituted.[12]

The call to his readers to replace the coarse language of the "sons of man" with a more refined and philosophically palatable one is made even before the text begins to take shape. The personal covering letter to his student, Joseph, is immediately followed by a quick succession of three biblical verses chosen to serve as independent quotations launching the book. Once the treatise in its entirety has been traversed, the student returns full circle to its originating moment and a personalized message crystallizes. Upon application of the Maimonidean lexicon and an appreciation for their biblical contexts, these verses combine in an epigraph that both invites and obstructs. The audience is clearly demarcated between those who are excluded and those who are included by means of the self-same aptitude that gains admittance to the divine realm—intellect.

The first verse, Psalm 143:8, "Cause me to know the way wherein I should walk, for unto Thee I have lifted up my soul," is a petitionary prayer for the success of his venture. Knowledge, in its truest form, leads to a contemplative life having little to do with directional movement. Hebrew terms for both "walking" and "way" appear in a key biblical verse whose directive is the emulation of God.[13] "And thou shalt go in His ways" (Deut. 28:9) is, according to Maimonidean metaphor, a mandate for "living a good life without in any way moving a body" (*GP,* I:24, p. 54). The only life that does not entail corporeal movement is that of the intellect, which man cultivates by virtue of the "form" he has been endowed with at creation. In nurturing this form man becomes godlike, since "in the exercise of this, no sense, no part of the body, none of the extremities are used; and therefore this apprehension was likened unto the apprehension of the deity which does not require an instrument . . ." (*GP,* I:1, p. 23). This is precisely the nature of the *imitatio dei* called for by Deuteronomy 28:9, which involves no anatomical reflexes.

The measure of the success in achieving *imitatio dei* is guaranteed by the second half of the verse, "for unto Thee have I lifted up my soul." The genuine soul *(nephesh)* for Maimonides connotes the "rational soul, I mean the form of man" (*GP,* I:1, p. 23). "Soul" is also an equivocal term that can denote more mundane aspects of man such as the "animal soul" that is shared by all living and mobile beings or the common life force of blood (*GP,* I:41, p. 91). "Walking in God's ways" requires a transcendence, a "lifting" (*GP,* I:41, p. 91), which denotes an elevation of degree and rank rather than in space. The pursuit of intellectual ideals "lifts" or elevates man's soul from its cruder sense of a bodily organism to the more noble human form that "remains of man after death" (*GP,* I:41). As the book's sole concern is with the sciences of physics and metaphysics, the author qualifies himself by way of Psalm 143:8 as adequately equipped to expound on topics that transport the human soul to that realm where the human and the divine intersect. The following verse in Psalms (143:9) is noteworthy, as it hinges on a term that literally translates as "concealment": "Save me from my enemies[,] O Lord[,] for to you I have looked for concealment." The device for preserving the integrity of one's soul is that of concealment, which provides a refuge from one's detractors and is instrumental throughout the *Guide* in tempering its radicalism. Already in the opening verses, the hermeneutic of concealment whose success depends on the prooftext is presaged and operative.

Once his expertise to expound on the most esoteric of topics has been established in the form of a prayer for divine assistance, Maimonides moves from his own prowess to that of his audience. Proverbs 8:4, "Unto you, O men *('ishim),* I call and my voice is to the sons of men *(benei 'adam),*" expresses a preference for one segment of the public over another. The main classical medieval commentators on the *Guide,* such as Efodi,

Abravanel, and Shem Tov,[14] are all in agreement as to the clear division drawn between two separate classes of humanity by the parallel halves of this verse. The first part of the verse is addressed to the more noble of the two, as the lowest intellect that governs the sublunar sphere is designated in the Mishneh Torah by the same technical term, *'ishim*.[15] Since this angel, commonly known as the Active Intellect in medieval philosophical circles, is the source of all knowledge in the human domain (as well as prophetic inspiration), *'ishim* can represent those who aspire to and are capable of receiving its emanative forces.[16] The term *benei 'adam* is clearly treated by Maimonides as denigrating the intellectually plebeian among men, or "the multitude, I mean the generality as distinguished from the elite" (*GP,* I:14, p. 40). The "sons of men" are also members of that community whose language is the graphic and anthropomorphic surface imagery of the biblical texts. The "Torah speaks in the language of the sons of man" so that a rapport can be established with the majority of men, who can never rise to the level of the elite *ishim*. The latter subscribe to the more sublime language that lies underneath the surface.

As the audience alternates, so does the mode of communication. In the case of *'ishim* it is a "call," whereas to the *benei 'adam* a "voice" *(qol)* is extended. There is another pedagogical moment depicted in the Bible and discussed at length in the *Guide* that also clearly distinguishes between two addressees being enlightened by the same source. While accepting the tradition that the entire nation of Israel was privy to the mass revelation at Sinai, the content of that revelation was not uniform to all its recipients. Though biblical terms used by Maimonides to capture the variant nature of this revelation are *qol* (sound, voice) and *qar'a* (call), they must be taken as metaphors for the sake of distinction and are in no way intended to express audible sound addressed to man by God. The collective revelatory medium is expressed by the term *qol,* which bears an auditory sense but not necessarily one of intelligibility. According to Maimonides, this is captured by those verses interposing Moses between the divine source of oration and the people: "Moses spoke and God answered him by a voice *(qol)*" (Exod. 19:19).[17] A divine cacophony required a decryption by Moses to render it intelligible for the people. Since it is the *qol* repeatedly mentioned as the sound heard and not "words," what is indicated is that Moses "was spoken to and that they heard the great voice but not the articulations of speech." Therefore "every time when their hearing words is mentioned it is their hearing the *voice (qol)* that is meant, Moses being the one who heard words and reported it to them."[18] The public *qol,* then, was one that lacked the clarity of the private communication heard by Moses, and necessitated his intercession for it to gain a communal semantic coherence. Moses himself is summoned to raise his mind to a higher level of consciousness and home in on a more sublime message by a "call" *(vayikr'a)* (Exod. 19:20).[19]

Proverbs 8:4 is an allusion to the variegated sounds of Sinai. The text will not be uniformly received by all its perspective readers, and its composition effects a discourse with a minority of them and a prevarication with the rest. The "voice" of Maimonides issues to the latter *(benei 'adam)*, pleading simply for caution when approaching their sacred texts. As the "voice" at Sinai substantiated the existence and unity of God to the general populace, so does the Maimonidean voice alert them to the metaphorical qualities of corporealisms in the Torah. These are also aimed at establishing the perfection of divine existence in their minds (*GP* I:27). The personalized "call," though, extends to the select disciple, who is expected to discover the significations that are submerged in the text.

The third verse, Proverbs 22:17, completes the dual-voiced welcome to the treatise extended by the previous verse; it enjoins, "Incline thine ear and hear the words of the wise, and apply thy heart unto my knowledge." Manifestly the two cola of the verse are parallel reiterations of the same instruction to attend to the teachings of scholars in whose company Maimonides would include himself. "My knowledge" would then be read as a specific case of "words of the wise." The parallelism can also be read as one between the two cola of this verse and those of the former verse, Proverbs 8:4, in a chiastic AB BA pattern. The instruction of the first half to pay heed to "the words of the wise" is directed to the *benei 'adam* of the latter half of Proverbs 8:4. Many of the theological positions expounded in the *Guide* on fundamental tenets of faith such as creation, prophecy, or providence are radical departures from those held by the rabbinic sages. Cognizant of the turmoil this may cause to the abiding faith of the masses, he encourages the harmonization of his teachings with the tradition that has preceded him. Those of his readers who qualify as confidants are adjured "not to comment upon a single word of it and not to explain to another anything in it save that which has been explained and commented upon in the words of the famous Sages of our Law who preceded me" (*GP*, introduction, p. 15). For those whose religious sensibility would be offended by change or innovation, the solution lies in hearing the "words of the wise *(chachamim)*," a term that commonly characterizes the rabbinic sages. The astute reader who is bound to discover novelty for which there is no precedent in the tradition is urged to suppress his discovery, for "whatever he understands from this Treatise of those things that have not been said by any of our famous Sages other than myself should not be explained to another" (*GP*, introduction, p. 15). What is publicly divulged is to be crafted so that, in the words of the biblical proverb, the *benei 'adam* only "hear the words of the wise."

In contradistinction, the *ishim* of Proverbs 8:4 are encouraged to implement their essential resources in the process of retrieving the author's unprecedented contributions from the text. They are challenged to apply their "heart," which, in this context, would most certainly signify its equivocal sense of "intellect" as assigned in *GP*, I:39. Devotion of this faculty leads to the singularity of the text ("my knowledge") as opposed to the mere parroting of traditional teachings ("words of the wise").[20] It is this knowledge which links up with that unique knowledge petitioned for in the first of the trilogy of verses ("cause me to *know* the way") that Maimonides wishes to impart. The targeted readers are those who are sufficiently possessed of intellect to withstand the religious turmoil this revolutionary "knowledge" may arouse.

This artful epigraphic combination of three biblical verses inaugurates the book with a paradigm of the prooftext hermeneutic that will be employed throughout the treatise. Appropriately, these verses lead into the very first sentence of the introduction, openly announcing the primary telos of the book: "The first purpose of this Treatise is to explain the meanings of certain terms occurring in books of prophecy." Recognition of the lack of univocity in prophetic God-talk is the motivating force behind his aim, and therefore prooftext citation imports that ambiguity extant in prophetic literature into the *Guide*. Paul Ricoeur's penetrating analysis of the enigmatic nature of metaphor in poetic contexts is instructive for an understanding of how Maimonides may have perceived biblical parables and what he hoped to achieve by incorporating excerpts into the *Guide*. Metaphor, taken literally in the codified lexical sense of the words of which it is constituted, creates a "semantic collision" that leads to a "logical absurdity where meaning would be annulled by incompatibility."[21] All anthropomorphic language regarding God fits this description, in that two wholly incompatible terms come together (such as "God sits" or "God stands"), producing what would normally be labeled a logical absurdity. Of course, for a medieval religious thinker such as Maimonides, the Bible could not possibly have been reduced to one pervasive logical absurdity whose language about God amounts to nothing more than gibberish. The task of the philosophically inclined exegete is to salvage some meaning in the text, a task that can only be accomplished by assigning its form to a genre of poetry ("language of the sons of man") rather than to science. Only then can the text maintain a rapport with the reader by transforming "an absurdity which destroys itself into *an absurdity* that *oversignifies.*"[22] On the face of it, the statement "God sits" joins a subject and predicate that resist each other semantically, for the subject is incorporeal and bears no trait that could account for the predicate. On the other hand, when read as metaphor, as we shall see in chapter 3, a whole panorama of signification discloses itself regarding such matters as stability, change, essence, modes, and relation. In short, the reader fashions a "surplus of meaning"[23] out of apparent semantic nonsense.

The focus in this book will be on how the programmatic use of prooftexts contributes to the volume of this surplus. Once the semantic parameters of a term have been broadened, prooftexts appear in the first instance to provoke fresh readings of their original biblical contexts. The Bible is thoroughly revamped for the mind that only sees absurdity. Secondly and just as importantly, the *Guide* itself undergoes a refashioning by the reader when the prooftext's germaneness to its context is questioned, when its originating context is retrieved and reinserted in the *Guide,* when its recurrence in the *Guide* or in other Maimonidean compositions is intertextualized, and when its rabbinic nuances are integrated. For the expression "God sits," the reader is obliged to attend numerous locales in the Scriptures as varied as Psalms, Lamentations, Malachi, and Isaiah and to rehabilitate them. He or she then must determine whether a series of disparate verses coalesce into some meaningful union. The resurfacing of a verse such as Lamentations 5:19 in chapters that may be critical to the issue of *creatio ex nihilo* (*GP,* I:9, II:26) might offer a clue as to how the lexical attribution of "changelessness" to the term "sits" alters one's conception of the relationship between the Creator and his creation. Finally, cryptic rabbinic statements culled from midrashic compilations such as *Genesis Rabbah* or *Pirke de Rabbi Eliezer* might supplement the esoteric puzzle that is being assembled. In this way, Maimonides' extreme apprehension about the dangers of public writing is somewhat allayed (*GP,* introduction, pp. 6–7), given that only very few will be capable of following the serpentine trail left by these prooftexts.

CHAPTER 1

Midrash on Midrash:
Self-Reflexive Discourse in the Guide

In this chapter I shall demonstrate Maimonides' artful use of midrash by analyzing three extracts from the *Guide*, each of which is constructed around a midrashic axis. All of these passages, when subjected to a detailed examination, will appear slightly skewed as a result of some incongruence arising from the manner in which the midrash is incorporated into the text. This unorthodox use of midrash is meant only for the philosophically trained eye, obliquely guiding it to reexamine the midrash both in its own context and in the context of the *Guide* as a whole. The outcome is an increasingly profound reading, deemed by Maimonides, for one reason or another, as detrimental to the simple piety of the masses. The thematic link between these passages is that each midrash is taken from *Midrash Rabbah* and forms the crux of a self-reflexive discourse about the nature and purpose of midrash itself.

Shir Hashirim Rabbah 1:8 and the Parabolic Method

Maimonides informs us at the start that the Jewish religion is practiced on various levels of the realm of intellect and thought in response to the equivocality of Scripture, "so that the multitude might comprehend them in accord with the capacity of their understanding and the weakness of their representation whereas the perfect man . . . will comprehend them otherwise" (*GP,* introduction, p. 9). The impossibility of an unequivocal narrative when discussing such obscure topics as the Account of the Beginning and the Account of the Chariot is illustrated by Solomon's maxim "That which was far off and exceeding deep; who can find it out?" (Eccles. 7:24).

13

Further on in the introduction, Maimonides quotes a midrash from *Shir Hashirim Rabbah* [1] that can be regarded as a direct response to the query in this verse, "who can find it out?" Solomon is portrayed as the inventor of the parabolic method, wherein the use of parables for the understanding of Scripture is likened to the joining of cords and ropes in order to draw up water from an exceedingly cold and deep well. Thus Solomon is credited with pioneering a method by which "the meaning of the words of the Torah would be understood." The image of drawing water (= knowledge) from a deep well soothes the Solomonic cry of despair in Ecclesiastes at the prospect of unfathomable depths. [2]

Maimonides elaborates on this idea by citing another midrash in *Shir Hashirim Rabbah* that compares understanding Torah by means of parable to using light provided by worthless material to find a valuable lost article in a dark house. Just as the material that provides the light is worthless, "so the parable in itself is worth nothing but by means of it you can understand the words of the Torah." At first glance both midrashim seem to convey the basic proposition that a true understanding of Torah can only be achieved upon the realization that its structure contains an external layer of parable whose aim is to conceal an internal essential truth. On closer scrutiny, a number of "divergences" [3] arise between the two that present us with the *Guide*'s first instance of midrashic duality. A parallel deconstruction of the two midrashic texts reveals a study in contrasts rather than harmony.

Well Parable	Pearl Parable
1. *Discovery* of meaning and attaining what was once unattainable (stringing cord together = Solomon's *mashal* methodology)	1. *Recovery* of what was once within grasp and lost (loss of pearl in house)
2. *Construction* of method to decipher biblical text	2. *Deconstruction* (lighting of material = dissipation of *mashal* to arrive at meaning)
3. Extolling virtue of *mashal*	3. Worthlessness of *mashal*
4. *Water* metaphor signifies message of biblical text	4. *Fire* eliminates outer layer, unveiling inner meaning of Scripture
5. Understanding conveyed by act of drinking	5. Lighting of lamp is act of comprehension

While the well parable vindicates the *mashal* as a vehicle ultimately leading to a comprehensive assimilation of meaning ("drinking water"), the pearl parable denigrates it as an aid that must be dispensed with in order to gain clarity. That clarity, signified by distinguishing a pearl at a distance from among household objects, would seem to indicate an apprehension inferior to the one symbolized by the actual ingesting of fluid.

The juxtaposition of these two midrashim reflects a variegated readership demarcated by different approaches to Scripture. The first midrash is directed at those who are philosophically adept enough to realize that a literal reading of Scripture can only lead to such absurdities as anthropomorphic images of the Deity, and therefore need a justification of the parable as a necessary instrument of truth. The nature of the subject matter— an ultimately unknowable Deity—mandates that Scripture take literary license of this kind in order to convey its meaning. On the other hand, the simple literalist belief of the masses values the prima facie above all else, and thus the anthropomorphic God is exactly the one prescribed by Scripture. For Maimonides, of course, this is tantamount to idolatry,[4] and widely held beliefs of this kind can only be dispelled by way of extreme corrective measures. The antidote is provided by the second midrash, with its radical call to discard the parable/literal altogether and regard the *mashal* as so much dross to be sifted out so that the true meaning can emerge. Although parables are a valuable medium of truth, as is made clear by the first midrash, they have, in fact, led the multitude into gross error, which the second midrash attempts to reverse with its derisive tone. Just as the golden mean, in the realm of ethics, can sometimes only be achieved by resorting to the habituation of an extreme trait,[5] so the acquisition of correct opinions, in the realm of thought, demands parallel remedial action.

Since the attitude can only aspire to a semblance of the truth, the imagery of lighting a fire out of the material that depicts the *mashal* represents an inferior form of knowledge obtained by the obliteration of the parable altogether. The unrefined reader gains insight, but only from a distance. This modicum of truth leaves them with certain indispensable notions of God (incorporeality, nonaffectability), described as "matters that ought to be inculcated, made clear and explained to everyone according to his capacity and ought to be inculcated in virtue of traditional authority upon children, women, stupid ones and those of defective natural disposition just as they adopt the notion that God is one, that He is eternal and that none but He should be worshipped" (*GP*, I:35, p. 81). Scripture's penchant for anthropomorphisms is the sole means of communicating God's existence to the multitude without revealing anything about His essence or the true reality of His substance. The understanding denoted by the act of drinking (ingestion), however, suggests a more profound level of assimilation and preservation. The association of the privileged few with the first midrash is further substantiated by the next passage, in which the water/well imagery surfaces (*GP,* I:30). A clever wordplay in the Targum[6] transforms the verse "With joy shall ye draw water out of the wells of salvation" (Isa. 12:3) to "With joy shall you receive a new teaching from the chosen of the righteous." Water is equated with knowledge, while the Hebrew term for "wells," *ma'yene,* is transformed to be "the equivalent of *me'eyne ha'edah:* I mean thereby the notables who are the men of knowledge" (*GP,* p. 64). The pairing of water/knowledge with well/notables in the context of the lexicographical analysis of the term "eating" in I:30 reflects on the metaphoric usage of the very same images in our first midrash as alluding to the process of "notables" acquiring "knowledge."

The final prooftext in this passage, "A word fitly spoken is like apples of gold in settings of silver" (Prov. 25:11), provides a synthesis for the ideas expressed in the two preceding midrashim by way of an expansive image of Scripture's heterogeneous meaning. "Silver" corresponds to the external meaning, which is "useful in many respects, among which is the welfare of human societies," while "gold," the internal meaning, "contains wisdom that is useful for beliefs concerned with the truth as it is" (*GP,* p. 6). The external represents the moral and political foundations upon which societal welfare depends, whereas the internal conveys the purely abstract and theoretical groundwork necessary for intellectual welfare. These two meanings are posited in addition to the starkly literal and vulgar reading,[7] and therefore the second midrash can be seen as prodding the masses to bypass the face value altogether in order to arrive at the "silver," the bread and butter of interpersonal and intersocietal relations. Though the Law aims at perfecting both conduct and thought, and is expounded with the goal of achieving widespread perfection in both, only the rare individual can truly hope to arrive at the ultimate perfection encased in "gold."[8]

Whereas the masses can only achieve the silver by discarding the vulgar meaning, the internal gold layer is attainable solely by assimilating the silver, as "its external meaning ought to contain in it something that indicates to someone considering it what is to be found in its internal meaning" (*GP,* introduction, p. 12). The tension inherent in the first two midrashim is resolved by Proverbs 25:11, which sets up two observers: one whose view from a distance leaves him with an illusion (although a useful one), and one who can traverse the distance and discern reality (though always ob-

scured by the illusory device of filigree work, indicating that a clear knowledge of God's essence is ultimately unattainable).[9]

When the three introductory verses of this passage (Hos. 12:11, Ezek.
17:2, Ezek. 21:5) are subjected to closer scrutiny, the choice of prooftexts
for the use of parabolic language by the prophets does not appear to be
random. Instead, a carefully constructed endorsement of the trivalent nature of Scripture has emerged thus far. When unraveled, the common thread
binding these three verses is that the truths of Scripture radiate out to respective audiences, satiating their diverse intellectual capacities on one of
the two levels of meaning beyond the bare literal. The middle verse (Ezek.
17:2) signifies the paradigm of parabolic exegesis in that it introduces a
chapter whose prophecy is marked by a duality throughout. It embodies a
poetic fable that is subject to a dual interpretation, first on an earthly plane
and then on a divine one. As Moshe Greenberg has pointed out,

> Duality pervades the prophecy: fable and interpretation, two eagles, two
> plants, two modes of punishment, two planes of agency (earthly and divine)
> doom and consolation. With this duality agrees the double command with
> which the oracle opens: "pose a riddle *(hidah)* and tell a fable *(mashal)"*—
> an indication that more is here than meets the eye.[10]

The schema of this chapter in Ezekiel precisely complements Maimonides' exegetical hierarchy as follows:

1. Verses 1–10 = eagle parable—vulgar literal, which in itself has no
   useful purpose and is pure poetry.[11]
2. Verses 11–18 = first level of interpretation, referring to political
   events of the day involving earthly entities Babylon and Egypt and
   consequences of breaching treaties—silver/external meaning, concerning "welfare of human societies."
3. Verses 19–21 = second level of interpretation, sets up first interpretation of earthly events as itself a parable alluding to the realm
   of ultimate truth—the divine, i.e., consequences of violating divine covenant = internal/gold, which is wisdom "useful for beliefs
   concerned with the truth as it is."

The great medieval exegete David Kimhi's distinction between the terms
hidah and *mashal* is enlightening, in that it may account for why Maimonides

chose this particular verse: "A *hidah* is an obscure saying from which something else is to be understood, while a *mashal* is a likening of one matter to
another—so the *mashal* in which the king is likened to an eagle is at the
same time a *hidah*, since none but the discerning *(maskilim)* can understand it."[12] The leap from the vulgar to the first level, where moral and
political lessons are derived, can and must be achieved by most. Advance-
ment to the second stage of theoretical speculation regarding the divine
sphere is barred to all but the few *(maskilim)*.

If Ezekiel 17:2 is emblematic of the structure of parabolic language,
then the two other verses relay the difficulty with which that language is
rendered comprehensible. Hosea 12:11, "And by the ministry of the prophets have I used similitudes," portrays God, in one sense, as bestowing the
allegorical method upon the prophets as a mode of communication. The
ambiguity of the Hebrew term for "have I used similitudes"—*'adameh*—
allows for another sense, and the midrash[13] and some medieval exegetes
take it to mean "I have assumed likenesses."[14] This wordplay and midrashic
gloss would most certainly have been familiar to Maimonides and may
explain his preference for the Hosea passage in this context. The elasticity
of the phrase conjures up an image of two very distinct domains: one, private and self-contained, playing itself out wholly within the confines of the
mind ("likenesses") of the prophet (i.e., philosopher/intellectual), and the
other, public and accessible, revealed in the prophet's popular pronouncements ("similitudes"). The "similitudes" are the means whereby the theoretical formulations conceived within the prophet's mind ("likenesses") are
relayed to the public, albeit in a very distilled fashion.[15]

Hosea 12:11 thus establishes two poles of humanity whose only hope
of rapprochement is by way of the parable. Ezekiel 17:2 affords us a typology of this literary device as a model for studying it. The third verse, "They
say of me: Is he not a maker of parables?" (Ezek. 21:5), when examined
contextually, reveals the failings of the parabolic device in actual practice
and how they can be overcome in order to salvage the original intent of the
parable. The sequence of the narrative surrounding the verse commences
with a prophetic vision to Ezekiel in which a fire is ignited and consumes
an entire forest; both fresh and dry trees are destroyed, and the fire is inex-
tinguishable. The prophet protests in 21:5 that the people will not acknowledge this as an authentic prophetic vision forewarning an impending historical disaster and will simply accuse him of being a spinner of riddles and
fables. God responds by rendering the prophecy as explicit as possible with
regard to the imminent destruction of Israel and Jerusalem; the consequences

of the destruction will be indiscriminately wreaked on both righteous and wicked.

Ezekiel 21:5, therefore, is the instrumental verse within a dramatic development that Maimonides utilized as a metaphor for what had unfortunately become the popular attitude toward allegory. The prophet realizes that the people will not see past the poetry—past the vulgar and literal— and this undermines his authority as a messenger of God. The parable is to be dispensed with altogether, and the people must be confronted with the unmediated political and social ramifications, which we have marked as the external/silver meaning of the original parable. Only then will they understand. This verse, which portrays the people as unable and/or unwilling to transcend the face value of the allegorical symbolism, provides the rationale for what we have demonstrated to be the moral of the second midrash, in which the *mashal* is deemed to be worthless. The devaluation of the *mashal* is a drastic measure to allay the fear expressed in the prophet's frustrated plea that the people will only view him as a "maker of parables" and not as a harbinger of the practical and theoretical truths implicit in his visions.

In summary, our analysis thus far has revealed this passage in the *Guide* to be a carefully crafted argument, constructed by manipulation of scriptural verse and midrash. The argument proposes a hierarchy of scriptural interpretation that parallels a pyramid-shaped model of human intellect. Ultimate meaning lies within the exclusive domain of the superior intellect. Inferior yet necessary truths are aimed at those less capable. For the former all planes of interpretation (poetic, practical-ethical, theoretical) coexist in a complex grid of truth that would collapse if any one component was lacking. For the latter the grid must be disassembled so that only what Maimonides calls the external meaning survives, while the literal is sacrificed altogether and the theoretical remains out of reach.

When the subtle interplay of midrash and verse is noted, a passage in the *Guide* purportedly advancing the simple proposition that Scripture relies heavily on parables as its parlance is rendered a more complex argument about such things as the nature of parabolic parlance, authorial intent and motivation, and composite readership. The stimulus for this reading is the incongruity of the two midrashim regarding the role of parable in recovery/discovery of the scriptural message, which then recasts the preceding and subsequent verses from simple prooftexts into a "generic pattern [causing] the verses to speak with each other and a kind of axiological code by which we can read the juxtaposition."[16] The reader to whom Maimonides is reaching out will discern the pattern leading to a true understanding of Scripture—"hermeneutic keys to the unlocking of the hermetic Torah"[17]—while others will be oblivious to it, gaining only very restricted access to Scripture's truths.

Genesis Rabbah 9 and Flash Technique

Another reason that compels Maimonides to adopt this writing style, particularly related to his use of midrash, is implicit in the nature of the subject matter (*ma'aseh bereshit* and *ma'aseh merkavah*), which obliges all who have gained any knowledge of it to transmit it to others by way of "flashes": "[E]very man endowed with knowledge who has come to possess an understanding of something pertaining to those secrets, either through his own speculation or through being conducted toward this by a guide must indubitably say something. It is, however, forbidden to be explicit about it. He must accordingly make the secret appear in flashes" (*GP*, II:29, p. 347). Maimonides' preference for the types of midrash that he employs in the composition of his treatise is expressed in terms of flashes: "Many such flashes, indications, and pointers occur in the saying of the Sages, may their memory be blessed, but these sayings are mixed up with the sayings of others and with sayings of another kind. For this reason you will find that with regard to these *mysteries*, I always mention the single saying on which the matter is based, while I leave the rest to those whom it befits that these should be left to them" (*GP*, II:29, p. 347). Only midrashim that conform with the strictures against disclosing such sensitive material by their usage of "flashes, indications, and pointers" in place of clear exposition will be incorporated into Maimonides' treatise on these matters. Therefore, as we have already seen, a reference to a midrash in the *Guide* should almost always alert us to a cautious reading of a text that is purposefully restrained and ambiguous regarding its message.

Indeed, the very midrash that provoked the discussion in II:29 is itself a case study in flash pedagogy. *Genesis Rabbah 9* is adduced as support for the prohibition against revealing these esoteric matters: "As from the beginning of the book up to here, the glory of God requires to conceal the thing" (*GP*, II:29, p. 347). Here the midrash relates a verse from Proverbs 25:2 calling for concealment of the scriptural account of the first days of creation. At first glance, this is simply a rabbinic endorsement of the confidential nature of esoteric topics. However, if we import meanings that

Maimonides specifically assigned elsewhere to the term "glory of God" *(kavod),* the midrash then flashes signals that have a different connotation. *Kavod* can equivocally signify either God's "essence and true reality" or "the honoring of Him by all men" (*GP,* I:64, pp. 156–57). Honoring God, Maimonides continues, is directly proportional to the extent to which one apprehends Him, and "man in particular honors Him by speeches so that he indicates thereby that which he has apprehended by his intellect and communicates it to others" (*GP,* I:64, pp. 156–57). Beings incapable of apprehension honor God only indirectly, simply by inspiring passively "him who considers them to honor God either by means of articulate utterance or without it if speech is not permitted" (*GP,* I:64, pp. 156–57). There appears to be an inconsistency in this line of thought. Honoring God is synonymous with apprehending His essence and communicating it to others. Surely such apprehension falls under the rubric of metaphysics, which is prohibited from being revealed. Ultimately, apprehension must lead to silence, which fails to qualify for the "honor" (as defined here) of "communication." Honor cannot materialize out of muteness. The resolution of this inconsistency may very well lie in the dual-voicedness of *Genesis Rabbah* 9. Proverbs 25:2 is not only a directive regulating future attempts to convey this material but is also descriptive of the Genesis creation narrative. The narrative in Genesis is itself a "concealment" in consonance with the glory of God, that is, there is a type of language that conforms to the prohibition against instruction, and that is the language of parable.

Maimonides may have had two reasons for not being overly explicit on this issue. First, by posing Scripture as a model for all future communications regarding physics and metaphysics, the implication follows that the Torah intentionally conceals truths from the masses (which was left moot in the introduction).[18] Second, the definition of *kavod,* when combined with this midrash, allows for very little hope that the vast majority of people can ever aspire to honor God. They cannot apprehend God; they cannot be taught by scholars; and the book to which they turn for guidance on all aspects of their lives intentionally withholds the truth from them. This extremely cynical and pessimistic stance is somewhat modified by the use of midrash that can be viewed univocally as simple instruction for the future or, upon deeper reflection and familiarity with the *Guide* as a whole, as a self-glossing discourse on the nature of Scripture itself. Only the few who have the prerequisite rigorous training[19] should be privy to Scripture's hidden agenda.

Another of Maimonides' evasive techniques is the art of omission. As with the passage in II:29, ambiguity or inconsistency should alarm the reader to cross-check any midrashic or scriptural quotation with its original source. The omission of part of the relevant reference or its context often provides a key to Maimonides' true intent. In II:29, only the first half of Proverbs 25:2 is quoted, whereas the entire verse is reproduced in *Genesis Rabbah* and reads thus: "It is the glory of God to conceal a thing, *but the glory of kings is to search out a matter*." In the original midrash, each half of the verse becomes a referent for different portions of the Genesis creation account. The first half characterizes the creation narrative up to Genesis 1:31, concluding with the creation of man, an account that must be shrouded in obscurity. The second half informs the narrative that follows, calling for study and clarity. This omission affords a liberal reading of the verse as colored by the midrash but is outside the strict confines of its original exegesis. For Maimonides, the opposing parts of the verse reflect the dichotomy of scriptural language and human intellect. Both parts refer to the same creation account, requiring concealment and revelation at the same time. The essence ("glory") and true reality of God are ultimately concealed, but it is the duty of those who are capable ("kings")[20] to investigate this matter insofar as it is intellectually possible. Scripture's parabolic Account of the Creation deters most from its mysteries but encourages the few to search on for its inner truth.

Genesis 1:31, the lead verse of *Genesis Rabbah* 9:1, is instrumental in the sifting out of Maimonides' message. For Maimonides, the words "And God saw everything that He made, and behold, it was very *good*" define the goodness that was revealed to Moses in response to his plea for knowledge of God's ways and glory. Moses' request to be shown God's glory was rebuffed as unattainable by any human being. Instead, God's goodness was revealed as the apex of human intellectual capacity, which "alludes to the display to him of all existing things of which it is said, 'And God saw everything . . . it was very good.' By their display, I mean that he will apprehend their nature and the way they are mutually connected so that he will know how He governs them in general and in detail."[21] The terms "glory" and "goodness" in this context are contrasting intellectual goals, the former unachievable, the latter to be striven for. This juxtaposition must be imported into an analysis of *Genesis Rabbah* 9 as quoted in II:29, and perfects its reading for the few as formulated by Maimonides.[22] Following our analysis, the mechanism for decoding the meaning of this passage can be traced as follows:

1. Contextually dissonant use of midrash (*Genesis Rabbah* 9:1) motivates the search for hidden meaning.

2. Discovery of partial omission of operative verse quoted by midrash (Prov. 25:2) and variant formulation of midrash by Maimonides inspires the search forward.

3. Lead verse (Gen. 1:31) assumes significations assigned to it in other chapters of *Guide.*

4. Derivation of meaning by intended audience regarding possible and impossible forms of knowledge ("goodness" and "glory"); language of Scripture (concealment); medium of instruction (concealment/parable) are all destinations of the search.

5. Intermeshing of midrash with discourse on nature of midrash ("flashes") results in intratextual illustration of "flash" technique.

Genesis Rabbah 27 and Prophetic Radicalism

Another instance of the interplay between midrash and textual dissertation regarding some aspect of the nature of midrash itself occurs in *Guide* I:46, where the midrash's preference for anthropomorphisms is rationalized. This is attributed to its mimicking of prophetic terminology: "For this reason you will find that in the whole of the Talmud and in all the Midrashim they keep to the external sense of the dicta of the prophets" (*GP*, p. 102). The sages felt secure that their adoption of this style could not possibly lead to error, since it is so obviously self-evident that it is not to be taken literally: "[B]ecause of their knowledge that the matter is safe from confusion and with regard to it no error is to be feared in any respect: all the dicta have to be considered as parables and as a guidance conducting the mind toward one being" (*GP*, p. 102). A midrash is quoted in support of this thesis: "Great is the power of the prophets; for they liken a form to its creator; for it is said: 'And upon the likeness of the throne was the likeness as the appearance of man' (Ezek. 1:26)" (*GP*, I:64, p. 103). The sheer audacity involved in describing God corporeally is sufficient proof "that they were innocent of the belief in the corporeality of God; and furthermore that all the shapes and figures that are seen in the vision of prophecy are created things" (*GP*, I:64, p. 103).

To corroborate Maimonides' understanding of the phrase "great is the power" *(gadol kochan),* a passage from the Talmud is quoted wherein a similar figure of speech constitutes a comment on the seemingly shocking action of a rabbi who performed the act of *halisah* (taking off a shoe to avoid levirate marriage) with a slipper and at night.[23] *"Another rabbi said thereupon: How great is his strength to have done it alone. How great is his strength* means *how great is his power.*" Upon closer examination of the original talmudic source, a startling discrepancy emerges between the phrase's contextual meaning and the meaning purportedly substantiated by Maimonides. Regardless of any textual variants or emendations, [24] the logical progression of this talmudic pericope seems to lead to the conclusion that the phrase is sarcastic and meant to be a declaration of disapproval of the actions at hand.[25] An expression advanced by Maimonides as one of praise and appreciation is curiously verified by one conveying denigration and mockery. Once again the cautious reader is alerted to an alternative approach to the midrash by an incongruity that could not have escaped Maimonides' attention.

The solution to this conundrum lies in the multipronged strategy of the *Guide* demonstrated thus far. Success in addressing the multitude is measured in terms of the extent to which they can be jolted out of their traditional acceptance of prophetic and rabbinic teachings at face value, thereby rejecting corporealisms and gaining closer proximity to a monotheistic belief. This is accomplished by a reductio ad absurdum implicit in the "great is the power" midrash. The perfect man, however, realizes that any particular section of the *Guide* can only be grasped in terms of the totality of the treatise, "connecting its chapters one with another . . . and also to grasp each word that occurs in it in the course of the speech even if that word does not belong to the intention of the chapter. For the diction of this Treatise has not been chosen at haphazard but with great exactness and exceeding precision" (*GP,* introduction, p. 15). For him each word of the quoted midrash and its talmudic counterpart gains significance beyond its specific context and attracts a network of allusions, definitions, and expositions that are scattered throughout the treatise.

Those who have "philosophized" and "have knowledge of the true sciences" (*GP,* introduction, p. 10) are aware that it is philosophically unacceptable to describe God in positive terms, as the prophets and rabbis have done. On the other hand, the alternative of utter silence and muteness regarding divine science would leave both the masses and the elite in a void, bereft of the guidance and instruction required in regard to such fundamental matters. The intellectually sophisticated reader, therefore, will be prompted to another level of understanding the "great is the power" midrash via the hidden message of its talmudic prooftext. The reference to levirate marriage and *halisah* conjures up Maimonides' theoretical formulations elsewhere in the *Guide*, suggesting that the form of the Torah's narrative and legal components is, in a sense, the lesser of two evils and necessitated by the unpalatable alternative of silence.

GP, I:26 is the operative chapter deliberating on the anthropomorphically charged narrative segments of the Torah, which are governed by the maxim, "The Torah speaketh in the language of the sons of man." Corporeal attributes convey the basic notions of existence and perfection to a general public whose only frame of reference is the physical world, "as the multitude cannot at first conceive of any existence save that of a body alone," and "everything that the multitude consider a perfection is predicated of Him even if it is only a perfection in relation to ourselves" (*GP,* p. 56). *GP,* III:32 is the complementary analogue to the I:26 argument with regard to the Torah's legislative component. The rationale it offers for much of the legislative content is divine recognition of human nature's weakness and general resistance to sudden and radical change. The law is motivated by primary and secondary intentions, the latter aimed at mutual abolition of wrongdoing and correctness of beliefs, and the former at intellectual apprehension of God.[26] Thus we are presented with a tripartite structure of scriptural law exactly paralleling what we have seen of scriptural narrative.

1. Literal/superficial = formal aspect of law
2. External = correct beliefs and moral-ethical guidance
3. Internal = true apprehension of the Deity

The external formal aspect of the Law, at its most stark and obvious level, means nothing. It is simply a concession to human frailty, "for a sudden transition from one opposite to another is impossible . . . therefore, He may be exalted, suffered the above-mentioned kinds of worship to remain [such as animal sacrifice] but transferred them from created or imaginary and unreal things to His own name" (*GP,* III:32, p. 526). Maimonides describes the outer form of the law as a "divine ruse" designed to establish God's oneness and existence, "while at the same time the souls had no feeling of repugnance and were not repelled because of the abolition of modes of worship to which they were accustomed and than which no other mode of worship was known at that time" (*GP,* p. 527). Just as there was no other language with which God could be discussed, previously pointed out in I:26, so there was no other legal modality whose praxis could lead to the same refined notions of God. "In anticipation of what the soul is naturally incapable of receiving, [God] prescribe[d] the laws that we have mentioned so that the first intention should be achieved, namely the apprehension of

Him" (*GP,* p. 527). Though much of this discussion centers on animal sacrifice, it can be read as an overall preface to the section dealing with the
rationale for the commandments and informs that entire discussion. Its thesis is applicable to the category of ritual law in general.

Critical for our purposes is the concluding paragraph of III:32, where
Maimonides fortifies his previous discussion with a midrash reporting that
at the waters of Marah, just after the exodus from Egypt, there was a revelation of a "first legislation" (*GP,* III:32, p. 530–31): that is, "The Sabbath
and the civil laws were prescribed at Marah."[27] Maimonides classifies this
revelation as one of "first intention concerned solely with correct opinions
as witnessed by the Sabbath (creation of world in time) and the civil laws
(abolition of mutual wrongdoing)"; "Accordingly it is already clear to you
that in the first legislation there was nothing at all concerning burnt offer-
ings and sacrifices, for, as we mentioned, these belong to second intentions."[28] Obviously, the perfect law is one that confines itself to first intentions and is not diluted by inferior secondary ones. For Maimonides, then,
the legislation promulgated at Marah is paradigmatic of this superlative
law untainted by formal ritual conforming to a defective human characteristic. The contrast of first and second legislations is indeed radical when
one considers that Marah preceded the Sinaitic theophany. The truly utopian law, it indicates, is not the one emerging from Sinai and presently
extant, but rather a pre-Sinaitic ideal that never fully materialized due to
the reasons outlined above. If not for the exigencies of human nature, the
final draft, as it were, of the Torah, as presented at Sinai, would have been
superfluous. *GP,* I:26 and III:32 form a sustained argument that the legacy
of Sinai is, in effect, a compromise. As a result, the potential religious philosopher is faced with an ongoing challenge to recover its original pristine
intentions aimed at the apprehension of the Deity.

In the passage under consideration, the inconsistency of the talmudic
prooftext on levirate marriage precipitates a revised reading of the "great is
the power" midrash in which the aggregate of these ideas planted throughout the treatise converge. The authentic student of Maimonides is directed
to the rationale for levirate marriage found in III:49 (*GP,* p. 603), which is
unique among the various reasons for other commandments in that it vali-
dates a custom that antedates Sinai: "As for the reason for the levirate, it is
literally stated [in Scripture] that this was an ancient custom that obtained
before the giving of the Torah and that was perpetuated by the Law." The
escape route for avoiding levirate marriage is *halisah;* according to Maimonides, this is a demeaning process providing an incentive to perform the

levirate. The reason provided for this commandment disrupts the pattern of the section dealing with the rationalization of the commandments. No actual reason is offered for its utility as either promoting a moral quality or right opinion or combating an idolatrous practice (*GP,* III:35). Instead, there is simply an appeal to some long-standing tradition of the Torah considered to be sufficient for its being adopted by and enshrined in the Law. A comprehensive analysis of this commandment would require a separate study, but what is important for our purpose is the signification it would bring to the mind of an attentive reader searching for a key to a difficult passage within which a seemingly inappropriate reference is made.

For Maimonides' true disciples, armed with the hints and clues interspersed throughout the *Guide,* the midrash at hand would emerge in a subtly nuanced form. In one sense, the expression "great is the power" truly praises the prophets for their ability to create a language where language is sorely inadequate. In quite another sense, the very same expression is critical of the prophetic choice of language when cast in light of the comments elsewhere about levirate marriage. Conclusions to be drawn from such disparate chapters as I:26 and III:32 converge on this expression and finally meld together in our passage in I:46.

This critique is bolstered by what we have seen to be the connotations raised by the levirate as emblematic of the law looking back to and embracing its antecedents. The "likening of a form to its creator" is not the telos and is really a practical submission to the weakness of the human intellect. The philosopher will be compelled to aspire to some pristine level of understanding beyond the language of the prophets. That level is one that prophetic speech, as embodied in the corpus of Scripture, cannot capture (possibly its level is the realm of pure abstract speculation). The demands of religious observance for the most, and of philosophical truth for the few, dictate that prophetic discourse will attract both praise and criticism. The astute reader can detect both notions in this midrash, while those not philosophically inclined will remain with the former. The notion that the Torah is not the ideal in the sense demonstrated would be too radical for the masses to absorb and yet continue to remain faithful to its content.

Marvin Fox's solution to the "contradiction" of maintaining both the duty to pray and the denial of divine attributes within the same Maimonidean system is most apropos our problem, as it deals with identical opposing demands. The doctrine of divine attributes is at odds with the traditional notion of prayer. Maimonides did not wish to explicitly reject the latter in favor of the former, for fear that unphilosophical but pious readers would not be able to cope. Instead, he synthesized the alternatives into a system that "enunciates the ideal of a form of worship that makes no use of language, but he also recognizes that this presents an impossible demand not only for common people but even for philosophers. His solution is to retain both the language of worship and the truth about divine attributes within a single system. These elements of the system live in dialectical tension, and it is a great art to keep them in balance."[29] The same balancing act must be performed by the religious philosopher who appreciates both the skillfulness of prophetic imagery and the nature of its sublime subtext.

CHAPTER 2

Intertextual Foils in the *Guide:*
Jacob vs. The Married Harlot

Parabolic Precision vs. Parabolic Flourish

In his introduction to the *Guide of the Perplexed*, Maimonides distinguishes between two types of parables that appear throughout the prophetic books. There are those in which each word is to be attributed a certain significance and those which are intended to convey meaning as a whole but within which words may have other roles to play than as individual signifiers. In the latter, words may "serve rather to embellish the parable and render it more coherent or to conceal further the intended meaning; hence the speech proceeds in such a way as to accord with everything required by the parable's external meaning" (*GP*, introduction, p. 12). The demands of literary style and cohesiveness dictate the usage of words that are devoid of inner meaning and operate solely on the level of the external catering to the purely aesthetic senses of the reader.[1] At the same time, the highly sensitive nature of the subject matter may require words that act solely as a subterfuge precisely so that the intended meaning escapes the attention of the unintended reader. That reader is to remain on the level of the external and never overcome it. The trained eye must determine which category of parable he is dealing with and, in the event it is of the second type, sift through the parable and weed out those words and phrases which are purely functional in contributing to its literary or esoteric success while superfluous to the core message.[2] If the first type is detected, then each word must be viewed as a signifier of the core meaning of the parable. The relegating of a word here to lower-level exigencies of style and embellishment would distort the true message.

Unfortunately, Maimonides does not provide the necessary criteria for determining which class a particular parable would belong to. What he does do is offer one illustration of each kind of prophetic parable with Genesis 23:12–13 (the dream of Jacob's ladder) exemplifying the first and Proverbs 7:6–21 ("the married harlot") the second. Though Jacob's dream of the ladder is the example par excellence of exacting language among prophetic parables, nowhere in the *Guide* is it subjected to any kind of systematic treatment that would unlock its meaning. This, of course, is in keeping with Maimonides' pedagogical methods and the *Guide's* purpose "that the truths be glimpsed and then again concealed, so as not to oppose that divine purpose which one cannot possibly oppose and which has concealed from the vulgar among the people those truths especially requisite for His apprehension."[3] The "glimpsing" Maimonides allows into the meaning of Jacob's ladder reflects that it is such a caliber that overt disclosure of its internal meaning would betray the divine agenda, which is purposefully obscure. If the Torah itself prefers riddles and parables as the appropriate mode of communicating highly sensitive material, how can Maimonides do otherwise? Indeed, he is driven uncontrollably to adopt the alternatives of parable and riddle or "obscurity and brevity," "drawn, as it were, toward this purpose by the divine will just as they were drawn by their natural circumstances" (*GP*, introduction, p. 8). There can be no clear exposition of Jacob's ladder, as of other prophetic parables dealing with the prohibited topics of the Account of the Beginning *(maaseh bereshit)* and the Account of the Chariot *(maaseh merkavah),* but we are led by the *Guide* to reexamine them in light of a new lexicography. The self-admitted use of diffuse and scattered organization ("you must connect its chapters one with the other" [*GP*, introduction, p. 15]) and contradiction must be taken into account as well as the subtle weave of text and scriptural prooftext where that prooftext points elsewhere than its own context.

My purpose in this chapter is primarily to suggest possible motivations for Maimonides' choice of these biblical examples of parabolic precision and parabolic flourish, respectively. The central characters of each are particularly suited to configuration as opposing philosophical tropes when juxtaposed and examined through the lens of the radically new Maimonidean biblical lexicon. The success of this exercise will, I hope, also further develop the thesis that the interplay of text and prooftext in the *Guide* transforms the prooftext from mere "proof" to actual "text." The *Guide* was primarily intended as a compendium of scriptural exegesis offering a distinct hermeneutic to be applied to the biblical texts.[4] It is a philosophical commentary that provides an exegetical master key allowing the devout

Jew to read his sacred texts comfortably alongside the current philosophical *Sitz im Leben.* In this particular instance the very juxtapositioning of
Jacob's ladder in Genesis with the "married harlot" of Proverbs beckons
the reader to apply a hermeneutic of intertextuality so that their original
biblical contexts are dislodged enough to allow for an accretion of meaning when cross-referenced.[5] The interaction between the two passages is
itself generative of a new synthetic parable. Maimonides will be seen to
have effected a parabolization defined by Paul Ricoeur as "the metaphoriza-
tion of a discourse."[6]

The *Guide* acts as a bridge, drawing the student out of the philosophical text into the sacred texts and back again, dissolving the divide between
the two in a perpetual hermeneutical crisscross.

Solomon's "Married Harlot" as Foil to Jacob

It is noteworthy that the *Guide's* introduction proffers Jacob's ladder as an
illustration of parabolic precision reflecting seven different subjects, but
the introduction is without any indication whatsoever as to what those subjects may be. On the other hand, the imagery of the parable of the married
harlot (Prov. 7: 6–21) that exemplifies parabolic flourish is interpreted in a
relatively detailed fashion, translating the central figure of the married harlot into "matter." The entire parable of adultery and seduction by the married harlot is an allegory "warning against the pursuit of bodily pleasures
and desires" (*GP,* introduction, p. 13), from which the lesson is derived that
man should not allow himself to become subservient to "matter" or his
"bestial nature" (*GP,* p. 14). The fact that we are left to our own devices in
deciphering the allegory of Jacob's ladder would indicate that the sensitivity of its subject matter precludes unfettered disclosure of its meaning. This
silence may itself intend a generalization regarding the kind of parable that
is outside the arena of public discussion and teaching. It is with regard to
this class of parable that "in some matters it will suffice you to gather from
my remarks that a given story is a parable, even if we explain nothing more"
(*GP,* introduction, p. 14). The first example of this appearing in the *Guide* is
the parable of Jacob's ladder, where simply noting that it is a parable "will
be like someone's removing a screen from between the eye and a visible
thing"(*GP,* p. 14), without further elaboration.

The very choice of Proverbs 7:6–21 as illustrative of the "literary parable" may serve to fill in somewhat the interpretive blank that accompanies

Jacob's ladder by acting as its counterpoint. The "harlot" who ensnares the naïve youth "void of understanding" is the "foreign woman" *(ishah zarah)* of verse 5, against whom "wisdom" *(chochmah)* acts as a protective shield. Without that shield the innocent, but ignorant, youth is vulnerable to the adulterous lures of the foreign woman. It is no coincidence that the vision of Jacob's ladder initiates Jacob's journey toward Padan Aram in search of the appropriate spouse. That journey is prefaced by a warning from Isaac not to take a woman from the *daughters of Canaan* but rather to confine himself to the women of his uncle Laban's household (Gen. 28:1–2). In other words, Jacob is directed, in no uncertain terms, to keep away from foreign women in favor of those who share a common lineage. The prophetic vision received by Jacob demonstrates that he has indeed assimilated his father's warning which, in the language of the Proverbs allegory, translates into the instruction that Jacob renounce "matter" and remain faithful to his true human "form" (intellectual apprehension).[7] This message of the married harlot as conveyed by Isaac qualifies Jacob to engage in the most sublime of intellectual activities, that of prophecy.[8]

Considered in this manner, the choice of texts for each type of prophetic parable is elevated from mere example to thematic substance. The juxtaposition of Jacob's ladder and the married harlot along with their originating contexts yields an allegorical construct regarding the ascent of man to perfection, a theme central to the *Guide* as a whole. This is achieved both from a notional and structural perspective:

1. Notional—Ignorance leads to a corruption of one's humanity and dooms one to the harlot's lair, making one forfeit the vast expanses of Jacob's vision. The acquisition of wisdom and the rejection of *foreign women* (Proverbs; Isaac's warning) pave the way for human enlightenment (Jacob's prophetic experience).

2. Structural—The parable whereby a *young man void of understanding* falls prey to the *adulteress* (matter) is, as a literary construct, figuratively impoverished; not every word has meaning. The literary unit of Jacob's ladder, on the other hand, is hypersignificant, with no words wasted through sacrifice to the vicissitudes of literary demands.[9] For Maimonides each parabolic type mirrors, in its structure, the human character type central to each. The *young man* in Proverbs is caught up in the material, sensible world, and therefore many of his daily activities are devoid of any significance, detached as they are from true intellectual activity. In stark con-

trast is Jacob, who has achieved a certain mastery over matter and is engaged in exercising that faculty which aspires to the human form. All his activity is fraught with meaning.

This portrayal of Jacob as the antithesis of the *young man* in Proverbs, who has renounced matter as his guiding life focus, is underscored by various references and allusions to Jacob throughout the *Guide*. In III:12 Jacob's "bargain" with God at Genesis 28:2 is quoted as capturing the essence of those excellent men who "keep the nature of that which exists, keep the commandments of the Law and know the ends of both, apprehend clearly the excellence and the true reality of the whole. For this reason they take as their end that for which they were intended as men, namely apprehension. And because of the necessity of the body they seek what is necessary for it, *bread to eat and raiment to put on*, without any luxury" (*GP*, p. 466). The biblical reference is excerpted from Jacob's response to the vision of the ladder. The plain sense of the verse is that Jacob is subjecting his faith in God to the condition that He provide him with the necessities of life. An unseemly "bargain" with God is transformed by Maimonides into an acknowledgment by Jacob that to attract God's providential concern one cannot pursue what is unnecessary or superfluous to the material human condition.[10] One must "restrict oneself to what is necessary." Jacob's fidelity to God will not be adulterated by any allegiance to the *foreign woman* beyond what is required for physical survival.

Another reference to Jacob appears precisely in the long-awaited chapter forecast in the introduction where the allegories of the *married harlot* and her antitype, the *woman of virtue* (Proverbs 31), are discussed. They respectively represent unbridled matter and subjugated matter, with Jacob configured as a model of the latter, since he quelled his sexual urges to the point of near emasculation. Consistent with this model is the midrashic address by Jacob to his son Reuben, where he is self-described as having "never had a seminal emission before [engendering Reuben],"[11] rendering him the human embodiment of the noble *woman of virtue* composite. The personality of Jacob is planted in the context of the promised exposition of Proverbs 7 and 31 in III:8 in order to assign new meaning to the juxtaposition of Jacob's vision and Proverbs in the introduction. Jacob is the archetype of the development from the married harlot to the "woman who is not a harlot but confines herself to attending to the welfare of her household and husband."[12] It is Jacob's sexual abstinence, the supreme gesture of victory over one's material substance, that leads to true harmony between "husband

and wife" or human form and matter.[13] The natural physical relationship between man and woman, in which the sexual component is generally a critical one, is inverted by Jacob's character to demonstrate that harmony between the male and female aspects of one's humanity is achieved by the virtual abnegation of sexuality.[14]

Though we are quite remote from having a full-bodied portrait of Jacob emerge out of Maimonides' writings,[15] Jacob's trait of austerity singles him out from other Patriarchs. The contrastive positioning of the married harlot parable with that of Jacob's ladder affords the first clue in uncovering the meaning of Jacob's ladder. The reader's attention is directed to radiate outward, to retrieve references such as these and assimilate them into the source biblical narrative, thereby liberating it from its most literal sense and[16] penetrating to its first level of significance. In this case, the stark anthropomorphic imagery of the dream and its mundane context of Jacob's first pit stop on the way to finding a wife give way to a level of meaning of utility in the social/political sphere.

This near-monastic construct of Jacob is critical to a reading of the biblical narrative within the parameters of language fixed by Maimonides. At the very outset of Jacob's journey, Isaac invokes Shaddai as the divine appellation necessary to ensure the success of his venture. Isaac, presumably at an advanced stage of intellectual perfection, exercises both his acquired knowledge and his familiarity with his own son to formulate a blessing that is most attuned to Jacob's character. The appropriateness of this particular name in this context is secured by the signification assigned to it in I:63 as *"He who is sufficient . . . He does not need other than Himself with reference to the existence of that which He has brought into existence or with reference to prolonging the latter's existence, but that His existence, may He be exalted, suffices for that"* (*GP,* p. 155). God is a wholly self-sufficient existence, not contingent in any way and not in need of anything external to its own essence. There is no deficiency or excess; in other words, there is no superfluity or extraneous dependence that would tarnish this essential sufficiency. Though the material world is His creation, He stands in total detachment from it in terms of His own existence.[17] The notion of self-sufficiency conveyed by this divine name is wholly in keeping with the character of Jacob, who suppresses his corporeal desires (sexuality) and who only seeks that matter which is the very minimum required to survive as a body ("bread to eat and raiment to put on"). Jacob's character development, therefore, is the human reflection of the ontological proposition regarding God captured by the name Shaddai. By eschewing the material aspects of the world, excepting what is needed for bare subsistence, Jacob comes closest to the ideal of self-sufficiency by casting off dependence on externals in the quest for his true form. It is quite fitting, then, that Isaac calls upon Shaddai to endow Jacob with the blessing to "make you fertile and numerous so that you become an assembly of people" (Gen. 28:3). The words "fertile and numerous" echo the original mandate of primal man to "be fertile and multiply" (Gen. 1:28) and therefore presumes sexual activity, albeit solely for the purpose of fulfilling a divine command. It is exactly in the sexual sphere that Jacob is most in need of the overarching principle dictated by the name Shaddai. The danger of falling prey to one's own corporeality is pronounced when one is involved in the most passionate and consuming of corporeal activities—the reproductive act.[18] The self-sufficiency symbolized by Shaddai will deter Jacob from allowing that act to be anything more than reproductive by imitating "God's ways" as far as humanly possible.[19] The midrash quoted above regarding Jacob's seminal emissions is of course evidence of the success achieved by Jacob in this endeavor.

The sign of circumcision that every Jew bears on his very body is, according to Maimonides, a permanent sexual prophylactic in that "sexual intercourse should neither be excessively indulged as we have mentioned, nor wholly obstructed. Did He not command and say, 'Be fruitful and multiply?' (Genesis 1:22). Accordingly, this organ is weakened by means of circumcision but not extirpated through excision" (*GP,* III:45, p. 611). Circumcision is the mean between unregulated nature and outright amputation for the sake of human propagation commanded by Genesis 1:22. The second part of Isaac's blessing, "and He shall bestow upon you and your descendants the blessing of Abraham," now enters the Maimonidean scene bearing the connotation of circumcision. It appears in the Mishneh Torah[20] within the context of the obligation of circumcision as a prooftext for the legal proposition, that the descendants of Abraham are restricted to his progeny through Jacob and specifically excludes those whose pedigree is traced to Esau. Therefore circumcision is the exclusive obligation of Jacob's descendants, designated as the bearers of the Abrahamic tradition by Isaac's testament. The bestowal of the "blessing of Abraham" is the antidote to the married harlot virus that circumcision provides. Both components of Isaac's blessing, when cast in the light of the married harlot parable and when infused with Maimonides' lexical nuance, are consistent with the allegorical journey of Isaac away from matter and toward intellect.[21]

The significance of the setting of Jacob's dream is also enhanced by its contrast with that of the *married harlot*. The youth who is *devoid of sense* wanders "in the twilight, in the evening of the day, in the pitch darkness of the night" (Prov. 9:9), whereas Jacob's journey is abruptly halted by the onset of nighttime.[22] The *youth* ventures into the blackness of night, while Jacob pauses and prepares for sleep so as to avoid the dangers night poses in favor of a state in which only his mind operates without the visual on-slaught of material representations, which would impede the revelatory process. Jacob escapes to the world that is devoid of matter when darkness looms, attracting a dream/prophecy.[23] The *youth* opts for the reality of the physical world and finds himself being embraced and kissed by the harlot (matter). When Jacob awakens he does not proclaim that he has had a dream but rather announces, "[T]ruly God is present in this place" (Gen. 28:16). This is the very verse that Maimonides cites as paradigmatic of those who have received true prophecy in a dream, as opposed to the lower levels of divine spirit experienced by the likes of Solomon, David, and Daniel. The latter awaken cognizant of a dream experience, whereas Jacob awakens and does not discern a dream but a reality. Jacob's denial of the material world in favor of the world of sleep offers up "reality," while the youth's somnambulism yields fake imaginings.

The meaning of the temporal setting of Jacob's dream is enhanced by contrast to that of the *married harlot,* and so is the meaning of its space. The place *(maqom)* of Jacob's dream is vital by virtue of the repetitive stress on the term *maqom*, "He chanced upon the *place* . . . he took a stone of that *place* . . . and he slept in that *place*."[24] The place *(maqom)* of Jacob's dream is a *Leitwort* to be read in conjunction with its recurrence in the postdream awareness of the place's significance: "Surely God is present in this *place* . . . how awesome is this *place* . . . He called the name of that *place* . . ." (Gen. 28:16–19).[25] There is a sense that this place is designated and fixed, a point of geographical focus giving way to a cognitive focus. Jacob's dream is anchored by its place, a site of aim, direction, and thoughtful awareness. The centrality of place yielded by the verses encourages a search in Maimonides' biblical thesaurus for further meaning. In I:8 we find that the literal-spatial connotation is extended to a qualitative one of "rank," "perfection," or "station," and can denote "an individual's rank and station . . . with reference to his perfection in some matter" (*GP,* p. 33). Jacob is now seen to be preoccupied with something more sublime than simply a location for bedding down. He has reached a metaphorical place of rank and perfection along the steady path of knowledge and prepares himself for further achievements of this nature. On this journey there is only one route and one destination, as the objects of true knowledge are absolute and static.[26]

The senseless youth of Proverbs, on the other hand, believes he is heading for a certain destination: "and he walks on the way to her house" (7:8). Since his goal, though, is the house of the *alien woman* or that which is related to matter, there is no fixed point of arrival as imagined, for "She is bustling and rebellious, her feet do not dwell in her house" (7:11). The state of matter is one of constant flux with no fidelity to one home; rather, "Sometimes she is in the street, sometimes in the squares, and she lurks at every corner." (7:12). The youth, like the primordial man before him, "inclined toward his desires of the imagination and the pleasures of his corporeal senses" (*GP*, I:2, p. 25), and as a result his focus is on the world of "generally accepted things" where there is no absolute standard of truth. The drama of Adam's original sin and rebellion demythologized by Maimonides to one of intellectual decline is reenacted by the senseless youth. The type of knowledge he aims for is always elusive and transitory, as the married harlot (matter) "never ceases to seek for another man to substitute for her husband and she deceives and draws him on in every way until he obtains from her what her husband used to obtain."[27] Since the youth is prone to ambush "at every corner," his seemingly assured goals are tenuous and his confidence delusional. Jacob, however, encounters a place (or *the* place)[28] that is exclusive and fixed (the domain of objective truth) for, as we have seen, he eschews the corporeal and turns his mind's eye to more abstract matters.

The austerity of lifestyle Jacob has come to represent is in sharp contrast with the luxuries that entice the youth of Proverbs. Jacob prepares to rest with the ground as his bed, and we are told in particular of his having chosen a rock as a cushion for his head.[29] The bare minimum in human comforts is afforded Jacob in preparation for a sleep that engenders a prophetic experience. The youth, on the other hand, is seduced (Prov. 7:21) by the lure of luxurious excess in the form of bedroom furniture; the couch is bedecked "with covers, with superior braided work of Egypt" and perfumed with "myrrh, aloe and cinnamon" (7:16–17). The attraction of that which is superfluous to basic human need leads to a night filled with "intoxicating lovemaking"[30] (7:18), the absolute antithesis of the divine communication that awaits Jacob's minimalist approach to materialism. The youth's mind is diverted toward "drink or copulation" so that he "has made use of the benefit granted to him applying and utilizing it to commit an act of disobedience with regard to Him who has granted the benefit and to transgress

His orders."[31] Jacob's contentment with the simplest and most basic of human requirements demonstrates, on the metaphorical level, his progress in dedicating his corporeal faculties (matter) to the service of the intellectual (form). He is thereby qualified to improve intellectually in consonance with that progress. The youth, to the contrary, reverses the master-servant relationship between matter and form, placing intellect at the command of body in defiance of the divine purpose for which intellect was placed at his disposal.[32]

Another point of departure augmenting our appreciation for Jacob's character here is what emerges from the respective attitudes toward sacred oaths expressed by Jacob and the harlot. One of her inducements offered to the youth is the puzzling declaration, "I have sacrificial meat *(zivhei shelamim)* on hand[,] for today I discharged my religious vows" (Prov. 7:14).[33] The fulfillment of a religious vow involving the sacrifice of a "well-being" offering from which a sizeable portion is reserved as a meal for the offerer[34] is here exploited to entice the youth into licentious behavior. Rather than a ritual of devotion to God, the leftover portion of meat is packaged as an opportunity for a feast accompanied by coital activity. The fulfillment of her vow is an occasion for gluttony that appeals to the youth. The harlot's attitude toward her sacrifice is a dramatic characterization of insolence and ingratitude. The very benefit granted by God (sacrificed meat) is utilized "to commit an act of disobedience with regard to Him who has granted the benefit" (illicit sexual activity). Such behavior stems from overlooking the sacral element of the sacrifice and perceiving simply excess meat.[35]

This portrayal of the seductress in Proverbs acts as a background against which that of Jacob is better understood. His vow of dedication to God is conditional upon being granted *"bread to eat and raiment to put on."* As we have seen, when taken in its Maimonidean sense it is expressive of an ideal diametrically opposed to that which materializes from the seductress's vow. It acknowledges the basic needs of the human body while rejecting its indulgence. The repression of matter's penchant for more than what it needs entails the choice of mind over body and is a sine qua non of the first part of the verse "if God will be with me and take care of me." In fact, Jacob's vow incorporates the very virtue that qualifies the laws concerning vows to be included in the thirteenth class of commandments enumerated by Maimonides alongside forbidden foods and Nazirites in describing the rationale for the commandments. The common purpose linking all three is "to put an end to the lusts and licentiousness manifested in seeking what is most pleasurable and to taking the desire for food and drink as an end."[36]

The seductress's vow results in a subversion of these aims by emptying the sacrifice of its representational value and viewing it as simply food. As it does not transcend its own materiality, it lends itself for use in the service of further bodily activities such as the sexual.[37]

Finally, the house *(bayt)* Jacob discovers as a result of his theophany stands in stark contrast to the one in which the senseless youth is ultimately confined. The intellectual journey away from his father's house to earn an independent perfection based on self-development inevitably leads back to the security of his father's house: "and I will return safely to my father's *house*" (Gen. 28:21). Jacob must at some point move beyond knowledge gained by tradition (his father's house) and engage in the lengthy and arduous process of speculation to achieve the true knowledge of rational demonstration.[38] His vision yields the cognitive realization that he has arrived at the "*house* of Elohim" (Gen. 28:17), which he designates as the "*house* of El" (28:19), and memorializes as the "*house* of Elohim" (22). This guarantees the return to his father's house, where tradition is now substantiated by demonstration. In Proverbs, the house from which the whole scene of debauchery is observed and in which wisdom is sheltered ("I glanced through the window of my *house*" [7:6]) remains aloof and detached. The witless youth has chosen the *house* of the harlot as his destiny (7:8), an image that is driven home by the repeated occurrence of house *(bayt)* in the parable (7:11, 7:19, 7:20), rising to the inescapable denouement that identifies that house with Sheol (7:27). The youth is ensnared in the very depths of depravity, while wisdom remains a hapless onlooker. The juxtaposition of the two parables generates an extreme polarity of two *houses,* between which Maimonides' readers must choose.

The objective spectator of all that transpires between the harlot and the witless youth is described as witnessing the drama by glancing *(nishkafti)* through his latticed window. The root of this verb is the very one that designates the operative hermeneutic posture requisite for deciphering prophetic parables. Silver "filigree" surrounding apples of gold, to which prophetically constructed parables are likened, is etymologically linked by Maimonides via Aramaic to the root *shakaf.* That Aramaic rendering then transforms the type of perception conveyed by a *glance* to one that is more probative and that penetrates through the silver to reach the gold.[39] Immediately preceding the illustration of Jacob's ladder and the married harlot, Maimonides cites Proverbs as typical of the silver/gold construction in prophetic parables that divulges an external meaning of social utility and a more profound internal meaning of "truth as it is" (*GP,* introduction, p. 12).

It is no coincidence that the detached observer (designating wisdom) surveys the entire drama with the selfsame discerning glance. Not only is he an actor within the dramatic setting of the allegory but, at the same time, he is the Maimonidean exemplar of scriptural hermeneutics. Any act of reading the biblical parable must be patterned after the perspicacious *glance* of the objective narrator/observer of Proverbs 7. Jacob's dream must also be subjected to the hermeneutic of the glance.

In summary, I have argued that the exemplification of the two types of biblical parables by Jacob's dream and Proverbs, respectively, is intended to draw the reader into a discourse between the two that yields antithetical archetypes of human virtue and profligacy. Though no light has yet been shed upon the meaning and significance of Jacob's dream per se, the setting and the dramatis personae involved become much better appreciated. The contrast forms a kind of preface to the actual explication of the dream yet to come in various places in the body of the text. This format is structurally sound, as we are not yet past the general introduction to the treatise as a whole, nor is even a hint dropped as to what each of the subjects in Jacob's dream, as sketched by Maimonides, represents. The senseless youth and adulteress of Proverbs 7 are meant to act as foils to the character of Jacob, in whom the dream of the ladder appropriately takes root. The two-column comparison of the two serves as a synopsis of the intertextual discourse in which we have seen that character fleshed out against the backdrop of Proverbs 7.

Maimonides succeeds in having the reader abandon an "interpretation internal to the text for a hermeneutic of the text's *referential intentionality*," whereby there is constituted "a network of intersignification, thanks to which the isolated texts signify something *else*, something *more*."[40]

JACOB'S LADDER Genesis 28	MARRIED HARLOT Proverbs 7
—Jacob —Warning to steer clear of women outside the family (vv. 1–2) = Renunciation of "matter"	—Senseless youth Youth heading toward foreign woman/harlot *('ishah zarah)* = Preference for "matter"
—Jacob guided by the ideal of Shaddai in sexual endeavors (v. 3) = no excess; basic physical needs	—Sexual activity for sake of pure eroticism = excess
—Jacob is bestowed the "blessing of Abraham" (v. 4) = circumcision = sexual prophylactic allowing only for reproduction as commandment —Night = time for sleep (v. 11) = intellectual activity	—Husband absent from household (v. 19) = absence of legitimate sexual activity under rubric of Gen. 1:22; sexual activity as end in itself —Night = opportunity for lustful activity (v. 9)
—Certainty of destination; —*Maqom* (v. 11, 16–17) = world of truth and falsehood	—Confidence of destination (v. 8) illusory (11–12) = world of good and bad
—Ground for bed; rock for cushion (v. 11) = minimizing of material needs in preparation for "dream" (v. 12) = activity of human form	—luxurious bed (vv. 16–17) in preparation for activity of human matter = sexual (v. 21)
—Oath (v. 20) = expression of physical austerity as condition of being with God *(bread to eat and clothing to wear)*	—Oath (v. 14) = opportunity for gluttony and physical excess condition of pre- occupation with matter
—Jacob discovers *house* of God (Gen. 28:17); names and memorializes place as *house* of God (19:22); return to father's *house* (21)	—Youth headed toward harlot's *house* (Prov. 7:8); Wisdom observes from separate *house* (6); Youth ensnared in harlot's *house (she'ol)* (27)

CHAPTER 3

"The Lord hath forsaken the earth":

An Interlude on the Dilemma
of Providence in Maimonides

The ongoing debate regarding Maimonides' true position on creation extends to the issue of divine providence as well. The notion of a God who exercises a personal and particular providence over humanity, who watches over individuals *(hashgacha peratit),* is inconsistent with the rigid changelessness of the God whom Maimonides advocates. Such a being cannot be located in any administrative, regulative, governmental, compensatory, or caring context vis-à-vis mankind, a context that has been associated with traditional images of God as, for example, a being who "commands, prohibits, punishes and rewards his subjects and who has servants and attendants who carry out his orders and do for him what he wishes to be done" *(GP,* I:46, pp. 102–3). Scriptural and rabbinic license for such analogies stems from the "great is the power" authority to "liken a form to its creator" *(GP,* I:46, pp. 102–3, citing *Gen. Rabbah* 27 and B.T., *Yebamoth* 104a) which, as we have argued in chapter 1, provides license for a wide creative latitude to construct audacious portraits of God while calling for their deconstruction at the same time. A paternal notion of God is precluded by a fixed essence that bears no orientation toward what is other than its own essence. Maimonides offers us his most radical formulation of this divine essence quite early in the treatise in a lexicographic chapter. God is defined as "the stable One who undergoes no manner of change, neither a change in His essence—as He has no modes besides His essence with respect to which He might change—nor a change in His relation to what is other than Himself—since . . . there does not exist a relation with respect to which He could change. And herein His being wholly changeless in every respect achieves perfection" *(GP,* I:11, pp. 37–38). Changelessness is hammered home repeatedly, almost ad nauseam, compelling the reader to subject any theory of providence to its strict requirements.

All those qualities that traditional religious language attributes to God, be they in the scriptural, rabbinic, or liturgical traditions, such as compassion, mercy, and grace, are in truth descriptive of the creation and not of the creator. There is an implicit transference in all such language normally associated with divine providence from actions proceeding from God to God himself. The reason, once again, that the divine essence is immune from these attributes is that they harbor passions, motivations, reactions, arousals, and responsiveness—all of which God is incapable of, for "all affections entail change" (*GP,* I:55, p. 128). When one views the process of biological birth and subsequent nurturing, the religious impulse is to shower God with epithets of mercy, pity, compassion, and kindness for such thoughtful design and preservation of his creation. In truth they are fictitious representations arising out of a combination of the inadequacy of human language and the urge to capture God in a familiar moral dimension, for "actions of this kind proceed from us only after we feel a certain affection and compassion. . . . It is not that He, may He be exalted, is affected and has compassion. But an action similar to that which proceeds from a father in respect to his child that is attached to compassion, pity and an absolute passion proceeds from Him, may He be exalted, in reference to His holy ones, not because of a passion or a change" (*GP,* I:54, p. 125).

The traditional providential God exercises governance in accordance with moral and just principles. These call for responses to external events and phenomena of which God cannot even know,[1] let alone react to. The terms of reference for a traditional scheme of divine providence are feeling, change, and reaction, all of which are precluded by virtue of the negative theology propounded in the *Guide.* Its theology demands, as a religious obligation, that one not simply refrain from the use of such primitively naïve language, but actually to negate it when engaged in God-talk.[2] The process of negating all possible affirmations regarding God is a sophisticated philosophical one whereby each one is methodically and demonstrably ruled out. All language regarding God must be refined to the irreducible two-word sentence "He is." Any further elaboration on the divine essence is not only to succumb to "an indulgence in facile language" (*GP,* I:58, p. 134), but is in fact to invent some mythic existence that is no more real than a centaur (*GP,* I:60, p. 146). Any theory of providence that operates on the basis of a divine omniscience that charts human activity and reacts in tandem with its perpetual flux is tantamount to atheism rather than simple error.[3] Any trace of change in God's knowledge must be purged in favor of an incomprehensible assertion "that His knowledge of a thing before it has come into being and after it has acquired reality as existent and after it has ceased to exist is one and the same knowledge in which there is no change" (*GP,* I:60, p. 144). Even when positing a metaphor to which he is partial on the issue of governance, Maimonides is quick to retreat from its traditional implication. If the religious impulse's desire for concrete images is satisfied by Maimonides' portrait of God as "a captain to his ship," it is immediately dissatisfied by the caution that "even this is not the true relation and a correct likeness, for this likeness has been used in order to lead the mind toward the view that He, may He be exalted, governs the existent things, the meaning of this being that He procures their existence and watches over their order as it ought to be watched over" (*GP,* I:58, p. 137).

The full account of Maimonides' theory of providence offered in chapters III:17–18 of the *Guide* must be read in conjunction with his exposition of the book of Job in III:22–23. In between those two sections there is an extended discussion of the uniqueness of God's knowledge that is crucial for an understanding of his view on providence. His presentation of the five schools of thought on providence represented by Epicurus, Aristotle, the Asharites, the Mutazilites, and "the opinion of our Law" is highly problematic. Not the least of those problems is that the last opinion seems to be shunted aside by a further opinion classified as "my own belief." To compound the problem, this last opinion subscribed to by Maimonides is, according to Maimonidean interpreters, as early as those in the medieval period—such as Samuel ibn Tibbon,[4] Joseph ibn Caspi,[5] and Shem Tov ibn Shem Tov—indistinguishable from the Aristotelian position ruled out previously. As astute a reader as Shem Tov concluded unequivocally, "It has become clear from this that the opinion of Aristotle on providence is identical with the opinion of the Rav, nothing less and nothing more."[6] In the modern period no less a scholar than Shlomo Pines has followed suit in linking Maimonides' doctrine on providence to Aristotle's. [7] My intention in this work is not to enter the fray regarding those sections of the *Guide* explicitly dealing with providence. I would refer the reader instead to those who have conducted very competent studies.[8] I have approached this issue from an entirely different direction, demonstrating that a scriptural and rabbinic edifice has already been constructed in which the discussion of providence anchors itself. My goal is to map out a trail that, snaking its way throughout the *Guide* and littered with scriptural and rabbinic prooftexts, ultimately converges in the prophetic vision of Jacob's ladder—the imaginative substrate for the philosophical doctrine of providence.

The allure of the strategic prooftext, however, entices me at this point to focus on the single verse cited in the sketch of the Aristotelian position. Ezekiel 9:9, "The Lord hath forsaken the earth," is cited as the ideological rallying cry of those who subscribe to Aristotle's teaching on providence. As this book argues is often the case, and despite the stridency of its tone, the scriptural reference at this juncture may in fact have been inserted to alert the careful reader that the categorical rejection of this position must be reevaluated and qualified. The following indicators are suggestive of just such a maneuver:

1. The proclaimers of this scriptural refrain are characterized as "Those who, deviating from our Law, believed in this opinion. . . ." The "I account" or "my own belief" rendered later in the chapter supersedes the fifth opinion, which is ascribed to the "opinion of our Law." If this is indeed the case, then "deviating from our Law" may be transformed from a condemnatory assessment to a laudatory one connoting a disengagement from an incorrect opinion. In point of fact, there is an implicit encouragement to deviate from "our Law" on the doctrine of divine providence to arrive at the correct account (which Maimonides calls "my own belief"), which hinges on the principle that "providence is consequent upon the intellect and attached to it."[9] The correlation of the various schools in III:17 to each of the characters in the Jobian drama in III:23 associates the "our Law" position with Eliphaz, while "my own belief" must, by process of elimination, correspond to the superior Elihu position.[10]

2. The error in the Aristotelian position is traced to its stance on the eternity of the world, which rules out the possibility "of that which exists being in any respect different from what it is." Although the reference is to the point of contention between Aristotle and the Law on miracles, the two, as formulated by Maimonides, may not be as irreconcilable as they seem. Miracles are also considered in the rabbinic tradition integral properties of the natural order, since "when God created that which exists and stamped upon it the existing natures, He put it into these natures that all the miracles that

occurred would be produced in them at the time when they occurred."[11] While Maimonides may admit the potential for the miraculous, it is a potential never to be realized. For all intents and
purposes, the reference in III:17 to error on providence aligns with
that half of Aristotle's position on creation with which Maimonides
concurs in II:29: "[T]hat what exists is eternal a parte post and will
last forever with that nature which He, may He be exalted, has
willed. . . ." (*GP,* II:29, p. 346). The providential mechanism may
then operate accordingly, that is, as will be seen, naturally.

3. The verse from Ezekiel, "The Lord hath forsaken the earth," directs the reader, as demonstrated throughout this book, to its reap-
pearance at the very denouement of the *Guide*. In III:54 that verse
is the scriptural expression of the philosophical school on providence that posits "that His providence, may He be exalted, terminates at the sphere of the moon and that the earth and that which is
in it are neglected" (*GP,* p. 637). This crude and categorical negation of divine providence cannot be perfectly aligned with the more
refined version of the Aristotelian position expressed by the same
verse in III:17. The latter allows for some extension of providence
to the sublunar world, primarily to the species and subsequently to
individuals via inherent self-preservative faculties; "[T]here is likewise an overflow from the providence in question, which necessitates the durability and permanence of the species, though the durability of the latter's individuals be impossible. However, the
individuals of every species are also not neglected in every respect."[12] Once the reader discerns the discrepancy in the scriptural
representation of both an unconditional rejection of sublunar providence and a qualified acknowledgment of an extended providential scheme, he is compelled to reconsider the purported rejection
of the latter.

4. The verse cited at *GP,* III:54, p. 637 as the polar opposite of "The
Lord hath forsaken the earth" is "That the earth is the Lord's" (Exod.
9:29). The ambiguity of the position on providence that this verse
articulates allows it to be quite neatly superimposed upon the Aristotelian position presented in III:17: "He means to say that His
providence extends over the earth in the way that corresponds to
what the latter is, just as His providence extends over the heavens
in ways that correspond to what they are" (*GP,* III:54, p. 637). The

two antithetical verses intersect at the Aristotelian crossroads of providence. Jacob's ladder, anchored as it is on one end in the earth with the other reaching into the heavens, is the ultimate prophetic meditation on the enigma of providence.

CHAPTER 4

Divine Immutability and Providence:
Chapters I:10–15—Prelude to the
Secret of Jacob's Ladder

The dream of Jacob's ladder is directly dealt with on four separate occasions in Maimonides' writings: (1) *GP,* I:15; (2) *GP,* II:10; (3) Mishneh Torah, *Hilkhot Yesodei Hatorah* 7:3; (4) Letter to Rav Chasdai Ha-Levi.[1]

Since the last composition's authenticity is subject to serious doubt and is self-admittedly not penned by Maimonides' own hand, I will confine myself to the first three. All three are incomplete in terms of dealing with the entire dream and all differ in their representation of the "angels" within the dream. They either signify prophets in the case of *GP,* I:15, or the basic structural elements of the world in II:10, or concrete historical political entities in the Mishneh Torah. I believe that once the method of "disentanglement" mentioned above is applied along with attentiveness to the role Scripture plays as more than mere prooftexts, then all three will come to be seen as housing the same impenetrable "secret" *(sod).* In this instance, *sod* is God's providence, a subject listed among those that defy public discourse as "they are truly the mysteries of the Torah and the secrets constantly mentioned in the books of the prophets and in the dicta of the Sages. . . . They are the matters that ought not to be spoken of except in chapter headings . . ." (*GP,* I:35, p. 80).

The first extended discussion of Jacob's ladder appears in a chapter dedicated to the explication of the biblical term for "standing erect" *(natsov* or *yatsov).* In addition to its literal meaning it can convey the sense of stability and permanency, and it must be taken in this sense "whenever it occurs with reference to the Creator." The verse cited as exemplifying this meaning is Genesis 28:13, where God is seen in the dream as "standing erect" upon the ladder. The discussion then veers off into an interpretation

49

of that segment of the dream which envisions the angels ascending and descending, ostensibly having nothing to do with the subject at hand of the term *natsov*. We are then pointedly steered back on course by the open declaration, "I shall now return to our purpose." The phrase "stood erect upon it," Maimonides says, "signifies God's being stable, permanent and constant. . . ." The notion of an unchanging and immutable God dominates this chapter and cannot help but inform the message of the ladder. The ladder is also fixed *(mutsov),* and therefore the only movement that transpires in this image is that of the angels climbing. That angelic activity reflects the prophetic "in which *ascent* comes before *descent.* For after the *ascent* and the attaining of certain rungs of the ladder that may be known comes the descent with whatever decree[2] ('matter' or 'thing') the prophet has been informed of with a view to governing and teaching the people of the earth." Why the digression to the details of the dream itself and why at this particular juncture in the *Guide*?

The key to the solution of these questions, and ultimately to an appreciation of the dream's significance, lies in viewing I:15 as one component of a thematic unit that comprises the seven chapters of I:10 to I:16.[3] *GP,* I:10 opens with advice not to expect a comprehensive "treatise on language" in the lexicographical section; it says, "[O]f those senses we cite only such as we require for our purpose and no other" (*GP,* p. 35). The overriding purpose of the *Guide* is to be consistent with the "divine purpose," which demands that "those truths especially requisite for His apprehension" be "glimpsed and then again concealed" (*GP,* introduction, p. 7). The "truth" with which this literary unit concerns itself is the immutability of God, which allows for no change whatsoever either in essence or in relation to what is other than His essence. As we have said, this existence, defined as such, cannot possibly accommodate traditional devout notions of a God of history responsive to the world and man and all the concomitant beliefs of a supreme being who punishes, rewards, heeds prayer, and manifests providential concern for man. It therefore admits only of an esoteric treatment that, I will argue, assumes its imaginative pictorial form in the dream of Jacob's ladder. Awareness of the esoteric enterprise will lead to a determination that there exists a common ground in which the seemingly conflicting interpretations of the dream intersect. The easy resolution of this conflict would be that the interpretations are aimed at their respective audiences, which have different levels of intellectual sophistication. Though this may be true in some respects, it is not strictly the case for the highest level of readers. It will be demonstrated that once the latter distill the true metaphysical teaching of the dream, they can return to the lower teachings and reread them in light of the true message, producing an integrated whole whose subject matter is God and His relationship with His creation. The sociopolitical historical lessons of the dream are transformed into lessons in "divine science."

There is a methodical repetition of the notion of divine immutability progressively reinforced by the explication of the particular terms in I:10 to I:16. What links each of these chapters is a feature of God's essence that is absolutely crucial for a subscription to the unadulterated monotheism espoused by Maimonides. That feature is captured by the repeated appearance of such terms as "stable," "permanent," and "constant," all identified with the notion of changelessness. It is given its most radical formulation in chapter I:11, which defines this "stability" in terms of an irreducibly pure, nonrelational, modeless, and changeless essence "who undergoes no manner of change in His essence—as He has no modes besides His essence with respect to which he might change—nor a change in His relation to what is other than Himself—since . . . there does not exist a relation with respect to which He could change. . . ." The reader is confronted quite early in the book with a highly abstract and refined notion of the divine essence, a notion that is bound to have serious repercussions for any previous conception of providence that may have been taken for granted. The arena of human activity, to which the faithful adherent of the Torah would normally expect the attendance of the watchful eye of God, becomes extremely problematic, since that arena is one that is characterized by temporality and change. Change, acquired knowledge, and familiarity with the fickleness and erratic behavior of humankind are indeed repellent to Maimonides' God as defined, since they would imply change in His essence. The "stability" that dominates this series of chapters and is equated with immutability is a seemingly impenetrable barrier, virtually denying the level of access required of a God who "acts" and "responds." Temporality, history, and causality associated with the realm of human conduct, and constituting the mainstay of biblical and classical rabbinic conceptions of providence, are all anathema to the radical immutability that lies at the core of the divine stability and constancy posed in these chapters. Every chapter broadens that notion of changelessness in ways that would not sit well with traditional tenets of divine providence. Ultimately, the climb up Jacob's ladder leads to an existent who is "stable and permanent," and therefore the parable of Jacob's ladder would remain inexplicable without an examination of each chapter in this unit.

I:10   Punishment as Cipher for Pre-eternal Will

The term "descent" when referring to the Creator can denote "a calamity befalling a people or a terrestrial zone in *accordance with His pre-eternal will*." (I use the somewhat ambiguous term *pre-eternal will* in accordance with the Pines translation. I believe what is intended by this term is a will that is eternal *a part ante* with no beginning.) The clue that directs the reader to link this offhand remark with the discussion of providence is the prooftext quoted in support of God's indifference to man: Psalm 8:5, "What is man that thou art mindful of him and the son of man that Thou should visit him, etc. *For this verse refers to this notion*." Though the verse is definitive of an unresponsive will here, it is projected as an expression of prophetic wonderment as to how man can be an object of divine concern in III:17 during the course of an argument *in favor* of specific providence.[4] Why raise a verse that can only dampen the force of the argument being made?

The answer lies in Maimonides' method of flashing discrete signals at the reader not to take what he is purporting to say at face value. One of the initial tools of that method is the provocative use of scriptural prooftexts. In this instance, Psalm 8:5 interrupts the flow of the argument being advanced in support of specific providence, and forces the educated reader to inquire whether Maimonides is truly a proponent of providence in the traditional sense or whether the term must be reevaluated. The verse then acts as a signpost pointing back to its appearance in the context of I:10, where its function is to render an equation between "punishment" and "pre-eternal will." Whereas Scripture portrays a calamity as "punishment," Psalm 8:5 dictates the replacement of the loaded term "punishment" with "pre-eternal will." "Punishment" as descriptive of divine retribution consequent to man's actions is simply inconsistent with the philosophical ramifications of Psalm 8:5. Bearing this in mind, III:17 is revisited for a fresh look at those scriptural prooftexts that endorse the belief of individual providence and are offered as "explicit statements concerning providence watching over human individuals and exercising a surveillance over their actions" (*GP*, p. 472). Each of the four verses quoted casts God in a retributive mode in response to man's malfeasance. No source is included that indicates reward for virtuous deeds, even though there would be no lack of such to draw on and even though it would strengthen the case for specific providence as more encompassing in its scope. The choice of punishment as the exclusive expression of providence nudges the reader to grasp the teaching of I:10, which dictates that the type of providence advocated here is one that is manifest "in accordance with His pre-eternal will." The individuals to whom these verses are directed are the "ignorant and disobedient" who "have been relegated to the rank of the individuals of all the other species of animals" (*GP,* III:18, p. 475) and therefore fall outside the sphere of providence.[5] Their lack of intellect confines them to the same domain inhabited by animals, which is subject solely to the rules of natural governance. Combine this with the assertions in III:28 that scriptural expressions of divine anger and punishment are merely ones of expedience rather than truth,[6] and the reader is left at a far cry from the caring, interactive God of the Bible and of rabbinic tradition.

I:11   The "Sitting" of Indifference

Chapter I:11 deals with the term "sitting" *(yeshivah)* which, in its figurative sense, means "firm and steady." It is in this sense that it must be taken when referring to God as "the stable One who undergoes no manner of change, neither a change in His essence . . . nor a change in His relation to what is other than Himself."[7] Though various verses are cited in which the verb "sit" is characteristic of God's immutable nature in an abstract sense, there is one verse that would indicate a certain relationship to a worldly historical event: "The Lord sitteth at the flood" (Ps. 29:10). This, again, is a metaphor for the static relation between God and the world, for "when the state of the earth is changed and corrupted there is no change in the relation to God . . . the relation remains the same—stable and permanent—whether the thing undergoes generation or corruption." Once again divine immutability, and once again the single verse in the chapter implying some relationship with a worldly event is one that evokes a mode of punishment (flood—*mabul*). The figurative construction of "sitting" in this context then is wholly consistent with that of "descent" in I:10—the world undergoes change, God does not.

The chapter then concludes with a proposition both extraneous to the analysis at hand and frustratingly ambiguous. Upon qualifying God's relationship with the world of "generation and corruption" as "stable and permanent," he posits that "this relation subsists only with regard to the species of the various things subject to generation, *not with regard to individuals.*" Does this mean that whatever relationship is indicated by "stable and permanent" only extends to the species, while individuals of the species are wholly outside the pole of any relationship whatsoever? Or does it exclude individuals from the providence entailed by "stable and permanent" but yet have them subsumed under some other type of providence? Whatever the determination of the first query, the same rule would apply to *all* individuals yet, in III:17, Maimonides clearly distinguishes between individuals of the human species who are subject to divine providence and those of the animal kingdom that are governed by chance.[8] At this juncture the inconsistency defies resolution, but it is clear that Maimonides is planting a seed of doubt as to whether his later espousal of specific individual providence is to be taken in its conventional religious sense.

I:12   "Rising" and the Role of Metatron

Chapter I:12 focuses on the equivocality of the term "rising" *(qimah),* which can move beyond its literal sense to "denoting the stability and validity of a matter" *(GP,* p. 38). An unequivocal proposition is then advanced: that whenever this term is applied to God it must, by definition, bear this meaning. Two biblical verses are then adduced as illustrative of this usage and are interpreted as follows:

> "Now will I rise saith the Lord" (Ps. 12:6 or Isa. 33:1). "Now will I carry out My decree, My promise and My menace."

And,

> "Thou will arise and have compassion upon Zion" (Ps. 102:14) = "Thou wilt carry out what Thou has promised as to having mercy upon her."

Were the chapter to simply end here, the philosophically figurative readings of "rising," while negating divine physicality, would still allow for traditional images of a responsive God. In both verses God is depicted as being moved by social injustice and political repression. The conviction of this position, though, is undermined by the further exploration of an alternative sense of "rise," resulting in an entirely new rendering of those verses.

The word "rising" can also be "used figuratively to denote the execution of God's decree against a people who have deserved punishment entailing their destruction." The suggestion is then made that the verses can accommodate this meaning as well, with the *"compassion upon Zion"* of Psalm 102:4 taking the form of the punishment of Zion's enemies. Once again Maimonides brings punishment into the picture which, as we have seen, is identified with a pre-eternal will that precludes reactions to temporal events. The rendering of "rising" as a punitive measure by God stimulates the qualified reader to draw on those associations intended to challenge the literalist view of a personal providential God, associations such as man's insignificance, pre-eternal will, and modelessness.[9] The materialization of the divine decree conveyed by "rising" in these verses will then be perceived as a kind of unfolding of primeval will, rather than a momentary response that would imply change in the divine essence.

The prooftext singled out to establish this second meaning is 1 Samuel 22:8, "That my son hath made my servant rise up against me." This verse is the conclusion to Saul's castigation of his entourage for not having divulged to him Jonathan's infidelity in assisting and forming an alliance with David. The "rising" in this instance is not to be taken literally, but rather is to be read in the sense that "As one who decides to do something marks his impulse to do it by rising, so whoever has revolted over some matter is said to rise up." Once this verse is examined in its original setting, the reader will be struck by the transitive (causative) form of the term—Saul's son has *caused* David to rise up against him. The peculiar choice of a transitive rather than an intransitive action of rising may prompt the reader to question further what it is that Jonathan is being accused of. Surely, in Saul's perception at least, David had already risen up against him and become his nemesis prior to any pact with Jonathan. The implication, therefore, is that since David had already assumed his adversarial position, Jonathan's role serves to reinforce that position.[10] Maimonides has carefully chosen a verse where the term "rising" suggests a relationship that already exists and is being perpetuated. This is the sense that would most approximate any divine "rising" as a manifestation of what has always been the case, as opposed to an "impulse" marked by abrupt change. It will come as no surprise, then, that with respect to God this word "denotes the execution of God's decree against a people deserving punishment," since punishment has become the code word for "pre-eternal will." God's impulse is always extant and is not conditioned by temporal events as man's is. Though the literal gives way to the metaphorical to convey human impulse, divine impulse is, in effect, an oxymoron. When God is the subject, the term "rising," therefore, must surrender both its literal and metaphorical nuances in favor of a wholly deconstructed meaning consistent with the language of negative theology.[11] The fickleness of human activity implied by 1 Samuel 22:8 forces the reader to investigate its context, negate that implication, and substitute the constancy of the divine character.

The context of the two verses cited as incorporating the sense of 1 Samuel 22:8 to "figuratively denote the execution of God's decree against a people" further substantiates the analysis thus far. Firstly, both Amos 7:9, "And I will rise against the house of Jeroboam," and Isaiah 31:2, "But He will rise against the house of the evil doers," are declarations of divine retribution for sin. Secondly, the punitive response is presented as the consequence of iniquity, the prevention of which requires some form of intervention. In the case of Amos, the natural flow of punishment is preceded by the withdrawal of such intervention—"I will no longer pardon them" (7:8)— allowing, so to speak, nature to take its course. The very same sentiment is expressed by Isaiah immediately prior to the cited text: ". . . and He brought evil and His words He did not retract" (31:2).[12] Unless there is "pardon" or "retraction," corruption and evil are automatically followed by disaster. Those verses that are indications of a natural law of governance are selectively introduced to sustain the truth of a philosophically immutable God, while at the same time catering to the sensibilities of the common religious devotee, who can read these very same verses and hold fast to a responsive God.

The chapter then concludes with a general rabbinic pronouncement that is evinced as proof for the rabbis' unmitigated disavowal of a God who bears corporeal traits.[13] The argument advanced in the chapter against a literal reading of the term "rising" with respect to God is said to be in accord with the rabbinic adage, "In the upper world there is neither sitting or standing."[14] Maimonides is aware that the term "rising" does not appear in this statement, and therefore he explains his peculiar choice of prooftext in a chapter whose key term is "rising,' saying "*standing* sometimes occurs in the sense of *rising*." The careful reader is alerted to the usage of this quote as a pretext for something other than its purported one by its wholly inappropriate reference. There happens to be a chapter dedicated to the term *sitting* (I:11) and one to *standing* (I:13), both of which appear in this and both of which proffer figurative meanings to dispel any traces of anthropomorphism as does chapter 12. Why then would Maimonides situate this prooftext in a chapter that lacks the terms of the prooftext, thereby compelling his defense of a weak tactic with the statement that "*standing* sometimes occurs in the sense of *rising*," when chapters 11 or 13 would have been far more welcoming of its significance?

Piqued by the problematics of inclusion in a chapter where it doesn't belong, the reader is impelled to subject the prooftext to closer scrutiny within its own talmudic context. This reveals an incongruity of a more serious nature, since it involves one of substance rather than one of mere form. The statement is one exclaimed by Aher (the rabbi who succumbed to some form of heresy as a result of his journey into the mystical realm of the Pardes) in shock at the sight of the angel Metatron being granted permission "to sit and write down the merits of Israel." To Aher this vision was contrary to the tradition, in Maimonides' version, that "on high there is no sitting and no standing and no division and no junction."[15] This, therefore, leads Aher to the possibility that there exist two godheads. Retrieval of this rabbinic prooftext within its original context yields an incongruity with the text of which it is supportive. Maimonides has purportedly discovered a rabbinic tradition inveighing against divine anthropomorphism, when in reality the subject of this tradition is not God but an angel.[16] The combination of a contrived placement, along with decontextualizing of a source with which Maimonides was surely familiar, argues in favor of authorial design on his part rather than error or sloppiness. Barring the latter, the reader must then proceed to discern the esoteric object of that design.

The discrepancy between the subject of Aher's astonishment (angels) and that of the chapter in the *Guide* that appeals to it as its chief supportive text (namely, God) is meant to be discovered by the privileged few. The subterfuge is necessary, since Maimonides is continuing to elaborate his view on providence that has surfaced in the previous chapters and from which the unphilosophical masses must be shielded. Once "angel" enters the scene, attention is directed toward the role assigned to angels by Maimonides as the bearers of divine providence in the sublunar world. Whenever actions are attributed to God in the Bible or elsewhere, one must always read in "angels," "for you never find therein that an act was performed by God otherwise than *through an angel*" (*GP*, II:6, p. 262). The subject of angels connotes a distancing of God from worldly affairs; they stand between God and the world, "for the Law does not deny the fact that He, may He be exalted, governs that which exists through the intermediation of the *angels*."[17] Angels are identified with separate intellects—"[T]he angels too are not endowed with bodies but are intellects separate from matter" (*GP*, I:49, p. 108)—and therefore constitute the fount of providence for the lower world. Maimonides' theory of angels, properly understood, precludes any immediate and direct divine presence that is accountable for the goings-on of this world. The only point of disagreement on this issue with Aristotle is with respect to the origins of the separate intellects, not with respect to the ongoing relationship of these intellects to the world: "There is then nothing in what Aristotle for his part has said about this subject that is not in agreement with the Law . . . we ourselves believe . . . that it was He who created the separate intellects and the spheres *and put in them the governing forces.* As to this we do disagree with him" (*GP,* II:6, p. 265).

Though the Maimonidean metaphor "angels" casts such a wide net as to represent virtually every aspect of natural causation[18] within the hierarchical design of governance, its symbolization of separate intellects is accentuated to the point of near exclusivity. Firstly, within the providential schema, they occupy the position of closest proximity to the originating will of the universe. The stream of governance flows down from the ultimate source of being to the intellects and subsequently to the spheres ending at the world of generation and corruption (*GP,* II:11, pp. 274–75). When separate intellects are first introduced by the *Guide* as the "face" *(panim)* denied to Moses in favor of the more remote "back" of God, they are appropriately designated so in virtue of the "power of the providence constantly watching over them" (*GP,* II:37, p. 86). The chapter on "face" then concludes with its connotation of "protection and providence," so that the verse "The Lord bear his face to thee and give thee peace" (Num. 6:26) "refers to His making providence accompany us" (*GP,* I:37, p. 87). It is via the face/separate intellect that this is accomplished.

Secondly, and more critically, angels are frequently distinguished as uniquely signifying separate intellects from among the host of other significations they may bear. The following assertions in the *Guide* serve to forge the identity between angels and intellects within the context of providence and governance:

1. At the beginning of II:6, Maimonides equates the characterization of God as *Elohim of the Elohim* or "the deity of the angels" in contrast to the *Lord of Lords* as "the Master of the spheres and the stars." *Angels* here clearly refer to the separate intellects.
2. This meaning of *Elohim of Elohim* is reinforced by further elucidation as the "Judge of the judges, *I mean to say of the angels*, and the Master of the sphere." Once again the contrast is between "angels" and "spheres," which can also be considered angels in other contexts.

3. The point of disagreement between Maimonides and Aristotle is characterized as one of terminology, "for he speaks of separate intellects and we speak of *angels*" (*GP,* I:37 p. 262).

4. The subject matter of his exposition in II:6 restricts the meaning of angels to separate intellects: "Now, our discourse here shall only deal with the angels who are separate intellects. For our Law does not deny the fact that He, may He be exalted, governs that which exists here through the intermediation of the angels" (*GP,* I:37, p. 262).

5. In the conclusion of II:10, a crucial chapter for explicating the vision of Jacob's ladder, all of existence is divided into three categories: "the separate intellects, *which are the angels;* the second, the bodies of the spheres; the third, first matter."

6. In the Mishneh Torah a series of ten "angels" constitutes the hierarchy of separate intellects, whereas the spheres and elements are not designated as *angels.*[19]

Armed with this notion of governance, of which angels are representative, the reader returns to our chapter and ponders the excerpt from the talmudic tractate *Hagigah* further. Since Maimonides' underlying concern in this chapter is for divine providence, as we have gleaned from all the verses quoted, and since providence is carried out via the agency of angels, it makes perfect sense to reference a text regarding angels. The question must still be posed as to what exactly are the implications of this reference now that we are cognizant of its true subject matter. Not only is God immutable and unchanging in the face of an ever-changing world, but so are the angels or the forces governing that world. Transitional movements such as standing and sitting are typical of corporeal beings, but wholly inappropriate when discussing incorporeal and static existents such as angels (intellects).

Once attuned to the subtext of angels, the reader is beckoned, so to speak, to search out reflections on the topic elsewhere, and specifically the mechanism of governance and its characterization as an "overflow." The choice of metaphor is prompted by the imaging of actions of a separate intellect that "spring forth from all directions and constantly irrigates all the directions" (*GP,* II:12, p. 279). There is no personal contact or indeed any direct consciousness of particulars below, but rather "*its action is constant* as long as something has been prepared so that it is receptive of the permanently existing action which has been interpreted as an overflow" (*GP,* II:12, p. 279). The waters of governance flow downward in a constant stream bearing no particular destination. The reception of that flow is a factor of the preparation initiated from below. I merely wish to demonstrate at this juncture what the chapter in the *Guide* is suggestive of and in what directions it stimulates the reader to follow. The metaphorical representation of a separate intellect's relationship with the world as "overflow" leads inevitably to its identification in III:17 as best capturing the theory of providence to which Maimonides subscribes: *"[D]ivine providence is consequent upon the divine overflow*; and the species with which this intellectual overflow is united so that it became endowed with intellect and so that everything that is disclosed to a being endowed with the intellect was disclosed to it, *is the one accompanied by divine providence* which appraises all its actions from the point of view of reward and punishment."[20] The flow of providence radiates down with no specific target, and the means by which man taps into that flow is this intellect. All others who fail to exploit this intellectual technique are abandoned and exposed to an impersonal law of nature; they are "given over to whatever may happen to befall them. For there is nothing to protect them against whatever may occur; for they are like one walking in darkness, whose destruction is assured." Their fate accords with that distant pre-eternal will that preprogrammed these ground rules into the fabric of the world.

The full import of this excerpt cannot be appreciated without, I believe, taking into consideration the specific angel whom Aher encounters— Metatron.[21] It is highly probable, as Gershom Scholem has pointed out, that Metatron warrants the title of "Prince of the World" *(sar ha'olam)* and that those passages in the Talmud referring to the *sar ha'olam* allude to this particular angel. It is also the case that Maimonides explicitly identifies the "prince of the world" with the Active Intellect from whose act all the forms derive (*GP,* II:6, p. 264). The Active Intellect is that force or angel under whose governance the sublunar world is subsumed.[22] The character of Metatron, therefore, is essential to any message regarding providence. As has been noted, the governance exercised by the intellect is constant and unfaltering. The qualified disciple of Maimonides, who is both philosophically adept and a proficient talmudist, will be led to a key verse in the *Guide* that is proffered as an apt description of the intellect's activities and that, in its talmudic context, is an allusion to the angel Metatron. *GP,* II:7 cites Exodus 23:21—"Take heed of him and hearken unto his voice; be not rebellious against him; for he will not pardon your transgression; *for my*

name is in him"—as supportive of the supposition that though the intellects apprehend their acts and possess "free choice with regard to the governance committed to them," they "always do that which is good, and only
that which is good with them . . . and all that they have exists always in
perfection and in actu since they have come into existence" (*GP,* II:6, p.
266). Clearly this concept of "free choice" is not consonant with a human
understanding of the term, since it is constrained to "always do that which
is good." The Talmud locates Metatron as the object of "My name is in
him," rendering it a prooftext for the proposition that "his name is identical
with his master's name."[23] Thus when the trained eye assimilates this verse,
it is infused with its rabbinic exegesis to yield the Metatron/Active Intellect
nexus.

Once again the eternal natural law of governance that was reflected in
the verses cited previously, Amos 7:8 and Isaiah 31:2, is attributed to its
source, the Active Intellect. Just as the absence of "pardon" (Amos) or
"retraction" (Isaiah) captured the inevitable consequences of iniquity in
accordance with the eternal will of God, so the absence of "pardon" is the
motivating factor stipulated by Exodus 23:21 for virtuous behavior. The
accomplished reader, having discerned Metatron's role as pivotal to the
Hagigah prooftext, then marshals his talmudic and biblical expertise along
with a thorough familiarity with the *Guide* as a whole to construct the following précis on providence encoded in this chapter:

1. *Biblical verses* denoting punishment = pre-eternal unchanging will
   of God.
2. Ruling out of "pardon" or forgiveness = code for impersonal in-
   frangible laws of governance initially set in motion by God.
3. Metatron = Prince of the World = Active Intellect.
4. God cedes governance of day-to-day affairs of world to Active Intellect.
5. Active Intellect operates via a constant inflexible overflow to the
   world.
6. Providence is *acquired* by man via the intellect and is not *endowed*
   from above.[24]
7. Failure to attain intellectual objectives = abandonment.

For obvious reasons, overt pronouncement of this radical theory on
providence is precluded as a viable communicative method.

There is one more aspect of the Aher/Metatron confrontation I believe Maimonides intends his learned audience to take note of. Metatron is said to be seated and occupied with "recording the merits of Israel." This image fits neatly into the logic of the metaphor as we have presented it thus far. Providence only accompanies those who have qualified intellectually to be those "with whom something of this overflow is united" (*GP,* III:17, p. 474). It seems also, from the analysis of the story of Job (*GP,* III:22, pp. 22–23), that wisdom is the only shield against calamity and misfortune, not moral virtue and righteousness. The "recording of merits" can only be an accounting for the sake of exercising providential beneficence to which, we have seen, only the perfected intellect can aspire. The bizarre portrait of Metatron tallying up merits conveys some sense of the philosophical notion as to what constitutes the point of intersection between man and the Active Intellect. That point can only be "merit" and, as defined in the Maimonidean system, that merit can only consist of intellect.

Aher's error can be brought into sharper focus if his intellectual odyssey is contrasted with that of his polar opposite, Moses. The latter may have initially sought the same ends as the former, but succeeded where Aher failed by first asking the proper questions. Moses, unlike Aher, cautiously requests that he be granted knowledge of God's "glory" *(kavod)* and "ways." The pause before advancing a request is in keeping with Moses' behavior at his first encounter with God, where the hiding of his face from the glare of the burning bush is an act of intellectual self-restraint (*GP,* I:5, p. 29). Acknowledgment of his own limitations allows Moses safe passage toward human perfection. Apprehension of God's *kavod*, equated with "His essence and true reality," is denied as being outside the bounds of human capabilities, while knowledge of His "ways," or attributes of actions, is granted as an attainable object of human contemplation (*GP,* I:54, pp. 123–28). The two responses find their expression in the anatomical gesture made by God of revealing His back *('ahor)* and concealing His face *(panim)*. The former signifies "all things created by me" (*GP,* I:38, p. 87), while the latter is "the true reality of My existence as it veritably is" (*GP,* I:37, p. 86). More importantly, for our context, is the added signification given to *panim* by Onkelos and cited approvingly by Maimonides, as the "great created beings which man cannot apprehend as they really are. *These are the separate intellects*" (*GP,* I:37, p. 86).

Aher, on the other hand, stumbles in a brazen attempt to exceed the human boundaries of reason. His lack of discipline, cautious reflection, and self-restraint result in a disastrous foray into a domain that is impenetrable to human advances (*GP,* I:32, pp. 68–69). The impatient arrogance of grasping the ungraspable lands Aher and his ilk, according to Maimonides, among those who are considered by the Sages as unworthy of ever having been born, those who gaze at "what is above and what is below, what is in front *(lifnim)* and what is in back *(le'ahor)*" (*GP,* p. 70, citing B.T., *Hagigah* 116). This rabbinic condemnation of speculative gluttony resonates with the precise objectives sought by Moses of *panim* and *'ahor.* Maimonides' interpretation of the revelatory interchange between Moses and God whereby *panim* was denied and *'ahor* granted is instructive to the reading of the Sages in *Hagigah.* What they abhor is an intellectual quest for a lethal combination of the two objectives signified by *panim* and *'ahor.* The latter is within reach, but when scrutinized in conjunction with the transcendent *panim,* who are the separate intellects, the speculative exercise deteriorates into the confused heresy of Aher. The consequences are most severe for the issue of providence, since the undiluted vision of *'ahor* entailed for Moses "the display to him of all existing things . . . I mean that he will apprehend this nature and the way they are mutually connected so that He will know how He governs them in general and in detail" (*GP,* I:54, p. 124). The conflation of the search for *'ahor* and *panim* by Aher resulted in the former being violated by the latter and generating a corrupt view on the source and mechanics of governance in the world. The final irony of the pariah existence Elisha ben Abuyah leads after his "heresy" is captured by the very name he is saddled with, Aher, echoing as it does the *'ahor* of ultimate human wisdom. Its ontological signification translates existentially into alienation from God, since it connotes "the beings from which I have, as it were, turned away and upon which, speaking in parables, I have turned my back, because of their remoteness from the existence of God, may He be exalted" (*GP,* I:37, p. 86).

Once all these associations and intratextual correlates are consolidated, the following Maimonidean exegesis of the Aher/Metatron episode emerges:

1. Aher's journey leads him into the Pardes, identified by Maimonides as the disciplines of physics and metaphysics.[25] This is not a mystical but a rational journey.

2. Aher, for Maimonides, is the archetype of the most egregious of human sins—aspiring to cognize things beyond human apprehension and being too hasty in the meticulous art of logical demonstration. Those guilty of this are said to have joined the company of Elisha/Aher.[26] Aher may have strained to grasp the mechanics of

divine providence, which "is not the same as the notion of our providence nor is the notion of His governance of the things created by
Him the same as the notion of our governance of that which we
govern" (*GP,* III:23, p. 496). Since the "word 'providence' is used
equivocally when applied to what we are provident about *and to
that of which it is said that He,* may be exalted, is provident with
regard to it" (*GP,* III:21, p. 484), human understanding of this subject matter is unattainable.

3. Aher's encounter with Metatron is the symbolic representation of
   the undue celerity with which he arrived at the Active Intellect in
   his quest to grasp providence.

4. Aher's error is the very perception of the intellect seated in an
   adjudicatory capacity. The Active Intellect is seen as divorced from
   the ultimate immutable source of being and acting independently
   and responsively in governing the world. Aher has lost sight of the
   notion that God is the ultimate form of the world. Not only is God
   a necessary existent but He is "the efficient cause of the world, its
   form and its end" (*GP,* I:69, p. 167). Aher has stopped short of this
   necessary existence and therefore becomes oblivious to what ultimately sustains the existence of this intellect. For Aher, there is a
   rupture between the Creator, who is "that upon which the existence and stability of every form in the world ultimately reposes
   and by which they are constituted" (*GP,* I:69, p. 167), and the forms
   of the world.

5. Aher, in his haste, has failed to comprehend the Active Intellect's
   modus operandi by ignoring the ramifications of the verse "My
   name is in him." In Maimonides' exposition of divine appellations,
   this verse (Exod. 23:21) is interpreted to mean "that he is an instrument of My will and volition. I shall make this statement clear
   when speaking of the equivocality of *angel*" (*GP,* I:64, p. 156).
   The reference is to his bone of contention with Aristotle and
   Maimonides' insistence that "it was He who created the intellects
   and the spheres and put in them the governing forces."[27] The chain
   of being must be linked back to its ultimate source. The name of *I
   Am That I Am* initially revealed to Moses is obscured to Aher. He
   has failed to grasp that name, which captures the essence of an
   "existent that is the existent, or the necessarily existent" (*GP,* I:63,
   p. 155), from whom the intellects draw their life force.

6. The flogging of Metatron demonstrates the notion above conveyed by "My name is in him." Ultimately all existents must be traced back to the Creator.

7. This parable of an intellectual quest whose success is undermined by fallacious reasoning and premature conclusions finds its denouement in the scene where a heavenly voice *(bat qol)* disqualifies Aher from the rehabilitative process of repentance. Convinced of his inexorable damnation, he surrenders himself to hedonism. Since a *bat qol* is of inferior quality when addressing "an individual who is not prepared for prophecy"(*GP,* II:42, p. 390), the message may be somewhat misconceived. Repentance is remedial for intellectual failure, as well as moral, as sin can result "by *professing an opinion* or a moral quality *that is not preferable in truth.* . . . If then the individual believed that this fracture can never be remedied, he would persist in his error and sometimes perhaps disobey even more because of the fact that no stratagem remains at his disposal" (*GP,* III:37, p. 540). This theory generated by repentance is the antidote to the fatal situation Aher sees himself consigned to (viz., the erasure of his merits). As we have seen, repentance promotes human initiative as the means to tap into providence, since the overflow itself is a constant dispassionate current of governance. Repentance epitomizes the "radical responsibility," as Jerome Gellman has coined it, implicit in Maimonides' theory, which is the sole route of divine providence.[28] Aher's interpretation of the heavenly voice constitutes a misinformed rejection of this worldview.[29]

I:13   "Standing on the Mount of Olives": The Intellectualization of a Messianic Vision

This chapter concerns itself with the term "standing" *('amidah)* and, as in the previous two chapters, it always assumes its metaphorical sense of "stable, durable, and unchanged" with reference to God. There is a progressive reinforcement of divine immutability that by now signals the reader to scrutinize the prooftexts for the purpose of ferreting out further consequences this may have on commonly accepted principles of religious tradition. The consistent theme in the chapters under discussion is the constraints a philosophically rigorous position on immutability imposes on divine providence.

The first verse among the series of verses appealed to in establishing the metaphorical sense of "stable and durable" that relates in some fashion to God is Psalm 111:3, "His righteousness *(tsedaqah)* standeth for ever." Those acquainted with the entire corpus of the *Guide* will be stimulated by the key term *tsedaqah* to reexamine the section in III:53 that justifies God's characterization as a *tsaddiq* (righteousness). It is befitting "because of His mercy toward the weak—*I refer to the governance of the living being by means of its forces*" (*GP,* p. 632). Elsewhere in the *Guide,* when surveying the full implications of the term "angel," these "forces" that govern living beings are located in an "angel": "[E]very force appertaining to bodily forces is an angel . . ." (*GP,* II:16, p. 264). All these individual microforces are themselves ultimately governed by that macroforce known as the Prince of the World/Active Intellect. *Tsaddiq,* as descriptive of God, is of course an "attribute of action" (*GP,* p. 262) and, by virtue of these assertions, is associated with the source of all living beings' governing force—the Active Intellect. Furthermore, in his discussion of the fifth opinion on providence ascribed to "the opinion of our Law," all human and animal activity is rooted in the individual will. This phenomenon itself derives from that pre-eternal will: "And He has willed it so; I mean to say that *it comes from His eternal volition in the eternity a parte ante* that all animals should move in virtue of their will and that man should have the ability to do whatever he wills or chooses among the things concerning which he has the ability to act" (*GP,* III:17, p. 469). The instrument of that volition is, as we have seen, that existent in which "His name" is embedded ("For my Name is in him" [Exod. 23:21]) or Metatron/Active Intellect. Thus the ethical tenor of Psalm 111:3 accedes to a metaphysical statement concerning the nature and manner of God's governance as follows:

1. *"His righteousness"* = attribute of action as manifest via the all-encompassing seat of governance for living beings—Active Intellect.
2. *"Standeth for-ever"* = that "once removed" governance is a constant variable operating pursuant to an originating distant will that generated the process with an act of will in eternity *a parte ante.*

The verse then chosen as illustrative of a God-referenced "standing" in the sense of being stable and unchanged expresses a vision of Zechariah: "And His feet shall stand in that day upon the Mount of Olives" (14:4). God does not possess limbs enabling a physical motion, and therefore the verse is transfigured to mean "his intermediate causes, I mean His effects, shall be established."[30] This verse is an apocalyptic prophecy that heralds the messianic era culminating in the universal acknowledgment of the nature of God in verse 9: "In that day shall the Lord be one and His name one." *"That day"* of verse 9 is the outgrowth of *"that day"* in verse 4. Verse 4 appears again in the chapter dedicated to the term *"foot"* (cause) where, in the same vein, "it signifies thereby the establishment of the things He has caused. I mean of the wonders that will then become manifest at that place and of which God may He be exalted is the cause" (*GP,* p. 59). Zechariah's vision then is one of cognitive achievement; it predicts an era when the true cause/effect relationship between God and the world will be grasped by mankind in toto.[31] The replacement of *"feet"* with "causes" and that of "will stand" with "stable and unchanging" produces a prediction of public cognitive achievement—*that day* will arrive when the chain of causation will be perceived for what it is: constant, enduring, and unchanging.

The importance of this realization lies in the authentic cognition of God's nature that it entails. The loss of a responsive interventionist God who lurks behind every material cause, thereby violating the fundamentals of unity and immutability, is more than compensated for by the cognitive preservation of those fundamentals, regardless of His remoteness in the chain of being that results. The biblical context of Zechariah's vision, molded by Maimonidean hermeneutics, further substantiates the intellectualist messianism it preaches. The cataclysmic event on the Mount of Olives paves the way for the universal declaration of verse 9, "the Lord shall be one, and His name one." According to Maimonides this is a corrective to the ignorant position that ascribes all actions directly to God and thereby has "produced in the fantasy of some men the thought that He has many attributes just as there is a multiplicity of actions from which these names derive" (*GP,* I:61, p. 148). The reversion to the invocation of one divine name "is indicative only of the essence and . . . is not derivative" (*GP,* I:61, p. 148). Traditional notions of a directly providential Godhead impede intellectual access to the divine essence, since they attribute ongoing governance to Him instead of its proper locus—the Active Intellect. The unity of God is perpetually under attack as long as man perceives His direct involvement with all worldly affairs, inviting a portrait of a polymorphous divine personality.

Demonstrative of this reading of the unification of the name expressed by Zechariah 14:9 is a reference to *Pirke de Rabbi Eliezer* that states: "Before the world was created, there were only the Holy One, blessed be He, and His name" (*GP,* I:61, p. 149). In primordial time God could not be associated with anything outside his own essence, and therefore there could be no mistaking the one articulated name that is bereft of all derivation and "gives a clear unequivocal indication of His essence" (*GP,* p. 147). The utopia of the messianic period is, for Maimonides, a reversion back to that pristine time when one could "envisage His essence as it is when divested and stripped of all actions and He no longer has a derived name in any respect whatever, but only one original name that indicates His essence" (*GP,* p. 149). This message from *Pirke de Rabbi Eliezer* is, for Maimonides, significant in that one must be transported to a time that is logically prior to creation for an ideal apprehension of God. The intellectualist goal of the messianic epoch is to recapture that Being who antedates the world. Of course, this can only be accomplished by envisioning a God who is a self-contained existence wholly detached from the world. One must dispel all traditional conceptions of providence, as they only serve to strengthen the ties between God and the world and disrupt the process of unification. The providential God of history reflects a variegated character prone to be quali-fied by attributes as a result of imputing all actions to Him. The God who is anterior to creation, and therefore transcends history, is incapable of being considered "active" except in the sense of pure intellectual activity or thought thinking itself, since there would be no external phenomena to which any act could correspond. The messianic era allows for the total abstraction of God from the world.

The chapter then concludes with further biblical examples of *stand* as "permanent," this time the references being to Moses. Deuteronomy 5:28, "But as for thee, stand thou here by Me," and Deuteronomy 5:5, "I stood between the Lord and you," both represent the durability and stability of Moses' capacity to focus on the ultimate truth of being. Deuteronomy 5:28 designates the rank of one from whom these truths are never concealed and who lives in "unceasing light" (*GP,* introduction, p. 7). This verse also ap-pears in III:51 as representative of that supreme state of intellectual con-centration in which one is outwardly engaged in human social activity, while inwardly the mind is wholly oriented toward God's presence. What is vital for our discussion is the providential effect this state of "union of intel-lects" has on those who achieve it: "[T]hese four [Patriarchs and Moses] were in a permanent state of extreme perfection in the eyes of God and . . . his providence watched over them continually even while they were en-gaged in increasing their fortune. . . ."[32] This very same chapter digresses somewhat to expound at length on the theory "that providence watches over everyone with intellect proportionately to the measure of his intellect" (*GP,* introduction, p. 7). Moses and the Patriarchs are models of the human, as opposed to divine, initiative requisite for providence:[33] "The providence of God, may He be exalted, is constantly watching over *those who have obtained this overflow*, which is permitted to *everyone who makes efforts with a view to obtaining it*" (*GP,* III:51, p. 625). These outstanding individuals are delivered from "the sea of chance" (*GP,* p. 625), because they have independently plugged into the intellectual overflow. The link to Zechariah's redemptive forecast above is the role these four were qualified to play in the formation of a religious community by virtue of their superior intellect: "Thus it has become clear to you that the end of all their efforts was to spread the doctrine of *the unity of the Name* in the world" (*GP,* p. 625). Those who have already aspired to the *vita contemplativa* endemic to the messianic community during conventional times are those who have grasped the philosophical import of "the unity of the Name." No more suitable candidates could be found, therefore, to indoctrinate mankind with this message which, in turn, escalates the arrival of the messianic era.[34]

The carefully crafted argument concerning providence submerged in the biblical prooftexts of chapter 13 can be synopsized as in the accompanying table.

"standing" *('amidah)* = "stable, durable, unchanged"

⇓

Prooftext

⇓

"His righteousness *(tsidqato)* standeth forever" (Ps. 3:3)

⇓

Links

⇓

"Tsaddiq" of *GP,* III:53 as descriptive of God = "forces governing living beings"
"Forces" = "angels" = Active Intellect (*GP,* II:6)

⇓

Prooftext

⇓

"And His feet shall stand that day upon the Mount of Olives" (Zech. 14:4)
= "intermediate affects shall be established"

"Foot" of *GP,* I:28 = "causation" => process of causation initiated by God will be
acknowledged (Zech. 14:4)

⇓

"That day" (Zech. 14:4) = "That day" (Zech. 14:9) = messianic age

⇓

"Lord shall be one and His name one" (Zech. 14:9) = articulated name (*GP,* I:61) =
essential, not derivative. No confusion with attributes of action

Pirke de Rabbi Eliezer—primordial existence of God prior to creation
—no attributes of action.

Cognition of God in messianic times = restoration of "name" of God detached from
world unfettered by attributes arising out of traditional belief in providence

⇓

Prooftext

⇓

"But as for thee stand thou here by Me" (Deut.5:28) = Moses
= permanent state of all-consuming mental concentration

⇓

Association

⇓

GP, III:51—Union of intellects = providence gained by intellectual human effort

⇓

Spread of Unity of Name among mankind

I:14 "Adam"—Situating Man in the Providential Scheme

It has already been noted by several of the medieval commentators that chapter 14 seems out of sequence.[35] This chapter deals with the equivocality of the term *adam,* and obviously does not pose the same anthropomorphic dilemma as do the terms in Maimonides' previous six chapters. As has also been noted, the chapter commences with the unique introductory formula, "The equivocality of the word."[36] I believe that the general theory on providence progressively developed thus far lends a certain logic to the order of this chapter. The idea of the commonly accepted focus of God's attention is now challenged. The highly selective use of biblical texts to distinguish the various senses of the term *adam* is unified to undermine the simplistic theory of providence. A construct of an ideal singular man as the true subject of divine providence in contradistinction to general mankind will provide its proper context at this juncture.

All six verses quoted in chapter 14 for the various usages of *adam* display a common denigrating attitude toward man in general. The first verse, "My spirit shall not abide in man" (Gen. 6:3), is the overriding principle of the chapter. The chapter that addresses the term "spirit" *(ruach)* *(GP,* I:40) exclusively assigns to it two possible meanings when applied to God:

1. "the divine intellectual overflow that overflows to the prophets and in virtue of which they prophesy" (*GP,* I:40, p. 90), and
2. "purpose and will."

The verse cited, which incorporates the second meaning, "Who hath comprehended the air *(ruach)* of the Lord" (Isa. 40:13), is translated into a pointed appeal that "he who knows the ordering of His will or apprehends this governance of that which exists as it really is, should teach us about it . . ." (*GP,* I:40, p. 90). That "teaching," I suggest, is to be extracted from Genesis 6:3. Since Maimonides admits of no exceptions in the use of the term *ruach* when God is referenced, its use in Genesis 6:3 must be confined to one of the two meanings posited by *GP,* I:40. As the term *adam* in this verse designates the species and not the individual, both meanings could coexist as complementary to each other. The divine intellectual overflow does not, of course, reach the species as a whole, since the vast majority never comes close to a prophetic experience.[37] It is also the case that exclusion from the divine intellectual overflow is synonymous with absence from the divine agenda of will and governance. The barrier to the divine over-flow can be found in the second half of the same verse, "since he too is flesh."[38] The ingredient of flesh poses an obstacle to that overflow.

The next verse, "Who knoweth the spirit of the sons of man" (Eccles. 3:21), can only be fully appreciated in its continuing context of "And the spirit of animals descends to the earth." This is a rhetorical query simply reinforcing the conclusions reached in the preceding verse, which fail to distinguish between the fate of man and beast: "[T]hey have one and the same fate[;] as the one dies so does the other and *both have the same spirit (ruach):* man has no superiority over beast. . . ." The general principle de-lineated in Genesis 6:3 is buttressed by the pessimistic expression of a shared destiny between man and beast. The "flesh" of Genesis 6:3 lands him in the company of the beasts, which are clearly outside the jurisdiction of divine providence (*GP,* p. 471). The third verse is simply the conclusion of verse 3:19 in Ecclesiastes: "So that man hath no preeminence above a beast." If the sum total of man is comprised of his "flesh," then he becomes an inte-gral part of the animal kingdom lacking in the protection of divine gover-nance.

The next designation selected for *adam* is the masses, "as distinguished from the elite," in support of which Psalm 49:3 is cited. It apparently juxta-poses the two: "Both the sons of man *(benei adam)* and the sons of an [outstanding] individual *(benei ish)*."

The contrast of *adam* and *ish* is taken as one between the multitude and the unique within the species of man. In its original setting, Psalm 49:3 constitutes a call to all mankind to heed the teachings of the verses that follow, climaxing in the abysmal assessment of Psalm 49:13 (repeated with a slight variation in v. 21) that "*adam*, unable to dwell in dignity, is like the beasts that speak not." The thematic comparison of man and beast is ex-tended to individuate the type of man from the "species." The very same verse is emblematic of the state primordial man plunged into as a result of his original sin. The distraction from the true objects of intellectual appre-hension to inferior levels of knowledge demanded the cessation of that which is the source of divine providence: "For the intellect that God made overflow unto man and that is the latter's ultimate perfection, was that which Adam had been provided with before he disobeyed" (*GP,* I:2, p. 24). The natural outcome, then, is abandonment to the forces of nature and being relegated to the level of beast conveyed by Psalm 49:13: "And God reduced him, with respect to his food and most of his circumstances to the level of the beast" (*GP,* p. 26). I would venture to suggest that the designation of *adam* as multitude and *ish* as elite in v. 3, and not vice versa, was based on its consistency with the usage of *adam* in v. 13 which, for Maimonides, would be decisive as the only credible option.[39] The elite could not possibly bear any resemblance to the beast.

The chapter concludes with two further illustrations of the multitudinous sense of *adam,* both of which, I believe, are intended to be read in conjunction, providing the rationale for God's judgment of Genesis 6:3 "My spirit shall not abide in man." The latter is the consequence of the next verse cited: "The sons of Elohim saw the daughters of man" (6:2). Here we are obligated to resort to the lexicon Maimonides has compiled so that the verse can unfold as a core component of this chapter's covert theme. The term *elohim* is an equivocal one determined by its particular context as either the Deity, or the angels, or the rulers governing cities (*GP,* I:2, p. 23). Clearly, for Maimonides, the context of Genesis 6:2 allows only for the last option. This is reinforced by the translation of the Targum Onkelos, to whose authority Maimonides defers in establishing the sense of "rulers" within the verse "And ye shall be as Elohim, knowing good and evil" (Gen. 3:5). The identical Aramaic term indicating "rulers" in Genesis 3:5 *(ravrivaya)* is offered in 6:2 for *elohim.* The word "son" can also be a euphemism for a student, for "whoever instructs an individual in some matter and teaches him an opinion, has, as far as his being provided with this opinion is concerned, as it were engendered that individual. In this sense the prophet's disciples were called *sons of the prophets . . .*" (*GP,* I:7, p. 32). *Elohim,* in the parable of the Garden of Eden (*GP,* I:2), is representative of the cognitive deterioration experienced by post-sin man. He slid from an obsession with "truth and falsehood" to "fine and bad" or "generally accepted things," the latter being the domain of rulers and judges, who only exercise their imaginative faculties.[40] The phrase *the sons of Elohim* then can be transfigured to signify those who deviate from the rational faculty and become disciples of the imaginative.[41] There is a natural attraction between these individuals and the masses *(daughters of man)* whose *Weltanschauung* is defined by the imagination.[42] *Adam* (multitude) forms the constituency of *elohim* (rulers) in their mutual affiliation with the world of the imagination.

The final verse in the chapter is incomprehensible without conjoining it to the preceding verse, Genesis 6:2. Psalm 82:7, "Nevertheless you shall die as man," is directed to those who are addressed by God in the previous verse as "You are gods *(elohim)* and all of you sons of the Most High *(benei elyon)* " (Ps. 82:6). This is the very same verse that, according to Maimonides, contemplates the most superlative of human beings who "take as his end that which is the end of man *qua* man: namely, solely the mental representation of the intelligibles. . . . These individuals are those who are permanently with God" (*GP*, III:8, pp. 432–33). In what fashion are we to understand that these outstanding individuals share the fate of the multitude as forewarned in Psalm 82:7? The simple answer could be that although they have aspired to such great intellectual heights, nevertheless they must anticipate the ultimate fate of all mankind—physical demise. It seems more likely, though, that the peculiar combination of Genesis 6:2 and Psalm 82:7 envisages a complementary reading, each being an indispensable unit in an integrated whole.[43] The key lies in the apposition of the term "sons" rendered as adherents of a certain school of thought (viz., *sons of the prophets* above). The construct *sons of the Most High* in 82:6 intimates the dominant essential characteristic of this class. The image of procreation is adapted to the world of thought, with the progenitor being the one who imparts knowledge and the progeny the one imbued with knowledge. Consequently *sons of the Most High* are those who have assimilated the array of concepts and beliefs generated by that being which occupies the highest rank in the scale of existence. This is what is definitive and what gains their proximity to that being. Any other ascriptions are mere corollaries of that essential definition, which is where the term *elohim* (gods) in its political sense fits in. The verse then captures the degree of excellence in man that finds its expression in the prophets who are focused on God *("sons of Most High")* yet also engaged in daily affairs of administrating and guiding the general populace (*elohim* = rulers, legislators). The prophet is the embodiment of *elohim* and *benei elyon,* in whom the rational and imaginative faculties operate in tandem. The combined traits of intellectual ardor and social commitment result from an overflow of such intensity "that it moves him of necessity to compose works and to teach" and "compels him to address a call to the people, teach them, and let his own perfection overflow toward them" (*GP*, II:37, p. 375).

The purposefulness in juxtaposing Genesis 6:2 and Psalm 82:7 crystallizes as the overtures to the paradigmatic story of the downfall of the first Adam become more and more obvious. The seduction of the *children of Elohim* (followers of the imagination) by the *daughters of man* (multitude) intervenes as the Achilles' heel of the ideal man *(son of the Most High)* described in Psalm 82:6. The latter, as was the case with primal Adam, is always vulnerable to the lure of the imagination and apt to suffer the same fate: "[W]hen he disobeyed and inclined towards his desires of the imagination and the pleasures of his corporeal senses . . . he was punished by being deprived of that intellectual apprehension" *(GP,* p. 25). Adam's stature deteriorated to the point that he reverted back to origins (the name is derived from earth, *'adamah*), being forced into a dependence on the *adamah* for his sustenance. The expulsion from Eden marks the transition from the contemplative life to an agrarian one, accompanied by an all-consuming preoccupation with the soil. One of the verses quoted by Maimonides confirming Adam's disgrace is Genesis 3:23, "And the Lord God sent him forth from the Garden of Eden, to till the ground *('adamah)*." This drastic corrective measure is also intended to impede access to the "tree of life," thereby alleviating God's concern in Genesis 3:22 that Adam will "take also of the tree of life, and eating live for ever." Within the parameters of the intellectual parable set in the mythic Garden of Eden, the death that is anticipated is the death of ignorance, given the equivocal meanings set out in the chapter on *living:* "[C]orrect opinions are called *life* and false opinions *death.*"[44] Adam is condemned to the death that consists of intellectual impoverishment, while the *tree of life* offers a possible route to regain the life of the intellect it represents.[45] Psalm 82:7, "Nevertheless ye shall die as man," then refers to this death that arises out of the ever-present danger that even those who have achieved the rank of *children of the Most High* must face. Despite their achievement they can always lapse into the world of "bad and fine" *(benei elohim),* losing their unique identities to the amorphous mass of humanity *(benot ha'adam)* (Gen. 6:2), and subsequently be confined to an existence replete with "false opinions" (the death contemplated by Psalm 82:7). The double verse finale of *GP,* I:14 is informed by the Garden of Eden exposition of I:2 which, in turn, is elevated by I:14 from a parochial episode in one man's life to an all-embracing one of the human condition.[46] The intellectual collapse sketched by these final two verses exactly parallels that of *Adam the first,* virtually effacing the literal rendering of that event, as shown in the accompanying table.

I:14		I:2
Ps. 82:6		Garden of Eden
elohim + benei 'elyon		
= ideal of human		Pre-sin Adam—engaged
perfection "permanently with God"		only in "truth + falsehood"
and extraneously involved with man	$\Rightarrow \Rightarrow$	(intellectual perfection)

⇓ ⇓   ⇓ ⇓

Gen. 6:2

benei elohim see benot ha'adam = turn to the world of the imagination enlists them in the ranks of the multitude $\Rightarrow\Rightarrow$	Adam turns to the imagination; involved with "fine + bad"; loses unique status and relegated to rank of animal kingdom

⇓ ⇓   ⇓ ⇓

Ps. 82:7

"die as man" = death of intellectual deterioration $\Rightarrow\Rightarrow$	Expulsion from Garden and access to "tree of life" (intellectual perfection) impeded

The contribution of *GP,* I:14 to the central issue, already detected in this series of lexicographical chapters, is where to situate man within the Maimonidean complex of providence. Essentially, man must transcend the "species" and "multitude" connotations of the generic label he carries (i.e., *adam*) in order to gain any advantage over the animal world in that respect. This serves to illuminate the initial etymology the chapter offers for the term as accorded the first man of history: "[A]s the biblical text states, it is derived from the word *adamah* (earth)." The biblical text in mind is Genesis 2:7, where the derivation of the term is implicit in its specification of earth as the basic formative ingredient of *Adam the first:* "And God formed *(vayitzer)* man *(adam)* from the dust of the earth *(adamah).*" The term for "forming" *(yetzirah)* in this verse is conspicuously excluded from the list of those four words indicative of "the relation between the heaven and God" assembled in *GP,* II:30.[47] The reason for this omission is that *yetzirah* (forming) does not occur in this sense: "[F]or it seems to me that *yesirah* is only applied to shaping and forming a configuration or to one of the other accidents, for shape and configuration are also accidents" (*GP,* p. 358). In contradistinction, a term such as *'assoh* (to make), included in the list, "is applied to the specific forms that were given to them—I mean their natures."[48] Although both terms apply to the creation of man, each constitutes entirely distinct aspects of man—the formal and the material. *Yetzirah* is used in conjunction with the material ingredient *('adamah),* which only accounts for the shape and configuration of man. These accidents of themselves are not constitutive of man qua man as distinct from any other living species. The term that is definitive of man, on the other hand, is "image" *(tselem)* and therefore is quite aptly generated by the activity denoted as *'assoh*

(make): "Let us *make* man in our image, after our likeness (Gen. 1:26)."
While *yetsirah* yields accident, *'assoh* yields essence, since "image" "is
applied to the natural form, I mean to the notion in virtue of which a thing
is constituted as a substance and becomes what it is. It is the true reality of
the thing in so far as the latter is that particular being. In man that notion is
that from which human apprehension derives" (*GP,* I:1, p. 22).

The derivation of the term *adam* from *'adamah* prefaces the entire chapter with its allusions to the creation and accidental attributes of man. Man
shares these attributes with the animals, and so the other meanings of the
chapter evolve naturally, since they never extend beyond that basic animality.
Adam as *'adamah* eludes God's providential concern, since it is that product arising out of a formative act *(yetsirah)* that is devoid of "relation between heaven and God" (*GP,* p. 358). The only other appearance of formation *(yetsirah)* with *'adamah* is in Genesis 2:19, which concerns the genesis
of the animal kingdom: "And the Lord God formed from the earth all the
animals of the field and all the birds of the heaven." Within the creative
process charted as formation *(yetsirah)*, earth *('adamah)* and shape, man
and animal, are replicas of each other. The world of *yetsirah* is populated
by creatures that are severed from the legitimate source of providence. The
creative act of *'assoh,* on the other hand, provides man with the one outlet
to that source—the intellect: "That which was meant by the scriptural diction, 'Let us make man in our image,' was the specific form, which is intellectual apprehension, not the shape and configuration" (*GP,* p. 22). The
preface to chapter 14 leads us to the original biblical text in support of the
adam/adamah etymology, which in turn conjures up all the associations
with *yetsirah, 'assoh,* shape and configuration, and image *(tselem)*. Man is
then bifurcated for the purpose of understanding his position within the
scheme of providence. Encoded in this chapter is the notion that man must
overcome the mundane world of *'adamah* and move to acquire providence
through the exercise of that faculty which is definitive of him as man. Unfortunately, the majority of mankind is mired in the provenance of *adam* as
species and never transcends it sufficiently to be no longer considered *adam*
but rather *ish* (unique individual). This is the reserve of the rare few who
are capable of surmounting all obstacles to survive as man qua man: "It
was because of this something, I mean because of the divine intellect conjoined with man, that it is said of the latter that he is *in the image of God
and in his likeness.*"[49]

I:15   Moses—The Paragon of an Elitist Providence

With chapter I:15 we arrive at the destination of Jacob's ladder. As has been noted, this chapter is dedicated to the equivocality of another term, that of "to stand erect" (*natzov* or *yatzov*), to which is assigned a figurative sense of "to be stable and permanent." It therefore qualifies as a logical member of the series of terms preceding it (sitting, rising, standing), all of which convey the same notion when alluding to God. The conceptual similitude of divine immutability uniting all these terms is the philosophical terrain in which Jacob's vision is grounded. In the terminology of prophetic mechanics, this vision is the concretization of a philosophical abstraction. The overflow emanating from the Active Intellect and inhabited by universal truths impinges on the prophet's rational faculty due to its preparedness.[50] At this stage it can either remain in abstraction or be filtered through the prophet's imagination, which deciphers it into a publicly accessible format, usually of a highly graphic nature. The ensuing prophetic utterance then communicates guidance on ethical or sociopolitical matters. Much of the audience will never surpass the external hyperbole. The majority may indeed discern the figurative language and cull the moral or political instruction that lies underneath. The task of the intellectual elite, however, is to sift through both those layers and retrieve the contents of the undiluted overflow vouchsafed to the rational faculty. Tracing back the prophet's mental processes leads to a state where "only intelligible beliefs will remain with you, beliefs that are well ordered and pleasing to God" (*GP,* II:48, p. 409). It will be demonstrated that in the parable of Jacob's ladder, the pertinent intelligible belief is divine providence.

The biblical references reveal that the chapter is bracketed by the figure of Moses. Of the first three verses quoted, two relate to Moses and are structurally parallel—those who "stand erect" observe Moses in anticipation of some information reflecting on his future. In the case of Exodus 2:4, "And his sister stood erect afar off," there is Miriam anxiously fixated on the wicker basket carrying the baby Moses as it floats down the Nile "to 'know' (*le de 'ah*) what would befall him." In that of Numbers 16:27, "They came out and stood erect," "they" are the rebels against Moses' authority who defiantly await Moses' challenge, which will determine the legitimacy of his leadership: "By this shall you '*know*' *(tede 'un)* that it was the Lord who sent me . . ." (Num. 16:28). These two are instances of the conventional literal use of "to stand erect." The last two verses of the chapter also concern Moses and illustrate the figurative use of the term.[51] Exodus 33:21,

"And thou shall stand erect upon the Rock," sets the scene for the very apex of human apprehension in the history of personal revelation—the vision of God's back (see *GP,* I:54). The last verse, "Behold, I will stand before thee there upon the rock of Horeb" (Exod. 17:6), is cited to draw an equivalence of meaning between the terms "standing erect" and "standing," and is the prelude to Moses hitting the rock in response to a hostile confrontation.

If indeed the vision of Jacob's ladder concerns providence, then it must incorporate allusions to the primary vehicle through which providence materializes—the intellect. The chapter is then overshadowed by that personality, which is the existential ideal of human intellectual aspirations venturing along that path "to the furthest extent that is possible for man" (*GP,* p. 123). The exploratory chapter of the substance of that discipline stretching the very limits of human intellectual capacity focuses on Exodus 33 as its core text. It consists of Moses' plea for supreme ontological enlightenment and God's response in accord with man's diminished capacity. The motivational function of Moses' request, "Let me *know (hode'ani)* thy ways that I may *know (ve'edo'acha)* you that I may find grace in Thy sight" (Exod. 33:13), is the subject of a slight but crucial digression in *GP,* I:54 that prefigures the extended discussion of providence in the third section of the treatise. The latter third of the verse "indicates that he who knows God *finds grace in his sight* and not he who merely fasts and prays but everyone who has knowledge of Him. Accordingly those who know Him are those who are favoured by Him and permitted to come near Him, whereas those who do not know Him are objects of his wrath and are kept far away from Him. *For His favour and wrath, His nearness and remoteness, correspond to the extent of a man's knowledge of ignorance.* However, we have gone beyond the limits of the subject of this chapter" (*GP,* I:54, p. 123). This prologue channels the middle third of verse 33:13 into those sections of the *Guide* which deal with the attainment of individual providence and its exclusive instrument of admission—intellect (*GP,* III:17, III:51). The chapter then continues to identify the contents of this revelation as a comprehensive grasp of "attributes of action." Moses' private perfection lies in the understanding that these attributes have nothing to do with God's essence, and that to gain proximity to God is to divorce God from all material realia.[52] In consonance with Maimonides' negative theology, Moses accomplishes the total and unmitigated negation of attributes from God.

On the other hand, a phenomenological analysis of these attributes as manifest in nature gains for Moses his public perfection, as expressed in the final third of verse 33:13: "*and consider that this nation is Thy People,* that is a people for the government of which I need to perform actions that I must seek to make similar to Thy actions in governing them" (*GP*, p. 125). Note that what conditions the general community as *Thy people* is not their direct contact with God but rather their subjection to the governance of the prophet. The two-tiered identity of the prophet is epitomized by Moses and dominates *GP*, I:15 since, as we shall see, this is precisely what the imagery of Jacob's ladder hints at with the ascent and descent of the prophet.

The repetition of various forms of the root for knowledge *(da'at)* in the contexts of the opening and closing verses categorizes it as a *Leitwort* that equates Moses with knowledge.[53] He is a bedrock of knowledge to whom all eyes turn for education. Miriam follows him attentively to "know" (Exod. 2:4). The participants in the coup against Moses listen to Moses to verify how he will "let them know" (Num. 16:27–28). God responds positively to Moses' request for "knowledge" of His ways so that he will "know" Him (Exod. 33:13). Finally, the very last verse of Exodus 17:6, "Behold, I will stand before thee there upon the rock in Horeb," is excerpted from a scene that concludes with classic metaphorical language of knowledge—the provision of water to quench thirst. The second half of the verse is God's direction to Moses to hit the rock so that water *(mayim)* will flow and "the people will drink." Water, in the Maimonidean lexicon, is so common a metaphor for knowledge "that it has become, as it were, the first meaning[;] the words meaning hunger and thirst are likewise employed to designate lack of knowledge and of apprehension" (*GP*, I:30, p. 64). Here too, then, the natural consequence of having attained that supreme level of knowledge represented by God standing before Moses is that Moses in turn overflows to the rest of the community to provide the requisite knowledge they lack. Whatever relationship exists between God and man in these verses, however, is restricted to one individual, who alone is the object of God's concern (Exod. 17:6) because God is the sole object of his concern (Exod. 33:21). This is the paradigm of God's very limited nexus with the world and is one aspect of Jacob's dream, in which the ladder and God are fixed and any activity establishing a rapport between the world and God is that of the angels.

The figurative meaning of "stable and constant" is demonstrated by the use of the term *natzov* in the verse "Thy word stands erect *(nitzov)* in heaven" (Ps. 119:89). Speech bears no physical stature, thus ruling out as absurd a literal reading of this verse. Since the referent of the term "word" *(davar)* in this verse is God, it lends itself to philosophical allegorization of a metaphysical nature. The reader searches the lexicon and discovers a chapter dedicated to speech-related terms such as "speaking" (*GP,* I:65). Any such term applied to God must be taken exclusively in one of the two following senses:

1. "either will and volition" or
2. "a notion that has been grasped by the understanding having come from God" (*GP,* p. 158)

Meaning (2) is the mode of communication between God and prophet, which although of a purely abstract nature is conveyed to the public at large by familiar speech terminology. The oral dimension of the speech is absent from the world of incorporeal beings, and "predicating speech of Him is similar to predicating of Him all the actions resembling ours" (*GP,* I:65, p. 158). Meaning (1) is mandated by the repetition of speech acts in the Creation account or *ma 'aseh ber 'eshit,* which can only express "volitions" and not articulated sounds. The prooftext in support of this use bears a striking resemblance to the verse Psalm 119:89 cited in *GP,* I:15: "By the word of the Lord were the Heavens made" (Ps. 33:6). Maimonides argues that the obvious anthropomorphic hyperbole of the second half of the verse "And all the host of them by the breath *(ruach)* of His mouth" reflects on the figurative sense of the first half—that is, God has no "mouth" and no "breath," and therefore no "word."

The two meanings assigned to God's speech acts converge in the prophetic arena. We have already shown that the overflow acting as the catalyst for prophetic activity is a constant and unfluctuating phenomenon originating in that primal creative will of God. Therefore every prophetic communication can be thought of in some remote sense as having come from God. Psalm 33:6 itself, by incorporating both the terms "word" *(davar)* and "breath" *(ruach),* produces a biblical parallelism on the notional level as well as the literal. Just as *davar* contains (1) and (2), so the term *ruach* (air) can connote either "purpose and will" or the "divine intellectual overflow that overflows to the prophets" (*GP,* I:40), depending on the particular context. Though the context of Psalm 33:6 admits of meaning (1), the terms resonate with the prophetic implications. Literal temporal communication between God and man is not viable within the Maimonidean system. The prophet merely tunes in to the "hosts of the heaven" from which the divine overflow emanates *(ruach)* and receives understanding *(davar).* That which allows for this human enlightenment is the other plane of meaning in which *ruach* and *davar* reside—the will and purpose of God. Thus, whatever message the prophet receives from the intellectual overflow can be qualified as revelatory of God's pre-eternal will.

The other key term in Psalm 119:89 is "heaven," which is where the verse locates God's word. The chapter on "sitting" (*GP,* I:11) offers a rationale for situating God's word in the "heaven." There Maimonides notes the pervasive scriptural location of divine "sitting" in "heaven" and finds the geography most suitable, since the heaven is "changeless and without diversity; I mean to say that the individuals existing in it do not change as do the individuals constituted by the terrestrial things, which are subject to generation and corruption" (*GP,* p. 38). *Heaven* connotes those existents who reside in it, assumedly being the spheres and intellects.[54] The combination of "word" and "heaven" effects a double entendre reflecting both God's relationship with the world and with man:

1. "Thy word stands erect in heaven" = God's will remains stable, constant and changeless. The domain in which the will persists in its stability is that of the intellects and spheres. Their governance of that which is below them is in consonance with that eternal will and is itself not subject to change.

2. "Thy word stands erect in heaven" = the understanding that seeps down to man via the prophetic process is rooted in "those individuals existing in it [heaven] that do not change." The prophet accesses a constant overflow from an intellect that is a product of an eternal and unchanging will.

This verse, then, portends the dual aspects of Jacob's vision, with the ladder mirroring (1) and the angels ascending and descending in accordance with (2). Moses, whose presence looms large in this chapter, penetrated to the very heart of the ladder's secret by gaining enlightenment as to how all the various structures and components of creation interconnect. Moses, then, is the standard by which the nature of the message of Jacob's vision must be assessed. Though the descent bearing its message of "governing and teaching the people of the earth" is subsequent to the ascent of individual perfection, it is clearly inferior, as the term descent implies, being oriented "toward a very near object" (*GP,* I:10). The core message of the dream is alluded to at the very conclusion of *GP,* I:15 prefaced by the words "I shall now return to our purpose." While the "purpose" is ostensibly a general lexical treatment of the term "stand erect" (*natzov* or *yatzov*), the term's characterization of both the top and bottom of the ladder widens the scope of the "purpose" to encompass the essential messages of the ladder. God's ontological erectness (at top of ladder) and standing (Exod. 17:6, *"I will stand before thee there upon the rock in Horeb"*) are complemented by Moses' intellectual erectness (Exod. 33:21, *"And thou shalt stand erect upon the rock"*) and "standing" (Deut. 5:28, *"But as for thee, stand thou here by me"*) of Moses. Moses' *standing erect* is dependent on an enduring grasp of *standing erectness* of God. It is the structural beam without which Moses would suffer intellectual collapse.

CHAPTER 5

The Seven Units of Jacob's Ladder
and Their Message

In the previous chapter it was argued that chapters I:10 to I:15 of the *Guide* form a kind of prelude to the actual vision of Jacob's ladder itself. These chapters constitute the philosophical setting out of which the message of Jacob's ladder emerges. The masterful interplay of text and biblical prooftext has provided the philosophical underpinnings for a new perspective on God's relationship to his creation that runs counter to the plain sense of the prophetic texts. Utilizing the same methodology, this chapter shall now proceed to an analysis of the vision itself that follows Maimonides' breakdown of its essential components into seven distinct units.

1. "Ladder"

In the *Guide* Maimonides exhibits a propensity for citing *Genesis Rabbah* more than other midrashic collections.[1] His familiarity with this midrash is evidenced throughout the *Guide,* and it is quite reasonable to assume that his interpretation of Jacob's ladder is based on *Genesis Rabbah* 68, though loosely so. I would agree with Sara Klein-Braslavy that this is the case, though I would not restrict the source text to subsection 12 of that chapter, as she does. Maimonides may have been more prone to roam through the midrash and liberally choose those sayings and opinions that suited his particular purpose. The fact that the midrashic literary genre is that of poetry and that it has a nonbinding authoritative status lends it an interpretative pliability that halakhic texts do not allow.[2] *Genesis Rabbah* 68 deconstructs Jacob's dream into a series of individual exegetical units such as "ladder," "ascending," "descending," "angels of the Lord," and so forth as Maimonides does, and then proceeds to identify each with a symbolic counterpart. The vision is thoroughly transfigured, portending various events in Israel's destiny, with the ladder alternatively representing Sinai, the Temple altar ramp, or Nebuchadnezzar's statue. The midrashic identification of angels with prophets, the calculation of the dimension of an angel as one-third of the world (based on a verse in Daniel 10:6), and disclosure of one and a third worlds to Jacob—all strongly indicate that Maimonides drew on *Genesis Rabbah* 68 in its allegorization of Jacob's dream. Sara Klein-Braslavy favors *Genesis Rabbah* 68:12 as Maimonides' urtext in light of its sevenfold division of the dream that parallels Maimonides'. As far as the ladder *(sulam)* is concerned, I believe *Genesis Rabbah* 68:13 offers a more credible representation for his purposes. *Genesis Rabbah* 68:12 deems *sulam* a representation of Sinai, since "the letters of this equal the letters of the other"—that is, their numerical values are equivalent, each adding up to 130. *Genesis Rabbah* 68:13 voices another opinion that projects the *sulam* as an allusion to the giant statue *(tselem)* of Nebuchadnezzar's dream in Daniel 2:31. The midrash bases itself on the letter correspondence between ladder (SLM) and the Hebrew for statue (SML) *(semel),* where the order of two characters is simply reversed.[3] Given the choice between a symbolization based on *gematria* (numerical equivalences) as the *sulam/sinai* is, or one fashioned by a wordplay, as is the case in *sulam/semel,* I conclude that Maimonides would have opted for the latter. In *GP,* II:43 Maimonides outlines three methods of decoding prophetic visions, and says that pictorial images can

1. form an integral part of a parable,
2. "point to what is called to the attention by the term designating the thing seen because of that term's derivation or because of an equivocality of terms," or
3. stimulate association "through the use of a certain term whose letters are identical with those of another term; solely the order of the letters is changed; and between the two terms there is [in] no way an etymological connection or a community of meaning" (*GP,* 392).

The SLM/SML equation of *Genesis Rabbah* 68:13 is a construct of precisely this third method. There is no provision, however, for resorting to the science of *gematria* in deciphering a prophetic vision as *Genesis Rabbah* 68:12 did to contrive the *sulam-sinai* equation. The reader is therefore drawn to the former (Gen. 68:13) to determine the signification of "ladder" for three reasons:

1. The term *sulam* is absent from the Maimonidean lexicon;
2. *Genesis Rabbah* 68:13 is a rabbinic precedent that adopts one of Maimonides' approved interpretative strategies; and
3. the last strategy is introduced as being "stranger" (or more wondrous) than the previous two, and "through this method very strange things appear which are likewise *secrets* . . ." (*GP,* 383). This type of wordplay seems to be best suited for plumbing the depths of cryptic visual objects that are encoded with *secrets* or matters pertaining to *ma'asseh ber'eshit* and *merkavah*. Images susceptible to this method abound in the opening chapters of Ezekiel *"and in other passages."*

The rare biblical term *semel*[4] is taken by the midrash to be synonymous with *tselem,* which is the applicable term in Nebuchadnezzar's dream of Daniel 2:31. The visualization of an actual ladder instigates an associative process that commences with abstracting the linguistic term SLM from the object it represents. The term is then subjected to an examination that determines its place within the logic of the parable. Its literal sense may be discarded, which leaves the prophet with simply three letters—S, L, and M—rather than a word. Various permutations of those letters are tested, resulting in a restructured term of an entirely different meaning. In this instance the following course is followed by the midrash: ladder *(sulam)* ⇒ SLM ⇒ SML *(semel)* synonym ⇒ ZLM *(tselem)*. *Tselem* (image) does appear in the Maimonidean lexicon in *GP,* I:2 as referring to a substance's "natural form," which accounts for its "true reality." The reason we are told that *tselem* is a common term for idols in the biblical tradition is "that what was sought in them was the notion that was deemed to subsist in them, and not their shape and configuration" (*GP,* p. 22). The word *semel* is exclusively reserved for idols in Scripture, as is the *tselem* of Daniel 2:31. This aspect of an idol's reality is in itself a neutral one, conveying the philosophical notion of "form" as opposed to "matter." *Semel* as a transmutation of *sulam* is isolated from its concrete manifestation as a statue and simply connotes "form." The ladder linking the earth and God, Who stands above it and is not part of it, defines God's relationship with the world as analogous to that of form to matter; "God has therefore, with reference to the world, a status of a form with regard to a thing possessing a form, in virtue of which it is that which it is. . . . In this respect it is said of Him that He is the ultimate form and the form of forms; that is *He is that upon which the existence and stability* of every form in the world ultimately reposes . . ." (*GP*, I:69, p. 169). At this juncture in our analysis of the dream the SLM/ SML/ZLM word association casts the ladder in its symbolic representation of the relationship between the Deity and the world. The fact that the ladder is anchored in the world, while not quite coming into contact at the end with the Deity, denies the Deity/world, form/matter analogy its perfect fit. While the world gains its true reality from God, He is not connected to or part of it.

2. *"Set up on earth"*

"Earth" *('erets)* is considered by Maimonides to be an equivocal term, with a general sense of "all that is beneath the sphere of the moon—the four elements," and a particular sense of the element "earth" (*GP*, II:30). In either case it connotes that which is an exclusive property of the sublunar world and to which all material existents owe their physical makeup. All such existents are an amalgam of one sort or the other of the basic four elements of earth, air, fire, and water.[5] Its location at the bottom of the ladder bespeaks a qualitative distance from the source of all being; it is "lowly" and "remote from His light and splendor" as opposed to the "sublimity and high rank" of the heavens (*GP*, II:26, p. 331). The architecture of creation segregated the heavens from the earth by virtue of their constituent ingredient, whose qualitative difference is analogous to that between life and death: "[T]he heavens are living bodies and not dead ones like the elements" (*GP*, II:5, p. 260). The elements in and of themselves are not conscious or self-aware, have no independent self-control, and are subject to a preprogrammed fixed and unalterable law of nature that governs their activity.[6] The hierarchy of existence bottoms out with structures that lack any faculties entailing some modicum of intellectual activity. In their static elemental state they are incapable of establishing any rapport with the superlunary world where intellect reigns supreme. In the figurative antonymical sense of the term "living" that connotes "acquisition of knowledge" (*GP*, I:42, p. 93), they are considered "dead" bodies.

God is also considered the form of the world in the sense that He "continually endows it with permanence in virtue of the thing that is spoken as an overflow" (*GP*, I:69, p. 169) and is not to be confused with the typical form/matter relationship of material bodies. *'Erets,* as emblematic of the elements, lacks form and lies inert at the foot of the ladder, which is in turn its form *(sulam=semel=tselem)* only in that it is responsible for its existence.[7] The directional movement of "form" as signified by the ladder is two-way, downward being the form that entails God's *endowing* the world with "being" and upward, the form *acquired* by material realia. Communion with the ultimate form of the world is directly proportional to the attainment of form by matter. Devoid of form, *'erets* (matter) remains at ground level subject to the perpetual monotonous natural laws promulgated at the Creation.[8] The ladder (form) is pegged *(mutsav)* in the earth, indicating the static relationship between God as the "form of forms" and the sublunar entity composed of *'erets* or the four elements. At this stage of the dream, providence and governance are mechanical, impersonal, and prohibitive of any interactivity between the above and the below. It must be borne in mind that God occupies the most distant link in the chain of being that culminates in the material creation. Therefore, even the ladder, in its role as "form" of the world, never actually comes into direct contact with the ultimate form. Whatever static governance accrues to the earth, as implied by the steady fixation of the ladder in the ground, is further diminished by the incalculable remoteness of God as the ultimate cause of all being.

3. "And the top of it reached heaven"

"Top of it" (R'osho)

Each of the three terms that comprise the third subunit in the terse yet exacting description of Jacob's ladder is afforded some treatment in the *Guide* outside the context of the ladder vision. The first of the group is the possessive form of the noun *r'osh* which, within the logic of the literal image, acts as a spatial referent—the top or uppermost extremity of the ladder. Our reconstruction of the vision, which pivots on "ladder" as some sense of "form," precludes any spatial dimension in favor of more abstract allusions. Though there is no specific analysis of the word *r'osh* on its own terms, it does enter significantly into Maimonides' interpretation of the very first verse in Genesis, which commences with *r'eshith*, a derivative of *r'osh* (*GP,* II:30, pp. 348–49). In order to dispel the notion of any temporal beginning to the world as implied by the commonly accepted translation of "in the beginning," Maimonides suggests an alternative reading of that phrase. That alternative rests on the distinction between "first" in the sense of temporal priority and that of the sense of ontological priority, the former translated by Pines as "first" and the latter as "principle."[9] Something may be the principle of something else without preceding it in time, as in the statement "the heart is the principle of the living beings." That distinction is borne out by the Hebrew vernacular, which indicates temporal priority by *tehillah* and "principle" by *r'eshith*. For our purposes what is most pertinent is the etymological rationale for *r'eshith:* "For it derives from *r'osh* (head), which, in view of its position,[10] is the principle of the living beings" (*GP,* p. 348). The head is the source that sustains the life of the rest, the body.

The extension of this metaphor to Jacob's dream indicates that responsibility for the ladder's existence lies at the top. The ladder is anchored at the summit and derives its existence from it. Within the human species, that activity which leads to the achievement of man's natural form is located in the head. It is through the exercising of the rational faculty that true human form is acquired in virtue of which man is constituted as man and becomes what he in reality is (*GP,* I:1). The ladder as "form" is generated by that which constitutes its principle source of being, "its head" *(r'osho).* I therefore propose the following reading of the phrase under examination: *R'osho* = its head = the ladder's source of existence consists in the activity represented by the remaining two terms "reaching [touching] heaven." That principle *(r'osh)* which constitutes its form lies in a lofty pursuit that ultimately links up with the heavens.

"Reached" (magi'a)

The term *nago'a* (touch) is treated as one of a group of three terms, all of which convey some sense of spatial proximity (approach, touch, come near). The metaphorical signification of all three is the "union of cognition with what is cognized" (*GP,* I:18, p. 43), substituting intellectual for physical activity. The verse cited as exemplary of this epistemological meaning for the term *nago'a* is Jeremiah 51:9, "For her judgment *(mishhpat)* toucheth heaven." The subject of the verse is the Babylonian empire that has suffered devastation of such magnitude as to rule out any hope of recovery. The metaphor conveys the extent of retribution which, if measured, would extend all the way to the heavens.[11] Though we are explicitly instructed on how to incorporate the sense of "union in knowledge" into the verses cited for the other two terms,[12] we are afforded no such aids for the reading of Jeremiah 51:9. There remains the vexing question as to precisely how one can read *nago 'a* in this sentence with any logical coherence. The subject of the verb "touch" is judgment, and the object is "heaven." Once "touch" is rendered "union in knowledge," the transformed metaphor becomes incomprehensible. What does it mean to say "judgment" gains knowledge of or unites cognitively with heaven? All the prooftexts in the chapter, illustrative of the nonliteral signification for the other two terms, have either God or man as the subject of some knowledge acquisition, whereas Jeremiah 51:9 is composed of a subject and object between which any cognitive interplay would seem to be nonsensical.

The key to deciphering this puzzling verse lies in its context of punishment and retribution.[13] We have seen that this particular context generally guides the reader toward the notion of God's immutable governance of the world, a notion that is at odds with traditional beliefs in a providence that is specific and responsive. This is especially pertinent to discussion of "union in knowledge," since it is precisely due to the ontic uniqueness of God's knowledge that those traditional beliefs must be rejected. Since God is an intellect *in actu* devoid of any potentiality, "He is always the intellect as well as the intellectually cognizing subject and the intellectually cognized object" (*GP,* I:68, p. 165). God knows all things perpetually and admits of no transitions or change normally consequent to timebound consciousness. "For this reason no new knowledge comes to Him in any way."[14] Within the particular historical context of Jeremiah, Babylon has experienced its collapse sequentially in time according to human perception. God, on the other hand, simply knows eternally without any regard for the phenomenal event that transpires before human eyes. The reactive image of God gives rise to nomenclature associated with traditional divine providence, such as decree, reward, and punishment. There is no better vehicle with which to overcome such primitive language than that of the philosophical notion of God's knowledge. History is irrelevant to a being that never "acquires" knowledge, whose knowledge never increases or decreases and whose apprehension "does not require an instrument" (*GP,* I:1, p. 23). All information normally accessed by man ex post facto is available to God eternally by way of a faculty constituted by His essence and not extraneous to it.[15] The ceaseless unity of intellector, intellected, and intellecting in God renders the language of reward and punishment obsolete; the only legitimate vocabulary is simply "God knows."

Jeremiah 51:9 then, is a restatement of the philosophical "God knows" via the license of prophetic speech. The particular manifestation of a judgment *(mishpat)* is known to God by the notion implicit in "touches," "union of cognition with what is cognized." That it is "heaven" that is designated as the recipient of the knowledge is significant, since it is the prime representative of a substance that is "changeless and without diversity" *(GP,* I:11, p. 38). It is therefore deemed the most appropriate location of divine sitting by the prophets, as it admits of no instability. The metaphor of God "sitting in heaven" provides the occasion for some of Maimonides' boldest statements concerning God's relationship to the world. The emphatic assertion is made that God is

> the stable One who undergoes no manner of change, neither a change in His essence—as he has no modes besides His essence with respect to which He might change—*nor a change in His relation to what is other than Himself— since . . . there does not exist a relation with respect to which he could change.* *(GP,* I:11, p. 38)

On the face of it, Jeremiah 51:9 is an expression of insurmountable devastation—an event of historical geopolitical ramifications. When it imports the lexical nuance assigned to it, there appears a statement of metaphysical proportion: from God's perspective there is no new materialization of turmoil but rather something always known to Him by virtue of the "union of cognition with what is cognized."[16] The esoteric reading of Jeremiah 51:9 intended for the scrutinizing reader reveals what is in effect an assertion regarding how God knows what transpires in the world. That knowledge is not acquired but is eternally present as a result of the unceasing identity of intellect, intellected, and intellecting that forms an integral part of God's essence. Its judgment *(mishpato)* is known to an absolutely immutable being *(shamayim)* in an exclusively noetic manner whereby cognition is forever united with what is cognized *(nago 'a).*[17]

The route that has led to extracting a lesson in divine epistemology from Jeremiah 51:9 is as follows:

1. noting the context of retribution within which the literal resides acts as a cue that the issue of divine providence may be lurking behind the scenes;
2. a straightforward incorporation of the figurative sense of *nago 'a* into the prooftext yields an incomprehensible reading;

3. the figurative meaning echoes notions that are dealt with elsewhere in the *Guide* (e.g., I:68);
4. the prooftext is transfigured into a dictum regarding divine noesis and its consequences for providence.

The curious structure of the chapter attests to the fact that the term *nago'a* is being singled out from the three terms for some covert motive. After introducing the three terms and assigning to them concrete and metaphorical meanings, the chapter continues to expand on the metaphorical meaning only with respect to the other two terms, *qarov* and *nagosh*. It then reverts back to *nago'a* by citing two further verses utilizing a form of the term, the purpose of which is puzzling. The interjection of these two verses is both interruptive to the thematic flow of the chapter and, as interpreted, incongruous with the two exclusive meanings allowed for the term within the chapter. The verses are inserted and intersect as follows:

> As for its dictum, *Touch the mountains that they may smoke* (Psalms 144:5), Scripture signifies thereby in parabolic language: let Thy decree come to them. It says in a similar way *And touch Thou him himself* (Job 2:5), meaning "let Thy infliction come upon him." (*GP*, I:18, p. 45)

Although there are those who argue that these two verses are cited as exceptions to the general figurative sense of intellectual apprehension,[18] neither at the commencement of the chapter nor at the conclusion does Maimonides allow for any other meaning but intellectual union or physical contact. Furthermore, "touching" in the sense of the manifestation of a divine decree is equally applicable to other biblical verses than these two alone.[19] The chapter closes with an invitation to approach every appearance of "touching" in any grammatical form "in a similar way": "Sometimes the word is intended to signify the approach of one body to another and sometimes union through the cognition and apprehension of a certain thing." Only two senses of the term are accounted for.

As with Jeremiah 51:9, these two last verses concern actions associated with God that are of a punitive nature. Physical contact is immediately ruled out, as both involve a divine touching—that leaves only the option of cognition. In both cases the wrath of God signifies the materialization of some divine decree. The elements of providence, wrath, and noetic activity coalesce in these verses, signaling the reader that there is an encoded subtext.

The key to recovering this subtext lies in the supplicating form of the verb "touch" that appears in both verses. They are both pleas to God originating from a subdivine perception rather than descriptive of some godly action. Maimonides' campaign to eradicate any traces of anthropomorphism extends to the forum of man communicating with and addressing God. At the very minimum, a vocabulary is provided that allows the petitioner to overcome any image of a Being possessed of human features. This overcoming is accomplished by converting "touch" to "decree" or "infliction." The pure philosophical notion of God, however, mandates the rejection of even this parabolic language, since it presupposes a kind of reciprocal relationship between Him and inferior entities that, as we have seen, is inadmissible.[20] This level of philosophical sophistication envisages a Being that is immune to affectability and impervious to entreaty. The use of the term "touch" as cognition in a supplicatory form serves as a reminder that even when engaged in any kind of traditional discourse with God, such as prayer, the sole means of contact between Him and all that is external to Him is via union of intellect. For God there is an eternal, ever-present knowledge of past, present, and future. For man the sole entrance to the divine sphere of influence is through a union of intellects. The intellectual connotation of "touch" frustrates any conventional sense implied by its supplicatory form and, in fact, drains it of its utility as a mode of imploring.

The specific biblical contexts of these verses further substantiate this message. Psalm 144:5 is preceded by two verses that are prominent affirmations of man's inconsequential nature within the general scheme of things. Psalm 144:3, "What is man that Thou takest knowledge of him," is one of the verses quoted by Maimonides as tending to exclude man from divine interest, "man being too insignificant for providence to watch over him" (GP, III:17, p. 472). Psalm 144:4, "Man is like unto vanity . . . ," is a lugubrious expression of man's insignificance that is "of no value at all in comparison with the whole that exists and endures" (GP, III:12, p. 442). In truth, any events befalling man result from his own misadventures and have nothing to do with God's intervention in human affairs. Psalm 144:4 is reflective of this reality contra to man's misperception that attributes them to God (GP, III:12, p. 443). Psalm 144:5 must therefore be read as a logical continuation of what directly precedes it—a prophetic dirge at man's isolation from any divine concern. The realization of a "decree," as Psalm 144:5 is taken to imply, is in effect a declaration of nature running its course.[21]

Job 2:5, when framed within the eisegetical parameters set for Job's prologue in III:22 of the *Guide*, operates in tandem with the message of

Psalm 144:5. The entreaty to "touch" Job is uttered by the character of Satan, who has been cast in the role of issuing a challenge to God to test Job's faith. Satan, clearly the personification of all evil in the world,[22] is estranged from the divine retinue and cannot be associated in any direct fashion with God's governance of the world. His transient existence is restricted to the terrestrial realm, and his appearance in divine company is "without having been for his own sake the object of an intention or having been sought for his own sake" (*GP,* p. 487). That which Satan represents cannot be an object of divine thought, as "there is no relationship whatever between him and the upper world in which there is no road for him." Satan's presence is not enjoined by God but is a consequence of the human choices made by Job in conducting his life. It is a life replete with moral virtue yet devoid of intellectual pursuits: "The most marvelous and extraordinary thing about this story is the fact that knowledge is not attributed in it to Job. He is not said to be a wise or a comprehending or an intelligent man. Only moral virtue and righteousness in action are ascribed to him" (*GP,* p. 487). It is a lack of intellect that attracts Satan and alienates from the divine provenance.[23] Therefore Job 2:5 is a plea that issues from an existence (Satan) incapable of communicating with God; the substantive response elicited by the plea (touch = harm) cannot possibly be accommodated by God; the subsequent calamity that befalls Job does in fact originate with Satan and not with God. Everything about this verse serves to vacate God from the picture and place responsibility for ensuing tragedy squarely on the shoulders of man. The "touch" of Job 2:5 resonates with the radical Maimonidean position regarding divine providence and its very limited jurisdiction over human affairs.[24] There remains only one channel that links up with God, and that is what the "touch" in 2:5 is meant to evoke. The intention is to lead one into 2:6, where God warns Satan to "spare his soul," meaning "that he has been given dominion over all terrestrial things but that he is kept away by a barrier from the soul" (*GP,* p. 488). For "soul" read "the thing that remains of man after death" (*GP,* p. 488), which in turn designates the "rational soul."[25] The "touch" addressed to God intimates the severance of any link with the phenomenal world—the vestiges of any contact with God reside in the "union of intellects." The realm of "intellect" is impenetrable to Satan's forays, since it is precisely the absence of intellect that provides the breeding ground for evil.[26] When evil is located God is nowhere to be found.[27]

This completes our analysis of the second term, "reaches" (touches), in the three-term unit *and the top of it reached to heaven.* As stated previously, our rendering of this part of the verse constitutes *reached to heaven* as the ladder's *top*. The "principle" of "form," or that which lends form its existence, resides in the enterprise that leads to a cognitive union of intellects with that which the remaining term in the unit, *heaven*, represents. The acquisition of "form" in this manner, as the exclusive channel to God, relegates God's involvement with the world to the very narrow confines of the remotest efficient cause. Divine providence in human destiny is diminished in favor of a self-initiated cognitive process that grounds man within the constant and unchanging divine purview. The terminus ad quem of this human initiative will now be shown to be signified by *heaven*.

"Heaven"

"Heaven" is the destination toward which intellect aspires in its quest for self-perfection and fulfillment of its formal function. One of the primary goals of the human intellect is to demonstrate rationally to itself the existence and unity of God, beyond which its capacity ceases and enters the world of negation.[28] The term "heavens" is an equivocal one that can, at times, be a generic designation of all that is above the earth and at other times can refer to a specific level in a hierarchy of spheres beyond the earth.[29] That heaven which is responsible for all the movement in the heavens is the uppermost one: "For all the heavens move as parts of the movement of the highest heaven, that is, the diurnal movement" (*GP,* I:71, p. 175). This latter movement constitutes the "greatest proof through which one can know the existence of the deity."[30] This outermost heaven is the requisite object of contemplation and provides the most definitive evidence of God's existence.[31] Therefore, to assimilate God's existence is to achieve cognition of the workings of this heaven, which in turn reflects on the ultimate precursor of its movement. In the language of the ladder imagery: form *(sulam)* is grounded *(r'osho)* in the cognitive attainment *(magi'a)* of what heaven has to offer *(shamayim)*.

In our discussion of the chapter dedicated to the term "sitting," the appropriateness of its common use in conjunction with "heavens" is attributed to the latter's characteristic of "being changeless and without diversity." Of the three verses cited in support of the figurative sense of sitting with reference to God, two explicitly situate that sitting in the heavens and the third does so by implication. "Thou, O God, sittest for all eternity" (Lam. 5:19) is followed in the same verse by "Thy throne is from generation to generation." In *GP,* I:9 (p. 34), the heaven is identified as a throne, and is a focus for "those who have knowledge of them and reflect upon them the greatness of Him who caused them to exist and to move, and who governs this lower world by means of the overflow of their bounty." The corollary of the most substantive evidence of God's existence, the heavens' movement, is the nature of divine governance that extends to the earth by proxy. The figurative parameters of the term "throne" are then expanded to include an attribute of God himself that is part and parcel of His essence— "greatness and sublimity." Scriptural support for this usage is found, curiously enough, in the context of God's everlasting crusade against the evil empire of Amalek: "For my hand upon the throne of the Lord."[32] The verse then continues: "[T]he Lord will be at war with Amalek from generation to generation." How does the unceasing battle to eradicate Amalek attest to the divine attribute of greatness and sublimity?

The fact that Exodus 17:16 casts God vis-à-vis some facet of the creation or, more particularly, a subgrouping of the human species (Amalek) in an adversarial vengeful mode may, once again, direct the reader toward the mechanics of God's interest in the world. The divine epithet chosen to designate the occupant of the throne in this verse is Yah. This name captures "the notion of the eternity of existence" (*GP,* I:63, p. 155), one that "has never been, or ever will be, non-existent" (*GP,* I:63, p. 155). This perpetual being is an existence in whom all attributes such as greatness, will, and wisdom simply collapse into an identity of essence (*GP,* I:69, p. 170). This utterly simple existence is blind to all external factors, as they would entail affectability and change. All manifestations of divine governance traced by the shortcomings of human language to a myriad of sources inhere in the simple, eternal, unified divine essence. The infinity of "*generation to generation*" is that of Yah, resulting in Exodus 17:16 being a redundancy, as are all attempts at describing God.[33] By substituting the philosophical vocabulary of divine immutability, the verse simply narrows God's relationship to the world as a whole, indicating it is static and monotonous.

Hand, throne, and Yah are all reducible to the identical notion: essence.[34] The characterization of the ensuing conflict with Amalek is really indistinguishable from the manner in which God relates to any other aspect of the world. Its duration is eternal *("generation to generation")* because essence is eternal and always *in actu*.[35] There is nothing but ever-present, ever-knowing essence incapable of any distinctive orientations toward the creation and its constituents. Though the hyperbole of the verse may be politically efficacious, its underlying metaphysical purport is to deny divine providence all its traditional connotations of a caring, involved God.[36]

Another verse is cited to remove any confusion regarding the possibility of the throne being extraneous to God's essence: "Thou, O Lord sittest for all eternity, Thy throne is from generation to generation" (Lam. 5:19). Maimonides views this verse as a parallelism in which the two hemistichs emphasize the same notion, leading to an equivalence between God and throne. Since they both share an eternal existence they must be identical; otherwise, a heretical dualism would result. The fact that Lamentations 5:19 incorporates the same synecdochical expression, *dor dor*, for eternity as the second stich of Exodus 17:16 regarding the eternal battle with Amalek must have motivated Maimonides in its selection. The first stich of Lamentations 5:19, "Thou who sittest in heaven," is an example chosen in *GP*, I:11 to convey the idea that there is no change in God's relation with what is outside Himself, since "there does not exist a relation with respect to which He could change." The throne of the second stitch, being the equivalent of God's essence, repeats the same notion. This notion is carried back into the usage of *dor dor* in Exodus 17:16 with respect to throne and battle. Since God transcends time, does not change, and does not admit of relation to anything external to Himself, there can be no personal involvement with the world, let alone a part of it such as Amalek. The metaphysical subtext of the verse thoroughly subverts its plain sense. The interventionist God is replaced by an indifferent one.

Critical to our discussion of heaven is the confusion that arises as to what throne represents, particularly in the context of Lamentations 5:19, "Thou O Lord sittest for all eternity. Thy throne is from generation to generation." In a highly controversial chapter, *GP*, II:26, Maimonides introduces a rabbinic statement from *Pirke de Rabbi Eliezer* that tends to undermine his own self-declared position on the sui generis creation of the world ex nihilo. There is no need for our purposes to enter the scholarly debate that has raged on regarding where Maimonides truly stood on this issue (namely, whether in the Aristotelian, Platonic, or Jewish rabbinic tradition).[37] What is pertinent for our discussion is the conflicting use Lamentations 5:19 is put to in this chapter. Here the two stichs of the verse are viewed as two different subject matters, with "throne" being divorced from "God" as a separate entity ("heaven"), whereas *GP*, I:9 clearly cites this verse as evidence that the attribute represented by "throne" is integral to God's essence. Some medieval commentators on the *Guide,* such as Efodi and Shem Tov, have astutely identified this glaring discrepancy as an instance of the seventh type of contradiction for which in the introduction Maimonides had cautioned his readers to be on the lookout.[38] This is an intentionally conceived contradiction that escapes all but the most trained eyes. It is by no means clear to me, though, that Maimonides does indeed treat the throne of Lamentations 5:19 in *GP,* II:26 any differently than in I:9.

In *GP,* II:26 he is only canvassing various possibilities as to the meaning of Rabbi Eliezer's cryptic statement that the earth was created from the snow underneath the throne of glory. The implication is that the throne is uncreated and therefore can be consistent with a Platonic conception of creation that commences with some eternal substrate. Support for an uncreated throne is elicited both scripturally and rabbinically. The scriptural argument is based on the lack of any references to the throne as a created object (with the exception of one verse that can be discounted if taken figuratively); and the rabbinic allusion to the creation of the throne cannot be taken at face value, Maimonides says, since it is expressed "in a strange manner"—its creation transpires prior to the creation of the world, obviously ruling out a conventional understanding of the term. There may be another reason that accounts for the uncreatedness of the throne, since, as in the expanded meaning of the term in *GP,* I:9, it is a reference to God's essence. There are two indicators that this is the true implication of "uncreated" disclosed by Maimonides' argumentation:

1. Two out of the three rabbinic sources for a preconceived throne base themselves on the verse "Your throne is established of old; You are from eternity" (Ps. 93:2).[39] The structure of this verse mirrors the exact parallelism exhibited by Lamentations 5:19, which provided the requisite proof for the identification of throne with God's essence in *GP,* I:9. The nearly parallel form yields the following equation in both verses: You (God) = Throne = Eternal.

Lamentations 5:19	Psalm 93:2
(a) Thou O Lord sittest for all eternity	(a) Your throne is established of old.
(b) Thy throne is from generation to generation.	(b) You are from eternity

2. Maimonides continues to conjecture that, had Rabbi Eliezer subscribed to the eternity *a parte ante* of the throne, then "throne" must be determined as an attribute of God. Yet, he countermands, if this is the case we would remain with the absurd result that something has been generated from an attribute. A second look at Rabbi

Eliezer's statement with respect to the throne's involvement in the creation renders this a specious retort to the possibility that throne is an attribute of God. The earth was created from "*the snow under the throne of His glory*" and not from the throne itself. There is no problem of generating something from an attribute, since it is the snow (whatever that may represent) out of which the earth emerges.[40]

The contradiction detected by Efodi and Shem Tov would then be resolved by the reconciliation of the two throne representations of Lamentations 5:19 to one idea of pure divine essence. Evasiveness is called for, since *GP,* II:26 deals with the issue of creation—the forum that provides the strongest nexus between God and the world. "Throne" as representative of God's sublimity signifies an otherness that, while somehow responsible for creation, is, at the same time, set wholly apart from it. Throne/essence simply exists for all eternity (for lack of any term that would capture atemporality), impervious to change and immune to any disturbance. Creation as a transformative event would constitute such a disturbance if directly related to God, and all the more so would the subsequent functioning of creation and its attendant maintenance.[41] The ongoing relationship with the creation is mediated by another existent that immunizes the Deity from any violation of His unitary essence by detaching it from the sphere of flux and change. Heaven is also called "throne" because it attests to that exalted incomprehensible essence. It indicates to "those who have knowledge of them and reflect upon them the greatness of Him who caused them to exist and move and *who governs this lower world by means of the overflow of their bounty.*"

Unadulterated pure essence, in which all attributes refer to one and the same notion, vitiates even the conventional sense of will, and therefore situates God with respect to heaven in a relationship of necessary causation.[42] Thus, contemplation of the heavens leads to the somewhat paradoxical conclusion of a creator with total detachment from the creation. Yet this is precisely what Maimonides considers intellectual achievement of the highest order—the most irrefutable of proofs for the existence of the Creator ("heavens") is also, in its role of distancing that Creator from his creation, the strongest evidence for determining the nature of that Creator. As with negative theology, the more one detaches God from the world of matter and the more one restricts His involvement with that same world, the truer a portrait of His essence is gained and the more human a form is acquired.[43] In the terminology of Jacob's ladder, human form is cultivated upon the intellectual grasp of what the heavens attest to: an inscrutable divine essence whose integrity is safeguarded against relational change and affectability in a withdrawn state preserved by the intervention of the heavens. The heavens, while presenting the greatest testimony to God's presence in the Creation,[44] act also as an impenetrable barrier to the relationship and familiarity that traditional belief in providence entails.

It is no coincidence, then, that in the chapter dedicated to a lengthy exposition on the machinations of the fifth all-encompassing sphere (heaven) and how governance of the lower world is its exclusive domain we find the following expression of bafflement:

> For the governance and the providence of Him, may He be exalted, accompany the world as a whole in such a way that the manner and true reality of this accompaniment are hidden from us; the faculties of human beings are inadequate to understand this. On the one hand, there is a demonstration of His separateness, may He be exalted, from the world and of His being free from it; and on the other hand, there is a demonstration that the influence of His governance and providence in every part of the world, however small and contemptible, exists. May He whose perfection has dazzled us be glorified![45]

The heavens, to which all forces of nature, motion, and preservation of species can be traced and whose function within the world as whole is analogous to the heart in a living body (*GP,* I:72, p. 187), are so all-pervasive that God's connection to the world is virtually eviscerated. On the other hand, they also attest to God being "the principle and efficient cause of all things other than Himself" (*GP,* I:16, p. 42), albeit every action in being is referred to God only in the sense that "God, considered as efficient cause, is then the remotest one."[46] The connective forces of the heavens that unite all of creation into one body are also "most necessary or most useful for the demonstration that the deity is one."[47] But, of course, we have seen that this oneness eludes all rational categorization. The very body that establishes His existence and unity, thereby inviting God into the world, also disengages God from it both by relieving Him of all control and stripping him of any rational categorization other than "He is." The heavens capture what moderns would term the existential tension that is endemic to the man of faith who fluctuates between nearness and alienation from a God who is both evident in all phenomena and yet abides in an almost unbridgeable remoteness.

"Heaven" is also featured prominently in chapter I:70, where the term "ride" *(rakhov)* is assigned the equivocal sense of "dominate and rule." "Heaven" enters the picture since it, and alternatively the *araboth*, is depicted scripturally as the vehicle of God's equestrian talent. The *araboth* is identified as that heaven which occupies the apex in the heavens hierarchy and "refers solely to one heaven: that which encompasses the universe" *(GP,* p. 172). Whatever traces of God's providence we detect in the world emanate from the relationship that has been forged between Him and this body, for "it is His instrument by means of which He governs that which is existent" *(GP,* p. 173). This relationship is said to be captured most fittingly in near-mythological terms by the midrashic comment on the geographic coordinate that set the scene for Jacob's dream: "He chanced upon a *place.*" The term "place" *(maqom)* evokes a sense of textual association that furnishes Deuteronomy 33:27—"The eternal God *(elohei qedem)* is a dwelling place *(me'onah)*"—as proof for the sublime notion that God "is the dwelling place of His world, His world is not His dwelling place."[48] God defies location within the geographical boundaries of the world because he precedes the world and supersedes it as an "eternal" existence that, we have seen, connotes a steadfast, immutable, and unaffected presence. Once again we find punishment as a backdrop for the eternal God of Deuteronomy 33:27, which continues, "He drove out the enemy before you, By His command destroy." Punishment is prefaced by a divine characterization *(elohei qedem)* designated to obviate any primitive notions of an intercessionist deity. The command to destroy of Deuteronomy 33:27 is figuratively ascribed to God, as it cannot possibly issue from that static existence that preceded the world.

Though omitted by Maimonides in his recitation of the midrash, this notion is further buttressed by an additional prooftext in Psalm 90:1 that addresses God as a "dwelling place" *(me'on).* This entreaty to God is ensconced in a context thoroughly imbued with the idea of "eternity"; the full text reads: "O Lord, You have been our dwelling *(me'on) in every generation (bedor dor). . . .* Before you brought forth the earth and the world, *from eternity to eternity (me'olam ad 'olam)* You are God."[49] Thus, when Maimonides quotes Deuteronomy 33:27, the portrayal of God as a dwelling place *(me'on)* is suffused with the idea of abiding eternality accentuated by the threefold repetition synonymous with it *(qedem, bedor dor, me'olam ad 'olam).* Such a ceaseless atemporal eternity within which the Deity abides renders a hermetic existence immune to the vicissitudes of world history and human affairs. Any association with the temporal would be anathema to an existence that is unsusceptible to the change and affectability appurtenant to it. The "place" where Jacob's dream materializes, when invested with this midrashic purport, is transformed from a geographical to an intellectual destination toward which Jacob is guided by his dream.

God's relationship to the heaven, or the fifth all-encompassing sphere, is further refined by casting it in the image of a rider and his horse. It is the "horse that is subsidiary to the rider," and not vice versa. The heaven "is His instrument by means of which He governs that which is existent" (*GP,* p. 173). The analogy of horse to rider, then, preserves God's ultimate control of the world, thereby providing some solace to the fundamentalist religious mentality that perceives all worldly phenomena as subordinate to a divine will contemporaneous with them.[50] The equestrian image would seem to indicate that the Creator holds tight rein on his creation, albeit mediated by the heaven. The verse quoted by the midrash, though, to validate the horse/rider relationship quickly retreats from the kind of control suggested by the metaphor. "That Thou didst ride upon Thy horse" (Hab. 3:8) addresses God's role in vanquishing Israel's enemies, specifically the Egyptians at the Red Sea. The first cola of the verse expresses God's anger with bodies of water, which is vented at the chariots of the second cola. This verse is cited as one of a host of examples in which prophets employ graphic hyperboles that merely reflect human sentiments of joy, fear, approval, and so forth. Though they express radical upheavals of natural phenomena (blackening the stars, shaking the earth, bloodying the moon, melting the mountains, etc.) (*GP,* I:29, p. 343), they in no way are to be taken as contraindicating the permanent, unalterable nature of creation. Even miracles are part of nature in that they are preprogrammed at Creation (*GP,* II:29, p. 345). Maimonides subscribes to the rabbinic motto that "The world goes its customary way,"[51] even with respect to miracles such as the very one alluded to by Habakkuk 3:8. At the very moment God's intervention seems most manifest, Maimonides, by his scriptural reference, directs us back to the role of heaven and God's disengagement from history.

In support of the notion that the heaven (fifth sphere) is God's delegated representative to which all governmental authority over the world has been ceded, Maimonides defers to a rabbinic view of the contents of the *araboth* (= *shamayim* = throne = heaven = fifth all-encompassing sphere). It is considered the repository of "righteousness, right dealing, justice, the treasures of life, the treasures of peace, the treasures of blessing, the souls of the righteous ones, the souls and the spirits that shall be created in the future and the dew by means of which the Holy One, blessed be He, will revive the dead."[52] The principle that lies behind this teaching is that all these things enumerated exist in the world "because they proceed from forces coming from the *araboth* of God, who caused [the *araboth*] to be their first origin and who situated them in it" (*GP,* I:70, p. 173). Three of the items on this list are then singled out for comment, the purpose of which, I shall argue, is to reinforce the proximity of heaven and the concomitant remoteness of the Deity from the realm of human affairs. They are as follows:

1. *treasures of life*—"every life existing in a living being only proceeds from that life" (*GP,* I:70, p. 173). The reference here is to the lengthy exposition contained in *GP,* I:72, which essentially locates the source of all forces responsible for life in the world of "generation and corruption" in the heaven—"Every motion existing in the world has as its first principle the motion of heaven and every soul existing in the beings endowed with souls that are in the world has as its principle the soul of heaven" (*GP,* I:72, p. 187).

2. *the soul of the righteous ones and the souls and the spirits that shall be created in the future*—Maimonides instructs the reader to carefully reflect upon this item and particularly to bear in mind the distinction between the soul with which man enters the world, which is "merely a faculty consisting of preparedness," and the actualized soul that survives death (see *GP,* I:40). The biography of man in its entirety from mortal to immortal soul is propelled literally and metaphorically by the motion of this heaven. In the first instance, it emanates the forces that generate the blank, impressionable soul. In the second instance, since intellectual function is what actualizes the soul and since the movement of the heaven is reflective of the Deity's existence—the highest object of intellectual contemplation—so the heaven is ultimately responsible for the perfected soul. From the soul's inception to its postmortem permanence, the heaven dominates both as the generative force for the former and the intellectual catalyst for the latter.

3. It is specifically pointed out that the Sages furnished scriptural prooftexts for each of the items enumerated, demonstrating their residence within the *araboth*. The only full text cited is the verse appropriate to righteousness *(tsedek)* and justice *(mishpat)*. There are two alternative explanations for why this particular item is singled out as opposed to the other. The first is simply that it is the one that leads the list and the first one so proven in the Talmud. We

therefore read "and so on." Alternatively, Maimonides wishes us to specifically focus on this pair as an additional indicator of the relationship between earth, heaven, and God. The reason I am persuaded by the latter is that the observation regarding the rabbis' attempts at grounding their description of the context of the *araboth* in Scripture arrives somewhat late in the discussion. The rabbinic statement is quoted; its allegorical tenor is noted; its inner meaning is somewhat penetrated, at least with respect to the details that interest Maimonides (see 1 and 2 above); and, finally, a general statement regarding the perception at large of fanciful midrashim is presented. His engagement with this particular rabbinic statement would seem to have come to an end, yet he reverts back to relate how it corroborated their "enigmatic presentation"[53] with scriptural proof, introduced by "I shall return to the remainder of what I have started out to explore" (*GP,* p. 174). Attention is being called to this pair of loaded terms, "righteousness" and "justice," and their role as the foundations of God's throne (read "heaven") in the words of the verse "Righteousness and justice are the foundation of Thy throne" (Ps. 89:15).

Once the reader's eye is caught by these terms, he or she is led to the main discussion of them in the very last two chapters of the *Guide,* III:53 and III:54, where they are infused with a metaphysical supplement to their ordinary political/ethical connotation.[54] God is described as possessed of those traits that qualify Him as a judge *(shofet)* and righteous *(tsaddiq)* only insofar as they reflect attributes of action. Man investigates the world and discovers that nature operates in consonance with the dictates of moral/ethical characteristics such as mercy, compassion, righteousness, justice, grace, and so on. These traits ordinarily give rise to certain corresponding actions in man, and they are consequently projected onto the personage of the Deity.[55] Both of the pertinent terms simply express natural causation; "righteous" refers to "the governance of the living being by means of its forces," and "judge" is on account "of the occurrence in the world of relative good things and of relative great calamities necessitated by judgment that is consequent upon wisdom" (*GP,* III:53, p. 632). Man predicates God with virtues by analogy. The analogy is of little utility with respect to attaining any semblance of knowledge regarding God. However, it is crucial for the proper conduct of human affairs in that "the purpose should be assimilation to them and that this should be our way of life" (*GP,* III:54, p.

637). A thorough understanding of nature and science ineluctably leads to the realization that attributes do not attach to God's essence but to actions. This serves once again to distance God from the world and dovetails with the theory of negative attributes. Unmediated governance of the world would justify attributes of essence which, of course, amounts to heresy in Maimonides' books. The only way one can escape positive attribution is to reject all traditional notions of providence that intimately tie God to the world.

"Heaven," then, as the repository of *tsedek* and *mishpat,* is intended to impose the necessary barrier between God and the world that the theory of negative attributes and attributes of action demands. There is an inverse correlation between attributes of action and negative attributes in the noetic quest for the ultimate source of all being. It consists of stripping God down to bare essence by shielding Him from the common inferences one would normally draw from a creation to its creator. The harmony and interconnectedness of nature act as a mirror for human ideals, thereby conditioning man for his ethical and political responsibilities.[56] The impulse to qualify God on the basis of His creation must be routed away from God and back to man himself in a process of self-discovery. The *imitatio dei* mandated by the obligation to "walk in His ways" (Deut. 28:9) is accomplished precisely by appreciating that these "ways," such as "mercy," "grace," "justice," "righteousness," and so on, are not descriptive of God but of the world.[57] The positing of attributes of action entails disengagement from divine existence and assimilation to the human, ethical, political constitution.[58] This then paves the way for a methodical process of negation, which is the sole method of gaining any knowledge of God. *Tsedek* and *mishpat* are isolated for domicile in the "heaven" to deter any divine attribution and promote negation that detaches God from the physical/historical context of the world.

As stated, in terms of the dream's imagery, human form and the form of the material world stem from the heaven. With respect to human form it is the acquisition of whatever heaven has to teach in terms of how God relates to His creation and the awareness that the cognitive process reaches its limits at the heavens *(magi'a hashamyim)*. When Maimonides analyzes the four terms that connote God's relationship with the Creation as a whole *(bar'oh, 'assoh, qanoh,* and *'el)*, they are introduced with the following instruction: "Among the things you ought to reflect upon are the four words that occur with reference *to the relation between the heaven and God*" (*GP,* I:69, p. 169; emphasis mine). What is striking is that even though all the verses quoted demonstrating the use of these terms encompass both the heaven and earth *(shamayim veha'aretz)*, the prefatory advice is to reflect on these terms as expressions of God's relationship solely with the heaven. When he deals with the term *'elohe* and *'el* toward the end of the chapter, he quotes only the part of the verse relating to heaven (*elohe hashamayim*—God of the heaven) and omits the second half of the title—God of the earth (*'elohe ha'aretz*) (Gen. 24:3). Finally, the closing comments concerning what aspect of God's relationship with the world these last particular terms allude to are confined to the heaven and not earth: ". . . He is Elohim—that is He who governs—and they are those governed by Him, not in the sense of domination— . . . but with respect to His rank, may He be exalted, in being and in relation to theirs. *For He is the Deity and not they—I mean heaven*" (emphasis mine). The cognomen God of Eternity[59] (*'el 'olam*) is cited as a purveyor of this concept, which restricts God's jurisdiction to the heaven and even then connotes not governance there, but rank in the hierarchy of being. This is the appellation by which Abraham introduces God to the world, being the appropriate connective to the idolatrous confusion the general population has fallen into.[60] The deity that Abraham has conceived is an implacable, immutable God who is attributeless and actionless and remote from the affairs of the world, yet acknowledged as occupying the highest rung of being.[61] This is the deity arrived at after studious observation of the heaven's rotation, its governance of the world of natural causation, and its imposition between that world and the Deity, thereby precluding any interventionist relationship between God and the earth.

4. "Angels of God" (elohim)

The metaphorical referent for the "angels of God" in Jacob's dream is explicitly identified by Maimonides as the prophets (*GP,* I:51, p. 41). Two verses are quoted to corroborate the identification of angels with prophets:[62]

1. "And He (YHVH) sent an angel" (Num. 20:16).
2. "And an angel of the Lord (YHVH) came up from Gilgal to Bochim" (Judges 2:1).

The conflict between the position taken here on the symbolism of the angels and that expressed in the discussion of angels proper in *GP,* II:10 has already been pointed out both by modern scholars[63] and earlier by disciples of Maimonides.[64] In II:10 these angels are identified with certain structural components of the world and not with human personalities.[65] Can the angels of the dream depict both at one and the same time? Though the ups and downs of a prophet's intellectual journey may be of interest to the general public, what exactly would be the utility of such a teaching to one who has already achieved prophecy, such as Jacob? In order to achieve prophecy the prophet must have, by definition, already ascended the "ladder of knowledge," since he must possess the requisite perfection of his rational and imaginative faculties in addition to a firm moral constitution.[66] The ascending stage of the dream, which represents "attaining certain images of the ladder," would be superfluous, since Jacob must have a desire to climb the ladder prior to obtaining a prophetic vision. So would the descending stage, which symbolizes "governing and teaching the peoples of the earth," since the bounteous overflow responsible for a prophetic vision compels the prophet to do so: "The nature of this matter makes it necessary for someone to whom this additional measure of overflow has come, to address a call to the people, regardless whether that call is listened to or not" (GP, II:37, p. 375). The lesson of the dream, as stated in GP, I:15, where angels are prophets, is a redundant one for Jacob personally and can only have been intended for a general audience. Yet Jacob still requires assistance in the conveyance of a public message. The level of abstraction operated on by Jacob demands the covertness of prophetic images so that he can teach in consonance with the median capacity of the general audience. The vision instructs him to be instructive. It legitimizes the prophet's capacity to govern and teach by stipulating from where the authority to do so derives. That authority is sanctioned by the prophet's intellectual capabilities and consequent success in gaining increased familiarity with the nature of the source of all being—God. Ironically, the initial internal process that crystallizes within the mind of the prophet and leads to his political/pedagogical mandate is driven by the science of metaphysics and not politics.[67]

Since Jacob already qualifies as a prophet, a parable whose ultimate lesson concerns simply a description of his vocation as teacher would seem to be a facile one indeed. The true message of the parable must involve that discipline with which the prophet is wholly preoccupied to the exclusion of all else. In the words of the Mishneh Torah: "When he enters Pardes . . . he advances and withdraws from the affairs of the general population . . . his mind is constantly preoccupied with what is beyond, found beneath the throne, in order to comprehend the pure and holy forms and delve into the wisdom of God in its entirety. . . ."[68] The stimulus for prophetic inspiration

is the psychic focus on "the pure and holy forms" or the separate intellects.[69] At this juncture the prophetic mental process is untainted by the
mundane considerations of everyday life. What the prophet gains for his
personal benefit results from intellect contemplating Intellect. It cannot be
shared with the common man, to whom any teaching in this domain would
be both incomprehensible and impertinent, and therefore remains exclusively for the self-edification of the prophet. The prophet is a metaphysi-
cian for himself and a moral-political tactician for the people. Who then
were the "angels" to whom Jacob was privy?

The clue in *GP,* I:15 for determining the "angel" metaphor is provided
by the slight incongruity between the purported allusion to "prophets" and
the prooftexts in support of it. We have already drawn attention to the two
verses cited, which establish the metonymic equation between angels and
prophets (Num. 20:16; Judges 2:1). There is a discrepancy, though, between the angels of these verses and those of the dream. The former are
emissaries of God, designated by the appellation YHVH, whereas the latter
are those linked to *elohim.* The cautious reader is thereby signaled to subject the current interpretation to further scrutiny. Since Jacob's ladder intrudes a lexicographical analysis of a single term in I:15, and given the
highly sensitive nature of its exacting imagery, its current rendering may
be tentative at best—an opportune occasion for resorting to the fifth type of
contradiction (*GP,* introduction, pp. 17–18). A fundamental matter that is
"easy to conceive," the various equivocal senses of the term "stand," is the
subject of *GP,* I:15. It is being elucidated by its use within a "certain obscure matter that is difficult to conceive," Jacob's ladder. Therefore there is
no attempt presently to "state the matter as it truly is in exact terms"; instead, it is given "in accord with the listener's imagination," which is insuf-
ficiently prepared to digest its full import. It is only when the reader reaches
a stage where he is sufficiently advanced "that the obscure matter is stated
in exact terms and explained as it truly is." That stage arrives later in II:10,
where the "angels" of the dream are entirely reinvented. At this earlier juncture, namely *GP,* I:15, Maimonides' primary purpose is to construct a lexicon from which the devout, yet unsophisticated, adherent of the biblical
tradition can draw to overcome primitive, anthropomorphic notions of God.
It is not Maimonides' intention at the first reading of I:15 to convey any
philosophically sophisticated theories of prophecy, be they directed toward
communal governance and welfare or individual perfection. The most basic reading of I:15 is to establish possible alternative meanings of the word
"erect."[70] Only after a comprehensive reading of the *Guide,* including II:10,

can the reader return to I:15 and extract its silver and gold. At the same time, a trail of clues intimating more esoteric doctrines are strategically planted in these chapters for the more advanced student. The "listener's imagination" at this point need only be attuned to the flexibility of the term "stand erect," which allows for metaphor, while those who have surpassed the preliminaries of avoiding anthropomorphisms are handed "a key permitting one to enter places the gates to which were locked" (*GP,* introduction, p. 20). The latter require more than the simple legitimation of prophetic authority, and they are steered in that direction by the discrepancy between the angels of *elohim* and those of YHVH.

The word *elohim* points to the discussion of angels proper, commencing in II:6 by the explication of the propriety of the term *elohim* as the biblical designation for angels. Since *elohim* can refer to "judges,"[71] it is an apt characterization of both God and the angels in the sense that they both govern that which lies below them. The prooftext cited suggests that the specific type of angel *elohim* refers to is a separate intellect. God is described in Deuteronomy 10:7 as the "Elohim of the Elohim—which *means the deity of the angels*—and the Lord of Lords *('adonei 'adonim)*—that is[,] the Master of the spheres and the stars." The *elohim* of the first cola of the verse is identified with simply "angels," whereas the second cola identifies *adonim* with spheres and stars. Though "angels" in the Maimonidean lexicon is so comprehensive as to virtually drain it of any meaning whatsoever,[72] it is distinguished in this particular verse from the spheres and stars and clearly represents the separate intellects. This is further substantiated by the concluding remark of the exposition on *elohim;* Aristotle is differentiated from the Jewish tradition only terminologically: "for he speaks of separate intellects and we speak of angels" (*GP,* p. 262).

After the reader has been led by the mismatch between the angels of the dream *(elohim)* and those of the prooftexts (YHVH) to II:6, the identification of the angels of the dream with the separate intellects becomes progressively reinforced. The list of things that "angels" can connote includes their appearance in prophetic visions, where they assume a more noble identity than animal forces or movements; as Maimonides says, the word "angels" "is furthermore said of the separate intellects that appear to the prophets in the vision of prophecy" (*GP,* p. 262). Maimonides then expressly states that his interest in the term "angels" at this point lies exclusively with its role as a signifier of separate intellects: "Now our discourse here shall deal only with the angels who are separate intellects" (*GP,* p.

262). Finally, the tripartite division of all creation, which is an endorsement of the midrashic dimensions assigned to angels—"a third part of the world"—is encapsulated as follows: "For all created things are divided into three parts: *the separate intellects, which are the angels;* the second, the bodies of the spheres; the third, first matter—I mean the bodies subject to constant change which are beneath the sphere" (*GP,* II:11, p. 273). The midrashic account of the number and size of the angels appearing in Jacob's dream implicitly adopts the medieval cosmological hierarchy of creation in which simple angels represent separate intellects.[73]

In addition to the textual evidence that the angels in *GP,* II:10 represent the separate intellects, the substantive presentation of the dream strongly suggests that this is the case. The parable of Jacob's ladder attracts far more scrutiny than other biblical parables due to its precise nature. If, as the medieval commentators have claimed, the central characters of the dream represent the four basic elements, then the parable is reduced to a lesson in physics. The subject matter would not measure up to the esoteric status of the parable. Separate intellects, on the other hand, dignify the portent of the dream by elevating it to the realm of metaphysics.[74] Furthermore, the internal consistency of the dream's imagery contraindicates the association of the angels with the elements. If the ladder represents some form of increasing proximity to God, as the image of God at the top suggests, why would the elements, the most remote component of creation from divine origins, occupy any space on it? The earth, the geographic domain of the elements, is already situated at the very foot of the ladder, thereby precluding any scaling of it by the elements. The ladder is restricted to the more eminent structures of being and inaccessible to the base elements.

The very first mention of separate intellects in the *Guide* arrives in the midst of the chapter dedicated to flushing out all the nuances of the term "face" *(panim)* (*GP,* I:37). That chapter is rife with allusions casting the separate intellects as pivotal players in the arena of providence. The chapter notes its frequent use "to denote the anger and wrath of God" (*GP,* p. 85). We have already argued that "God's anger" in the *Guide* is a subliminal code term for lack of God's providence and involvement with worldly affairs. Since God is immune from affectability and resultant emotions, one would have expected further elucidation as to the metaphoric sense of God's wrath and anger.[75] In the section devoted to the decorporealization of God, simply noting an alternative anthropomorphic sense (anger) for the term *panim* would seem to defeat the purpose at hand. However, God's anger and wrath have come to assume the connotation of man's insignificance and God's remoteness,[76] and they pave the way for an alternative source of providence also represented by *panim*—the separate intellects.

We are then introduced to the separate intellects in the course of considering the sense of *panim* in God's response to Moses' demand for direct revelatory knowledge of God's essence: "But my face shall not be seen" (Exod. 33:23). Here Maimonides defers to the Targum, which renders this verse "And those in front of me shall not be seen"; Maimonides says, "He indicates by this that there are likewise great created beings whom man cannot apprehend as they really are. These are the separate intellects" (*GP,* p. 86). *Panim* as indicative of "presence" is an especially apt term for the separate intellects, since they "are constantly in front of Him and in His presence because of the power and providence watching over them." Conversely, the term "back" *(ahor)* is rendered by the Targum as "that which is behind me," or that which lies beneath the realm of the separate intellects, which appropriately captures the total absence of God's interest in the lower world, on which He has figuratively *"turned His back"* "because of their remoteness from the existence of God". (*GP,* p. 86). Our understanding of the separate intellects as a barrier to God's unmediated providence[77] proscribes falling prey to the primitive, anthropomorphic tendencies that interventionism promotes. The cost of preserving the unitary essence of God amounts to relinquishing any belief in a divine governance that is analogous in any way to human governance. The separate intellect is therefore pivotal in maintaining the proper perspective and acting as a bulwark against lapsing into notions regarding God that are tantamount to idolatry. The latter is an idolatry that "bears upon His essence." Though there may be an allegiance to a God who is numerically one, an alien being has been set up as an object of worship if He is thought of as corporeal or subject to affectability.[78]

I believe that what misled the medieval commentators into identifying the angels with the elements was the emphasis on the number four. There are indeed four elements and more than that number of separate intellects. However, when configuring the structure of the universe into units of four, Maimonides manages to pare down the number of spheres to four, even though there are clearly more.[79] This is accomplished by adopting a classification that divides the spheres into "informed" ones—that is, those which contain stars. According to this enumeration, there are four such spheres, "namely the sphere of the fixed stars, that of the five planets, that of the sun and that of the moon; while above them all there is one empty sphere in which there is no star" (*GP,* II:9, p. 269). The notion of each of these spheres can in turn be attributed to four different causes: its sphericity, its soul, its intellect and, what is crucial for our purposes, "the separate intellect which is its beloved" (*GP,* II:10, p. 271). The desired number of four is achieved by lumping a number of spheres into one supersphere category (the five planets, each of which has its own sphere) and by discounting the diurnal sphere by reason of it being vacant of any stars and thereby "uninformed."[80] Since each of these four spheres is said to be propelled by a "separate intellect which is its beloved," it is consistent to associate four such intellects with this quadrispherical enumeration. The intellects constitute the objects of desire with whom the four spheres are infatuated.

5–6. *"Ascending and descending"*

Since the intellects are wholly incorporeal and abstract and do not occupy space per se, they are incapable of motion. They are arranged in a hierarchy of rank, not space,[81] and therefore their movement in the dream cannot transpire in a spatial dimension. Their sole activity is an intellectual preoccupation with the originating source of their being: God. This being the case, the ascending and descending of Jacob's ladder can only assume the metaphorical denotations assigned to them in chapter I:10 of the *Guide*. The relative integrity of intellectual objectives can be distinguished by ascending and descending as reflective of psychological sophistication. Descent connotes intellectual demotion—"a lower state of speculation; when a man directs his thought toward a very mean object"—whereas ascent conversely occurs "when he directs his thought toward an exalted and sublime object" (*GP,* p. 35). This intellectual progression and regression mirrors the Janus-faced direction of each intellect's gaze. Each contemplates that which is immediately superior and reflexively turns toward the next inferior intellect, both acquiring knowledge and being itself an object of knowledge. The knowledge uniting this chain of intellects is that of the divine essence, which becomes progressively diluted as it is traced down the ranks of the incorporeal beings. The intellectual exchange between the intellects manifests itself on the ladder, which is pure form, the domain of those "holy forms" unadulterated by any material substrate.

Why do the angels, according to the midrash, end up congregating on one rung of the ladder? For one thing, it serves to thwart any misconception that what distinguishes these beings is spatially related. Intellects composed of pure form do not occupy any unique space, and therefore the individuating factor separating them is the object of their thought. The more sublime the intellectual focus, the more noble the rank.[82] Their ultimate assembly on the same step facilitates conceiving of ascending and descending as abstract motion rather than as anything concrete. Since this movement does not achieve any spatial distinction relative to each other, as they all converge in the same location, it must convey a different type of activity. That activity, as we have shown, is determined by drawing from the lexicon of the first part and imbuing these terms with their cognitive implications. The intelligences (angels) are therefore capable of ascending and descending and yet remain stationary on one rung, since their activity is noetic rather than physical. They are permanently engaged in a divine enterprise, that of intellectual apprehension "which does not require an instrument,"[83] and the directional movement is a measure of the gravity of what is being apprehended.

What are we to make of the dimensions of each angel, emphasized as the equivalent of one-third of the world, and accordingly the midrashic calculation of the width of the ladder as one world plus a third (4 angels assembled on one rung $\times$ 1/3 = 1⅓). Firstly, the calculations do not offer up the desired equation. Maimonides informs us that the basis for the midrashic dimension of angel as one-third of the world is the threefold division of all creation into separate intellects, spheres, and first matter (*GP*, 273). If this is the case, then it is each class of existence that constitutes one third and not each individual in a class. Secondly, if the angels, who are explicitly identified as separate intellects, comprise one class (and there is no contraindication to this), then the ladder need not be expanded beyond one-third of the world, as it accommodates the angels of one class on one of its steps. Of course, if the angels do not correspond to an entire class, then we remain with less than one-third of the world. Finally, assuming that there is a solution to this mathematical conundrum, what kind of knowledge is gained from being exposed to something in excess of the world? If "the world" supposes the state of existence in toto, then any excess is either incomprehensible or simply redundant.

It is very possible that this built-in imprecision regarding measurement of being is intended to stimulate the reader's mind to a more abstract overview of the structure of being. Maimonides himself admits that although his fourfold schema of the universe may not precisely correspond to the views of contemporary physics, it is conceptually expedient, for "our purpose is to count all the forces that we have apprehended in a general way in that which exists without troubling to give a precise account of the true reality of the intellects and the spheres" (*GP*, II:11, p. 274). His primary declared purpose "is to show that the existents that are below the Creator, may He be exalted, are divided into three parts" (*GP*, II:11, 274). The tripartite division of the existents is paramount and concedes some latitude for contrivance of details. The dream itself, as depicted biblically, has the angels mobile but does not provide for any interaction. Maimonides introduces the midrash to supplement the biblical portrayal of distinct and disparate beings with a more uniform view of existence. This is accomplished by the angels converging on one step. The spatial accommodation that allows for this discloses the metaphysical cohesive force that brings the intellects into contact with each other—the "overflow." Width does not facilitate ascending and descending but accounts for how these beings come into contact with each other. Since they are not physical bodies, contact cannot imply spatial proximity. Width is a metaphor for that ideational connective thread between the intellects known as the overflow.

The overflow serves as the cohesive cosmic force that binds the universe into a unitary whole. Each successive rung on the hierarchy of being is imbued with its vitality by its predecessor. The overflow provides the medium of providence in the world by channeling governmental forces from the uppermost echelons of being to the lowest. This chain of command is summed up concisely as a predominant consequence of the cosmic regime Maimonides has constructed, which is intended

> to show that governance overflows from the Deity, may He be exalted, to the intellects according to their rank: that from the benefits received by the intellects, good things and lights overflow to the bodies of the spheres: and that from the spheres—because of the greatness they have received from their principle—forces and good things overflow to the body subject to generation and corruption.[84]

The separate intellects act as both the generative source for each other and the spheres[85] as well as the governmental seat of authority. Each angel on the ladder, therefore, can be said to represent its entire class in the sense that it is both the recipient of the fecund overflow from above and a transmitter of it to what is below. All of the intellects (and indeed all of being), converging into each other via the overflow, are conveyed by the image of the four angels congregating on one step of the ladder. This image also reinforces the perception of the world, as Maimonides formulated it earlier on, to "know that this whole of being is one individual and nothing else"

(*GP,* I:72, p. 184). The overflowing forces of interconnectedness in all of being account for a harmonious and holistic edifice that is "useful for the demonstration that the deity is one" and reflect that "the One has created one being."[86] Of course, when the unity of God is mentioned, much more than simple numerical value is implied. The same force that cements the universe into an integral unit is also responsible for its internal governance. It, therefore, as we have seen with the separate intelligences, is instrumental in immunizing God from the interventionism that personal providence entails. In this sense the unity of God, which defies affectability, attributes, change, and external knowledge, is immaculately preserved.

There is still one component missing from the scheme and can be accounted for by the surplus fraction of the world that the midrashic dimensions of the ladder reveal. The four angels are the four intellects who govern the four spheres (or the nine intellects that govern the nine individuated spheres). There remains one intellect who does not preside over a sphere but funnels all the forces of the superior intellects down into the sublunar realm—the Active Intellect. Because it is responsible for sublunar matter (*GP,* II:4, II:11), form (*GP,* II:12, p. 280), and human rational activity (*GP,* II:4, p. 257; II:37; III:8, p. 472) (including prophecy [*GP,* II:36]), it is the most relevant for man. The fact that it is, as Davidson characterizes it, "an eternal cosmic transmitter, broadcasting an undifferentiated range of forms as well as the substratum that can receive them," renders it the mirror of all being for man.[87] This angel constitutes that extra third which is the conduit between the higher elusive intellects and ultimately God. In its capacity as the conveyor of thought, form, and governance, by way of being the final outlet for divine overflow to the world of man, it enhances man's ability to glimpse into the divine realm. At the same time it defines the limits of human thought and maintains the distance required so that any conceptualization of the Deity remains free of anthropomorphic corruption.

Immediately following the calculation equating the width of the four angels with the world plus a third, a verse is cited from Zechariah with no obvious relevance to the context. Zechariah's vision of four chariots appearing from between two mountains of brass (Zech. 6:1) is deciphered for the prophet by an angel (within the vision itself) as "the four airs of the heavens which go forth after presenting themselves before the Lord of all the earth" (6:5).[88] The implication of this angelic elucidation of the vision is *"they are accordingly the cause of everything that comes to pass in time"* (*GP,* p. 273). The point of departure of these "airs" is identical with the "sons of God" *(elohim)* who are members of the divine retinue in the opening scene of Job. The latter also "present themselves before the Lord" (Job 1:6, 2:1), forming a quorum for the divine tribunal. The term "present themselves" (whose root is *natzov*—stand erect—the subject term of *GP,* I:15) bears two connotations regarding the status of these beings:

1. their presence is intentionally sought for their own sake and they do not arrive as an afterthought (*GP,* III:22, p. 487);
2. "they exist as subject to His order in what He wills" (*GP,* p. 488).

Zechariah's use of the phrase is then cited as evincing the same trait in his four "airs." This juxtaposition corroborates drawing an equivalence between the four "airs" and the separate intellects as follows:

1. God's associates in Job are the *benei elohim,* and we have seen that *elohim* in certain contexts indicates the intellects (*GP,* II:6, p. 261). The *"Elohim of the elohim"* of Deuteronomy 10:17 is identified as the "deity of the angels" as opposed to the spheres. Those beings that most closely resemble God in the sense that they are pure intellects are the separate intellects, and therefore qualify as His "children" *(banim),* as *images* and *likenesses* of Him.[89] The *benei elohim* are also specifically mentioned by Maimonides in the Mishneh Torah as one level among ten of separate intellects.[90]
2. When positing the intellects' roles as intermediaries of God's governance, the notion is reinforced by midrashic exegesis that rejects an autocratic God: "The Holy One, blessed be He, as it were, does nothing without contemplating the host *(pamaly'a)* above" (*GP,* pp. 262–63). There is no better graphic illustration of this midrashic assertion than the assembly that convenes in the opening scene of Job. Maimonides expresses particular delight in the wording of this midrash, as it captures the sense that "God looks at the world of the intellects and, in consequence, that which exists overflows from Him."[91] The two biblical instances of heavenly deliberation cited to illustrate this cooperative administration both relate to man as the ultimate repository of this intellectual overflow. Genesis 1:26, "Let us make man in our image," refers to that essential ingredient which endows man with his natural form—intellectual apprehension.[92] This is the intellect that "God made overflow unto man" (*GP,* I:2, p. 24), the most proximate benefactor of which is the Active Intellect. Genesis 11:7, "Come let us go down," contemplates

the confounding of the language of those responsible for the Tower of Babel. Language is, of course, unique to man and is the concrete linguistic expression of rational thought *(image)*.[93] The image of the Heavenly Council as depicted by these two verses defines the relationship of man to that council in terms of success and failure in receiving the divine overflow. Genesis 1:26 constitutes union with that flow which cascades down to man.[94] Genesis 11:7 envisages the alienation from God, manifest in the dissonance between internal reason and external speech, that the "confounding of language" entails.[95]

3. One of the verses quoted in the Mishneh Torah illustrating the versatility of angelic forms appearing in prophetic visions is Psalm 104:4: "He makes his angels airs *(ruchot)*" *(GP,* II:4). In this chapter "angels" are explicitly identified as the immaterial intellects *(GP,* II:3); hence "airs" *(ruchot)* is a metaphor for the separate intelligences.

4. One of the equivocal senses of the term *ruach* (air) discussed in *GP,* I:40 is that of purpose and will. Therefore, when it is apposite to God it assumes the sense of the "ordering of His will" and His governance. An alternative sense offered in the same chapter, the choice of which is determined by its context, is "the divine intellectual overflow that overflows to the prophets and in virtue of which they prophesy." It is no coincidence that the term connotes both senses, since the "divine intellectual overflow" and divine governance are synonymous. The *ruach* supplied by the intellects via the Active Intellect[96] catalytic of prophecy is also the embodiment of divine governance in the world. Superlative prophetic cognition consists therefore in apprehending God's all-embracing governance. Knowledge of divine governance is proportionate to the strength of the overflow culminating in the unsurpassed Mosaic revelation of the manner in which all existing things "are mutually connected so that he will know how He governs them in general and in detail" *(GP,* I:54, p. 124).

Divine purpose and governance are predetermined constants, being both monotonous and invariable. *Ruach* (air) is the key term that conveys this perpetual force within Ezekiel's vision of the Chariot. The movement of the *living creature* is ascribed to divine purpose, as in Ezekiel 1:12: "Whither the air *(ruach)* will be they will go, they turned not when they went." According to Maimonides, the combination of this verse and 1:20, "Whithersoever the air *(ruach)* will go, they will go thither, as the air to go," emphasizes the immutable nature of the divine purpose, since *ruach* remains unalterable. God himself resolutely acts in accordance with this pristine will: "Thus the direction in which God wished the *living creature* to go had been determined; the *living creature* takes the direction that God had wished it to take; and the will is constant regarding this direction" (*GP*, III:2, p. 419). The overflow that effectuates God's will is also a constant multidirectional flow accessible by way of orientation from what is beneath: "For its action is constant as long as something has been prepared so that it is receptive of the permanently existing action which has been interpreted as an overflow" (*GP*, II:12, p. 279).

The four airs of Zechariah's vision, therefore, are synchronous with the four angels of Jacob's dream. They both represent, at one and the same time, the separate intellects and the totality of existence that partakes in the overflow linking all three segments of the universe.[97] The meaning that *ruach* imports from other parts of the *Guide* reflects back on Jacob's angels, who are interchangeable with Zechariah's *ruchot*. What is revealed to Jacob is their pivotal role in transporting God's will, and being "accordingly the cause of everything that comes to pass in time" (*GP*, II:10, p. 273). Zechariah's vision, then, draws the reader's attention to Job, a parable whose central theme is providence, and then to the *ma'aseh merkavah*, where *ruach* is emblematic of divine purpose. Its very introduction within the context of determining the size and number of Jacob's angels suggests an identity between the *ruchot* and angels, transforming Jacob's dream into a discourse on providence and the structure of being. Jacob's vision is a minimalist version of the *ma'aseh merkavah* in Ezekiel.[98]

I have argued that since the Active Intellect is the conduit enabling the overflow of the higher intellect to trickle down to the sublunar realm, it is representative of its entire class. In this sense it can be viewed as being as expansive as one-third of the world. Another clue that tends to substantiate this inference surfaces in a diatribe against those who prefer to see tangible angels behind every natural phenomenon rather than as abstract natural forces. Seduced by the sensual, this class has a penchant for grotesque imagery that would have an angel be "a body formed of burning fire and . . . his size . . . *equal to that of a third part of the whole world*"(*GP*, II:6, p. 263). However, if this class was to be presented with a scientific account that substitutes natural causation for angels, "or that all the forms *derive from the act of the Active Intellect and that the latter is the angel*" (*GP*, pp.

263–64), they would deem it repugnant. In effect, Maimonides is admonishing his more learned audience to revamp any primitive angelology they may subscribe to so that it accords with contemporary science. Therefore, when one encounters graphic angelic imagery in the rabbinic corpus one must apply the rules of allegory and metaphor to escape the fatuousness of the literal. By setting up as alternatives a crude, oversized angel and a more refined "giver of forms," guidance is offered on how to approach one particular instance of rabbinic hyperbole. Any mention of an angel bearing the dimension of a third of the world is to be replaced with the Active Intellect and its role as informer of the lower world. It is precisely this function that is accomplished by channeling the overflow from the superior intellects down to earth, which we have claimed this dimension alludes to.[99]

7. "And behold the Lord (YHVH) stood above it"

All the movement in the dream transpires in the ladder, while that being which occupies the space beyond or at the top of the ladder remains inert *(nitsav)*. The austere and rigid philosophical connotations of this "standing erect" have already been thoroughly canvassed as signifying "God's being stable, permanent and constant" *(GP,* I:15, p. 41). He is distinguished from the vehicles of governance in the world, the intellects, who are the emissaries of *elohim* by his appellation YHVH. This name is singular in its "clear unequivocal indication of His essence" *(GP,* I:61, p. 147) by virtue of it being nonderivative. It is the sole name whose etymology, so to speak, cannot be traced back to anything in the world, whereas all others are "derived from terms signifying actions" *(GP,* I:61, p. 147). The only path leading to this notion is one of divestiture, in which God is dissociated from the world that mirrors His actions. Pristine in its immutable transcendent state, the God captured by this name must be methodically disengaged from the world so that it can be perceived as pure Form imparting form *(sulam)* to the world from the remotest of distances (above the *sulam).* "If you envisage *His essence as it is when divested and stripped of all actions,* He no longer has a derived name in any respect whatever, but only one original name that indicates His essence. In fact we have no non-derivative name except the one in question, namely, *Yod, He, Vav, He" (GP,* I:61, p. 149). Negative theology approaches that essence by preventing all terrestrial nomenclature from circumscribing it. Yet it must also be supplemented by a radical reevaluation of God's relationship to the world that does not disturb His immutability, as depicted by the static posture of "standing erect."

If negative theology demands eschewing any linguistic framework within which God can become familiar to man, then wherein lies the aperture through which God can gain any entry into man's life? I believe we are furnished with the key to that entryway by Maimonides' allusion to the Targumic rendition of this last segment of Jacob's dream. One of the numerous references to the Targum Onkelos's programmatic disavowal of biblical anthropomorphisms[100] is the reference to the "Lord stood erect upon it." In consonance with this general approach, the Targum Onkelos substitutes for God some other divine notion that is omitted from the verse. In this instance it is the "glory *(yekar'a)* of the Lord" that is doing the "standing" and not the Lord Himself. *Yekar'a* is the usual Aramaic rendering by the Targum Onkelos of the Hebrew *kavod* (glory) and may very well be the intended association appurtenant to singling out this component of Jacob's ladder as representative of the Targum Onkelos's method.[101]

The "glory of YHVH" *(kavod)* is a technical term in the Maimonidean lexicon, and its equivocation expresses the ambivalence of the *Guide* toward an absolute transcendence and a qualified transcendence concept of God.[102] The two relevant meanings are[103]

1. The essence and true reality of God, inaccessible to the human mind as expressed by the negative response to man's request for disclosure of God's glory, and
2. The "honoring of God" that "consists in apprehending His greatness. Thus everybody who apprehends His greatness and perfection, honors Him *according to the extent of his apprehension.*"

The two meanings together define the epistemological limits to which the mind is confined. Though the ultimate honor due God, consisting of an intimate acquaintance with His essence, is unattainable, there is a somewhat diminished honor that man can bestow upon God. Limited apprehension of God that falls short of "true reality" remains a viable ambition. Just as the measure of providence is extended to man in his intellectual achievement, so the honor yielded God is a factor of that very same endeavor. Honor is a reflexive consequence of providence directed back toward God. The glory of God, to which Jacob was privy at the top of the ladder, is not some divine aura that graces man but rather, as with providence, is a function of a human undertaking. The *kavod* that is the divine essence is insulated from mortal cognition by virtue of its *nitzav* state and all we have seen that is philosophically associated with that immutability. On the other hand, there is a *kavod* that man generates by way of intellect. It is only in this latter sense that one can say man "relates" to God. Though Maimonides does allow for a *kavod* that manifests as a sensual created realia,[104] it is merely as a concession to those of inferior intellects whose religious sensibility cannot thrive without some tangible divine presence. It is the lesser of two evils, since the alternative of direct anthropomorphic attribution poses a far greater danger to the religious credo. For those of Jacob's kind, however, the *kavod* is demythologized into a product of man's intellectually creative process.[105]

The *kavod* to which man can aspire is that which the angels declare fills "the whole earth" (Isa. 6:3). The earth is replete with *kavod*, not because of spatial occupation but because "the whole earth bears witness to His perfection" (*GP,* I:19). It "bears witness" solely by man's investigation and contemplation of it, which results in the intellectual glorification of God. The world is "indicative of [the] power and wisdom of Him who brought them into existence" (*GP,* I:64, pp. 156–57) to those who plumb its order and beauty. The intellects, who ascend and descend in the company of the overflow, are also ipso facto *kavod* generators in the sense that they contemplate God and communicate that activity which bears witness to God's glory via the intellectual overflow. That overflow, which extends to the human realm, stimulates rational thought and elevates man to the domain of the intelligibles, amounting to, for Maimonides, God's presence on earth. God's glory is a product of the intellectual process and has no independent subsistence. Isaiah 6:3, "The whole earth is full of his glory," is experienced as an intellectual objective and cited as an expression of the fact that what accompanies man is not a mystical presence but rather "the intellect that overflows toward us and in the bond between us and Him, may He be exalted" (*GP,* III:52, p. 629). The intellect is the overture to God and the progenitor of His presence on earth: "Just as we apprehend Him by means of that light which He caused to overflow to us . . . so does He by means of this selfsame light examine us; *and because of it He may He be exalted is constantly with us* examining from on high" (*GP,* III:52, p. 629).

The Targum Onkelos's approach is critical for determining the philosophical subtext of prophetic visions such as Jacob's. It compensates for omission in the biblical text by inserting its own divine genitive when all there is in the verse is simple divine presence, as in Jacob's dream, or to mediate divine activity in others. For Jacob, as has already been noted, the ladder merely extends to what the heavens represent, whereas there is no actual contact with the "standing" existent beyond it. Resort must be had to the Targum Onkelos's assertion of "glory" *(yekar'a)* as the focus of any rapport between man and God. The Aramaic rendering depicts the glory in a preparatory state[106] rather than the static, entrenched one of standing. This aspect of the diversity is predisposed to the human intellect and awaits its arrival to be fully configured. Jacob perceives that both divine providence and divine presence are creatures of the mind.

The Coalescence of Three Interpretations

Although the three interpretations of Jacob's ladder offered by Maimonides in the Mishneh Torah and the *Guide* vary, they do not conflict. Jacob, in his pedagogical capacity, cannot disseminate indiscriminately the personal teaching obtained, as described in *GP,* II:10, since this involves metaphysics (the Chariot)—a discipline whose open discussion is subject to halakhic restrictions. On the other hand, the communal message cannot be entirely incongruous with its esoteric core. The two inferior messages of the Mishneh Torah (historical prognostication) and *GP,* I:15 (political authority) are informed by the metaphysics of *GP,* II:10. Thus informed, they are, for Jacob, sublimated from mere sociopolitical guidance to corollaries of the structure of being represented by the ladder. All the layers of content—the political, physical, and metaphysical—reflect an ever-increasing esoteric domain and remain the provenance of those of prophetic stature. Even the political and physical/natural are subjects to which the public is not privy. At the same time, some of these restricted teachings filter down to the audience at large, albeit in a diluted format, via the pedagogical talents of the particular recipient prophet. Access to abstruse social, political, and metaphysical theory is provided through the legislation and practical guidance the prophet formulates on the basis of his theoretical maturity.

Chapter 7 of the Mishneh Torah introduces the essential tenets of a belief in prophecy that includes the qualifications necessary to earn the title "prophet" as well as what constitutes prophetic activity. Jacob's vision is adduced as one of six examples of prophetic imagery, the interpretation of which becomes immediately apparent to the prophet within the vision itself. Of the six, only the parable of Jacob's ladder is singled out for its parabolic referent to the future subjugation of Israel by various empires.

The allusion is to a well-known tradition, similar versions of which are to be found in a variety of midrashim.[107] As Sara Klein-Braslavy has already noted, the two key terms used to indicate kingdoms *(malkhiyot)* and subjugation *(shibud)* positively identify the midrashic source from which Maimonides draws, where both these terms appear.[108] Since the full import of Maimonides' comment cannot be appreciated without evaluating its midrashic predecessor, the full text as extant in the *Pesiqta DeRav Kahana* will be quoted here:

> R. Berechiah, citing R. Helbo who cited R. Simeon bar R. Jose in the name of R. Meir, said: The verse in Genesis teaches that the Holy One showed to our father Jacob the prince of Babylon climbing up and climbing down, the prince of Media climbing up and climbing down, the prince of Greece climbing up and climbing down, and the prince of Edom climbing up and climbing down. The Holy One then said: "Jacob, climb thou also." Thereupon Jacob grew afraid and said: Am I to suppose that as these princes are to have a come-down, I am to have a come-down too? The Holy One replied: "*Thou wilt not come down, O Israel* (Jer. 30:10). If thou climbest up, thou wilt never have a come-down." But Jacob did not believe God and did not climb up. In regard to Jacob's lack of faith, R. Berechiah citing R. Helbo who cited R. Simeon bar R. Yosina, said that R. Meir in expounding the verse *For all this they sinned still, and believed not in His wondrous works* (Ps. 78:32) attributed Israel's lack of faith [in other circumstances] to the example set by our father Jacob who lacked faith enough to climb up. [When Jacob would not climb up], the Holy One said to him: Hadst thou believed Me and climbed up the ladder's rungs, thou wouldst never have had to climb down. Since thou didst not believe and didst not climb up, the result for thy children in this world will be their subjection under the four kingdoms who will impose levies on entire communities of Israel, levies on crops and herds, and all sorts of exactions and poll-taxes. One might suppose that God was declaring that this subjection would last forever. But not so, for He went on at once to say [words that were addressed to Israel as well as to Jacob]: *Thou wilt not suffer a come-down, O Israel; for lo, I will save thee from afar* (Jer. 30:10).[109]

The choice of this particular variant may have been dictated by its narrative structure, which lends itself to Maimonides' view of the personal and public facets of prophetic vision. The vision of ascending and descending empires is presented as a forecast of shifts in the geopolitical map of the world with no particular bearing on Israelite history. The brunt of imperialistic hegemony by these kingdoms is then borne singularly by Israel as a punishment for a momentary lapse in faith by Jacob. Within the midrash,

Jacob's vision of the angels is primarily one of the waxing and waning fortunes of future political regimes. The decree that Jacob's descendants are to be subject to the oppression of these regimes is secondary, and only a reaction to Jacob's snubbing of God's invitation to scale the ladder. Mindful of the *Guide's* nonliteral approach toward midrash, how would Maimonides assimilate this midrash?[110]

Each angel of Jacob's vision is identified with the "prince" *(sar)* of the four successive empires and not with the empires themselves. We have already noted that all the imagery of Jacob's dream intimates a metaphysical teaching concerning the anatomy of being. This includes the tracing of all God's governance to the intermediaries of angels (separate intellects) *(GP,* II:6, p. 262) and locating the medium of that governance in the overflow *(GP,* II:12, p. 279). That stream of governance terminates with the Active Intellect, which in turn filters it down to earth. Rabbinic tradition recognizes this latter intellect as "the *angel* and the *prince of the world (saro shel 'olam)*" *(GP,* II:6, p. 264). What Jacob sees initially is consonant with the metaphysics of the ladder—the rise and fall of political fortunes and the survival of collective peoples are attributed to the "prince" *(sar)*, or the natural continuous governance of higher intellectual forces. Absent any human intellectual vitality, these regimes, driven by imaginative goals of power, wealth, and territory, cannot master their own destinies and are doomed to failure. Their ascent and descent are solely a function of arbitrary forces in that "they are given over to whatever may happen to befall them. For there is nothing to protect them against whatever may occur; for they are like one walking into darkness, whose destruction is assured" *(GP,* III:18, p. 476). Their demise *is assured* because they are merely at the whim of the ascending/descending movement of the "prince" who is the intellect.

Jacob, on the other hand, is addressed in his personal capacity. Jacob's ascent is not to be attributed solely to the movement of a *sar*, but must proceed due to his own initiative. Ascending, for Jacob, is an intellectual process that affords escape from the world of chance and fate, and opportunity to establish contact with the world of the intelligibles. Though Jacob's aspirations do not converge with the coarse ambitions of the empires, his hesitancy in scaling the ladder betrays a frustration that ultimately he will share their destinies. At this juncture in the midrash, Jacob cannot comprehend how the prophet can ever avoid this common fate, since he too must inevitably return from the coveted isolation of lofty pursuits to the cave of social reality. The providence he attracts due to his intellectual ascent will, of necessity, dissipate on resumption of his duty to govern the people. Social commitment detracts from the concentrated devotion of the mind requisite in maintaining the prophet's providential immunity against mechanistic forces. Jacob would rather not venture up the ladder at all than risk the pain of enjoying an ephemeral moment of blissful divine contact only to quickly fall back into the ranks of those who are estranged from that contact. If the end is to return to the fold, why not remain in it?[111]

God's response to Jacob's reluctance is vital, for it envisions a prophetic model that is at odds with the one predicated upon the Jacob's ladder imagery in *GP,* I:15. Jacob receives God's assurance that no descent will ensue from his ascent and that whatever heights are achieved will endure. *GP,* I:15, however, sees the order of ascending and descending on the ladder as paradigmatic of the prophetic agenda, in which descent is an automatic reflex of ascent. "For after the *ascent* and the attaining of certain rungs of the ladder that may be known come the descent with whatever decree the prophet has been informed of—with a view to governing and teaching the people of the earth." Although this is the message of the dream as processed by the prophets' imagination for public consumption, the divine guarantee of perennial ascent in the midrash imparts quite another message for Jacob himself. The midrashic challenge to the purported standard prophetic model as presented in *GP,* I:15 leads one in the direction of III:51, where both can be reconciled in the superlative degree of perfection realized by Moses and the Patriarchs. Their ascent was *essentially* permanent, while their descent was only apparent. These individuals display a behavior in which there is such an extreme dissonance between mind and body as to warrant a modern clinical diagnosis of schizophrenia. What may be classified as deviant by current psychiatric standards, though, is considered by Maimonides to be an ideal of human perfection, "in which he talks with people and is occupied with his bodily necessities while his intellect is wholly turned toward Him, may He be exalted, so that in his heart he is always in His presence, may He be exalted, while outwardly he is with people."[112] In this archetype of human perfection there is only an appearance of "descent," since only those ingredients not essential to man qua man are involved—the corporeal. The portrait of the prophet as a community activist presented in *GP,* I:15 is thereby preserved for the sake of enjoining public obedience to the prophet. However, since the true essence of man lies in the intellect, which is his true form, and since that intellect is oblivious to external reality and remains focused on the true objects of being, the true person has never really descended.[113] The private metaphysical teaching of *GP,* II:10 is thereby also reserved for Jacob personally.

Why are Jacob's fears of descent not allayed by God's assurances in the midrash? What can account for Jacob's lapse in faith (for "he did not *believe* and did not ascend")? After having described this state of union with God leading the Patriarchs and Moses into "a permanent state of extreme perfection in the eyes of God, [in which] His providence watched over them continually even while they were engaged in increasing their fortune" (*GP,* p. 624), Maimonides expresses some skepticism as to whether this can be held out as a realistic goal. Incredulity regarding its attainment is revealed in an unusual impressionistic assessment that "this rank is not a rank that, with a view to the attainment of which, someone like myself may aspire for guidance."[114] This rank of perfection is so foreign to human experience and so extends the boundaries of intellectual growth that it eludes any rational categorization.[115] Acceptance of this perfection as potentially attainable involves a leap of faith, since it may very well transcend any ratiocinative class and constitute what David Blumenthal has termed "postcognitive devotion to God."[116] Jacob is unprepared at this stage of his intellectual journey to accept so extravagant a possibility. The midrashic choice of disbelief is an apt one within the Maimonidean reinvention of its context. It is "belief" that is called upon to assimilate an objective of an abiding ascent, unsubstantiated by experience or logic.

Routinely the midrash correlates circumstances in its narrative to some biblical verse accounting for its occurrence and assigns it theological significance. In this instance, Jacob's flawed faith corresponds to that found in Psalm 78:32: "With all this, they still sinned, and they had no faith in his wondrous acts." The reference in this particular psalm is to the lack of faith demonstrated by the Israelites in the desert, despite having been miraculously provided with manna to sustain them in their trek through this barren terrain. Subjected to the Maimonidean interpretative lens, this would be a fitting rationale for Jacob's foible within the philosophical allegorization of the midrashic narrative. Manna is the perfect symbol of the utopian state reached by Moses and the Patriarchs. Manna is the solution to how one can be intellectually obsessed with God to the exclusion of all else and yet continue to thrive in the mundane world of physicality. The parable[117] of manna raining down on God's people in the desert represents, for Maimonides, the universal prescription that "those who wholly devote themselves to His service, may He be exalted, *are provided by Him with food in an unthought-of way*" (*GP,* III:24, p. 499). The lesson of the manna, as articulated by Psalm 78:32, is precisely that rebuffed by Jacob. The goal of a perpetual ascent need not be followed by the descent that physical survival demands. Continuous providence is a natural concomitant of this state in which all material needs are somehow negotiated: "[T]hat individual can never be affected with evil of any kind. For he is with God and God is with him" (GP, III:51, p. 623). Manna is the allegory of having an extraneous physical occupation while being intellectually engrossed in God's presence.

The final relevant exchange in the midrashic dialogue between Jacob and God, if taken at face value, impugns the inviolate justice characteristic of Maimonides' God. Punishment for Jacob's transgression is reserved for his descendants, who will be oppressed by those four imperialist powers. For Maimonides, vicarious suffering constitutes an injustice that is inconsistent with divine wisdom, which calls for consequences directly related to personal behavior. Reward and punishment are a function of individual merit and operate in accord with the apothegm "All his ways are judgment, a God of faithfulness and without iniquity" (Deut. 32:4).[118] The midrashic quid pro quo for Jacob's sin can become tenable if the literal is relinquished in favor of the figurative vocabulary provided by Maimonides' lexicon. In this case it is the term "children" that is in need of processing through that lexicon so that it is in fact a reference to some aspect of Jacob's own person. One of the figurative meanings assigned to the term yalod (bear children) is "with reference to happenings within thought and the opinions and doctrines that they entail" (GP, I:7, p. 32). By extension, the term "children" can designate something born of the mind, like opinions (GP, I:7, p. 32). The "children" who will bear the brunt of God's wrath are now identified with a facet of Jacob's personality. Jacob's thought processes and intellectual maturity will be frustrated to some extent by the natural progression of history as represented by the four kingdoms. Those processes will be subject to that domain, and not be entirely liberated from it, as they would have been had Jacob accepted the possibility of permanent ascent, which transcends the constraints of material history. The punitive reaction is now a measured one responding to a dereliction of the mind with retribution in kind. This may account for future regressions in Jacob's prophetic talents, such as transpired "during the time of his mourning because of the fact that his imaginative faculty was preoccupied with the loss of Joseph."[119] The midrash then concludes with the assurance that there will eventually be a resurgence of prophetic function with the liberation of "your progeny" (read: mind) from captivity.

Since the prophetic process follows the route of the overflow from God to the Active Intellect to the prophet's rational faculty and finally to his imaginative faculty (GP, II:36, p. 369), there must be a connective thread that can be traced through its transfigurations. The overflow's journey from its ultimate transcendent source cannot be so disjointed as to disengage the final repository of its contents, the imaginative faculty, from what has preceded it. Otherwise there can be no distinction between political and prophetic governance. What distinguishes the latter from all other authorities is the adroitness at transmogrifying the metaphysical truths to which he is privy into pronouncements the public can digest. Their speculative prowess "has a counterpart in their giving information regarding matters with respect to which man, using only common conjecture and derivation, is unable to give information. *For the very overflow that affects the imaginative faculty . . . is also the overflow that renders perfect the acts of the rational faculty . . .*" (*GP,* II:38, p. 377). Each stage of the overflow's transmutation en route to its final destination must bear the seeds of its successor. As it flows downward, the content becomes progressively diluted, undergoing a metamorphosis from objective truth (Active Intellect ⇒ rational faculty) to subjective (imaginative faculty = fine + bad). The people's yearning for guidance and comfort is sated by prophetic utterances that issue from the depths of the prophet's psyche but are clothed in the "language of the sons of man." All the while the prophet's own internal perspective is not occluded.

Jacob's ladder and its trivalent exegesis in the Maimonidean corpus discloses precisely the harmony between the rational and the imaginative. The prognostication of the Mishneh Torah's symbolization is of sociopolitical significance for the people. As a sanction for halakhic disobedience it also provides an impetus for conformity with the law. For Jacob, on the other hand, we have seen that it reflects the inevitable ebb and flow of history subject to the unalterable governing forces that impel it. The full midrashic context from which the Mishneh Torah excerpts its slant on the ladder imagery also adumbrates the interpretive shift advanced in I:15 of the *Guide*. Once again what is being offered the people is of practical import—the legitimization of prophetic authority. For Jacob, the ascent and descent of the prophet mirrors the orientation of the intellects as helmsmen of the universe sketched in *GP,* II:10. Howard Kreisel has noted the striking parallel between the activity of the prophet and that of the separate intellects,[120] both of which abide by the operative metaphors of "descent" and "overflow" and, I would add, "ascent." By virtue of intellecting their superiors (ascent), all that is inferior is governed (descent) by the overflow without ever having their intellectual focus on God disturbed. This is the paradigm from which Jacob extrapolates to the prophetic model of ascent and descent.

The prophet graduates to an intellectual sophistication in metaphysics (ascent) that instigates an overflow by which he governs others (descent). Ideally he remains unswayed from his primary vocation of contemplating the source of all being. While the metaphysical blueprint for the governance of the world allegorized by Jacob's ladder remains a configuration of the prophet's mind, it pervades his ethical and political stewardship of the community at large.

CHAPTER 6

Chapter III:24 of the *Guide:*
"Trial"—The Bridge between
Metaphysics and Law

This chapter will deal with another transformative event in the lives of one of the Patriarchs—the binding of Isaac *('aqedah)*—and its implication for the superlative prophet Abraham was. I will argue that Maimonides reads the *'aqedah* as he does Jacob's ladder, treating it as a parable of utmost philosophical significance rather than as a historical record. That parable once again can only be deciphered by maneuvering through the complex interplay of prooftexts to produce, in the end, a radically new conception of what the Bible refers to as "trial," of which the *'aqedah* is but one example, albeit the most portentous. In the previous chapter the argument was made that the parable of Jacob's ladder, when subjected to a reading that views text and prooftext as a collaboration of substance rather than mere reinforcement, yields a minitreatise on providence. The result is a radically new construct that challenges previously held traditional beliefs and impels the devout but philosophically inquisitive student to reread his revered texts. "Trial" is another link in the esoteric chain that binds the theoretical section of the *Guide* to the practical section on the commandments. Our prooftext methodology, though, will serve to blur the distinction between theoria and praxis, whereby the law itself can be considered a parable.

Chapter III:24 of the *Guide of the Perplexed* examines the notion of "trial" within Scripture and presents us with an exemplary case study in Maimonides' unique brand of exegesis. It purports to deal exhaustively with a particular concept by gathering all the relevant scriptural passages and assigning to them significations, which then converge in a reformulation of that concept.[1] Strauss, in his introductory essay to the *Guide,* constructs a schema of the entire work in which he places this chapter at the conclusion of the major heading entitled "Views" and describes it as the "teaching of the Torah on omniscience."[2] Although the notion of trial does raise difficulties with respect to God's knowledge, the issue of omniscience per se does not figure prominently in this chapter. It will be demonstrated that this chapter is a self-contained unit that traverses the boundaries of what Strauss calls "views" and "actions" and is strategically positioned as a transitional point between the two, arriving at the very end of the discourse on providence and preceding the section dealing with the rationale for the commandments.

Although Maimonides' notion of trial and the binding of Isaac, in particular, have been the subject of study by some scholars[3] no one, to my knowledge, has undertaken a detailed analysis of the underlying hermeneutic linking all the trial passages to produce a common conceptual theme. It will also be seen that Maimonides manipulates prooftexts to construct an esoteric exposition on the notion of trial that, when unraveled, provides a link between what has preceded and what follows and colors the entire ensuing discussion of the commandments. The combination of particular verses quoted as prooftexts for various propositions and supportive scriptural references, which both point beyond their contextual presentation and bear the imprint of significations assigned to them elsewhere in the *Guide,* are the literary devices of this esotericism. Through Maimonides' exegesis it will be shown that what he posits as the very crux of the notion of trial— namely, that it "consists as it were in a certain act being done, the purpose not being the accomplishment of that particular act, but the latter as being a model to be imitated and followed"—is itself an allusion to how one ought to regard the discussion of trial within the scheme of the *Guide.* That is, the purpose is not necessarily the understanding of the notion of trial within Scripture but rather of how that notion directs us toward the higher message that is integral to the *Guide.*

At the very outset we are forewarned of a probable esoteric discussion with the remark that the subject of trial "is one of the greatest difficulties of the Law." If the book does in fact contain esoteric discussions, as Maimonides makes clear throughout his introduction to the treatise, then surely an issue described as one of the greatest difficulties of the Law would require such a treatment.[4] The difficulty of the subject matter is accentuated by its strategic positioning within the book, sandwiched as it is between what Strauss has noted to be the two main divisions of the book: views and actions. It will be seen to be the bridge between philosophy and Law, between intellectual endeavor and religious observance. In order to arrive at our conclusions, particularly with respect to the striking manner in which Maimonides manipulates the various scriptural verses and references, we will adhere closely to the introductory directives: "[I]f you wish to grasp the totality of what this Treatise contains, so that nothing of it will escape you, then you must connect its chapters one with another; and when reading a given chapter, your intention must be not only to understand the totality of the subject of that chapter, but also to grasp each word that occurs in it in the course of the speech, even if that word does not belong to the intention of the chapter" (*GP,* introduction, p. 15).

The error that the masses are inevitably prone to make on the issue of trial is identified by Maimonides as being "that God brings sufferings onto the innocent man in order to increase his reward in the future" (*GP,* III:24, p. 497). This opinion, previously endorsed and presented as the doctrine of "compensation" by no less a thinker than Saadiah,[5] had previously been dismissed with the proposition that "for Him justice is necessary and obligatory, i.e., an obedient individual receives compensation . . . and [is] punished for all evil acts" (*GP,* III:17, pp. 470–71). This critique is reinforced by the identical rabbinical maxim "There is no death without sin . . ." both here and in *GP,* III:17. The only difference is that the part of the verse in Deuteronomy 32:4 that describes God as "a God of faithfulness and without iniquity" is cited exclusively in the chapter on trial. The rabbinical maxim appeals to the common man's most basic instincts regarding justice, while the biblical quotation is descriptive of God's nature. With this verse Maimonides ventures into the metaphysical realm, wherein the nature of the divine is contemplated with a view to grasping ultimate truths. That Deuteronomy 32:4 is pivotal for Maimonides can be seen from the fact that it is the biblical verse cited the most times in the *Guide.* It is also the verse that virtually brackets the entire section on the rationale for the commandments being cited in its introductory chapter, III:26, and its concluding chapter, III:49. The essential link between the '*aqedah* and the commandments to be developed in this chapter is reinforced by the strategic appearances of this verse.

We cannot fully appreciate what this verse (Deut. 32:4) conveys without viewing it as a continuation of a line of thought initiated with the first part of the very same verse: "The Rock—His work is perfect." In *GP,* I:16 the term "Rock," when referring to God, is rendered the philosophical equivalent of "He is the principle and efficient cause of all things other than Himself."[6] One who truly comprehends this philosophical premise will not fall into the trap to which most people are prey and which is the cause of the collapse (or origin) of their primitive theodicy—an anthropocentric view of the world: "[T]he reason for this whole mistake [evil + God] . . . [the] multitude considers that which exists only with reference to a human individual . . . and if something happens contrary to what he wishes he makes the trenchant judgement that all exists is an evil . . . according to us on the other hand what exists is in existence because of the will of its Creator."[7] That God is the principle and efficient cause of all things other than Himself lies at the very heart of the argument for a theocentric outlook and repudiates the arrogance associated with anthropocentrism.

The logical conclusion of the anthropocentric argument is a simplistic, mechanistic equation between man's conduct and reward and punishment in which God acts as mediator. Anything that upsets that equation raises the theodicy problem. In order to maintain the balance, therefore, the notion of "sufferings of love" is introduced, whereby the innocent suffer to increase reward. "Trial" is a pivotal link in the mechanism because trial, within the context of sufferings of love, is the response to the imbalance in the equation as perceived by the multitude. All answers are reduced to the framework of reward and punishment. The masses prefer to see Job's reward increased to preserve their simplistic beliefs rather than assimilate the highest metaphysical truth—the "Rock" or First Principle and efficient cause of all else, which demands a mammoth intellectual effort requiring a virtual mastery of the entire corpus of Aristotelian physics and metaphysics for its true comprehension.

It is the "Rock" principle that unites all the trial passages mentioned in this chapter of Maimonides and renders it a cohesive unit dealing with a primary metaphysical truth. The reader is confronted by an intricate weave of passage and text that obliges him to proceed with caution. On the one hand, Maimonides uses trial as an allegory of knowledge and truth regarding the divine nature. On the other hand, the danger of antinomianism becomes more of a concern, since ethics is no longer the sine qua non of reward and punishment. He, therefore, is conscious of the need to avoid so radically upsetting traditional notions of reward and punishment, which might lead people down that road. What awaits us at the end of this acrobatic act is not the demise of God but rather a heralding of His existence and absolute truth.

At the very core of the Maimonidean religious model is the intellect. The goal toward which man must strive is knowledge of the world and, subsequently, knowledge of the divine, with the end of knowledge being the outermost limit of human intellectual capacity. The pinnacle of human intellectual achievement is personified by Moses, who stretched the boundaries of the intellect to the extent humanly possible, arriving at the ultimate vision of God's "back." "Back" is an equivocal term that, when used as a referent to God, is but a metaphor for knowledge of that which "follows Me, has come to be like Me, and follows necessarily from My Will—that is, all the things created by Me."[8] Moses is the model for the rigorous training and painstakingly slow and meticulous research and study required to arrive at the ultimate truth. Moses initially demonstrates intellectual restraint at the burning bush by "hiding his face" (i.e., he does "not make categoric affirmations in favour of the first opinion that occurs to him") and is rewarded for this with looking upon the "figure of the Lord."[9]

Hastiness and straining of thought without proper preparation leads to imperfect apprehension. The "nobles of the children of Israel" are portrayed by Maimonides in stark contrast to Moses; because of this error, they were led to an inferior vision of God ("His feet") tainted by corporeality (*GP,* I:5, p. 30). Maimonides thereby concludes that it behooves all to "aim at and engage in perfecting our knowledge of preparatory matters and in achieving those premises that purify apprehension of its taint which is error. It will then go forward and look upon the divine Holy presence" (*GP,* I:5, p. 30). The consequence of their warped vision, Maimonides thinks, is that "their actions too were troubled because of the corruption of their apprehension [and] they inclined toward things of the body" (*GP,* I:5, p. 30), as is indicated by the end of the passage: "and they visioned God and did eat and drink" (Exod. 24:11). A supremely sublime apprehension is unfortunately debased by the supremely mundane—eating and drinking.

This very idea provides the key for understanding Maimonides' minitreatise on trial and its pivotal location within the *Guide*. The teaching that lies implicit in Maimonides' presentation on trial is that intellectual, and therefore human, perfection mandates a slow, deliberate, methodical thought process that will lead one to a correct understanding of the ultimate truth. Any wavering from this almost tortuous path will lead one astray and will result in perversion, both intellectually and morally. A careful analysis of each illustration and its accompanying passages in *GP,* III:24 will bear this out.

Trial Passages

False Prophet vs. Intellectual Conviction

We are told that the purpose of trial in the Torah is not the accomplishment of the particular act concerned but rather its "being a model to be imitated and followed." The first passage illustrative of trial is that of the sending of a false prophet or dreamer in order to test and to "know whether ye do love God" (Deut. 13:4). This trial serves to highlight publicly the certitude of the Jewish people's faith in God and commitment to His Law. The knowledge that is acquired here is not by God but by the "religious communities."[10] The analogy for this type of "knowledge" is offered by the prooftext in Exodus 31:13, where the reason underlying Sabbath observance is to "know that I am the Lord that doth sanctify you." The interjection of a Sabbath-oriented prooftext provides an allusion to a critical aspect of this trial to be emulated. Elsewhere in the *Guide* the scriptural justification for the cessation of work on the Sabbath—"and he reposed on the seventh day" (Gen. 20:11)—is grammatically transformed by Maimonides to mean that God "established" existence on the seventh day: "[E]very day of the preceding six, events occurred that did not correspond to the established nature that exists at present in the whole of existence, whereas on the seventh day the state of things became lasting and established just as it is at present" (*GP,* I:67, p. 162). The chapter immediately following *GP,* III:24 focuses primarily on the telos of divine actions in the production of the world. Its central prooftext corroborating the notion of an abiding purposefulness in every aspect of creation is the divine assessment at the very peak of creation, "God saw everything that He had made and behold, it was very good" (Gen. 1:31). This "good" is representative of the orderliness and design of all facets of creation originating in wisdom rather than pure arbitrary will (*GP,* III:25, p. 503). It is the same "good" that Moses views from the vantage point of God—that is, a firm understanding of how all the minutiae of creation coordinate and interconnect (*GP,* I:54, p. 124).

The creative process serves as a model for the thought process. The building blocks are laid over a period of six days, becoming progressively more entrenched, and it is not until the seventh day, after an arduous and methodical construction, that existence gains its permanence and is fixed for eternity.[11] That fixedness manifests itself in all details of existence being "well arranged and ordered and bound up with one another, all of them being causes and effects" (*GP,* III:25, p. 505). Thought that is similarly programmatic will endure and not lapse or revert to more base origins, because it emulates the process by which the consummate knowledge of Moses is obtained—the teleology of cause and effect. The Sabbath analogy fully understood, then, reflects on the moral of the false prophet trial. The false prophet attempts to deceive by way of a sign or miracle that, in reality, is simply the "quick fix" upon which people have come to rely. The Israelites, on the other hand, are a role model for "everyone who seeks the truth, for he will seek out beliefs that are so firm that when one has them one pays no attention to the man who tries to compete through working a miracle" (*GP,* p. 499). The conviction of true beliefs can be acquired only by "seeking" and not by relying on some extraneous phenomena such as miracles. If Israel's faith in God was based merely on miraculous wonderment, then that faith would be a tenuous one subject to attack by subsequent competing miracles. Truth acquired by a laborious process of education and logic has the strength to withstand the persuasive techniques of a false prophet. That process culminates in an understanding of the interconnectedness of the whole that is disturbed by the miracle of the false prophet. That miracle intrudes upon the orderly causality of the world and therefore subverts the notion of its underlying wisdom. The "competing" miracle is rooted in the vitiation of all order and chain of causation in favor of arbitrary will.

The Sabbath analogy assumes even greater significance when examined in light of Maimonides' particular view on miracles and their place within the natural process. According to Maimonides, miracles are not an interruption of, or intrusion into, that process but rather are an integral part of nature simply programmed at the time of creation to appear when they do.[12] In *GP,* II:29, a midrash is adopted as an expression of the idea that "when God created that which exists and stamped upon it the existing natures, He put it into these natures that all the miracles that occurred would be produced in them at the time when they occurred" (*GP,* p. 345). The prophet's "sign," then, is attributed merely to his "knack" for knowing when a certain thing that was already woven into the fabric of nature will occur. The Sabbath, which is the culmination of the creation, is the crowning event of nature. Once the Sabbath caps the creative process, the immutable laws of nature have been fixed and contain within themselves what we tend to view as miracles but that are, in reality, nothing more than rare and unique expressions of nature. The false prophet, therefore, cannot possibly manipulate his knowledge of these events to lend credibility to a message that refutes God's work. Properly understood, the miraculous event is simply a vindication of God's original word at creation, which remains constant. It would be self-contradictory to accept the false prophet's refutation of God's commandments, rationalized as a change in His will, based on a miracle that is, in fact, a confirmation of the immutability of His will.

Maimonides expresses this same opinion in a parallel exposition within his commentary on the Mishnah in *Aboth* 5:5, which lists ten things that were created by God in the twilight hours during the seven days of creation.[13]

He states that one should not think "that there are renewed manifestations of Will at every point in time but rather at the beginning of the formation of things, whatever would happen in the future was placed in their nature, whether it be frequent, i.e., natural or rare, i.e., a sign." It is significant that the six passages accumulated by Maimonides that mention trial all relate to phenomena that are listed in this Mishnah as having a special place in creation:

Passages Dealing with Trial	*Aboth* 5:5
1. Deuteronomy 8:2, 8:16; Exodus 8:2— All these passages refer to the receiving of manna in the desert.	Manna
2. Genesis 22:12—The verse that initiates the binding of Isaac episode	Ram of Abraham (this is the miraculous event occurring at the climax of the *aqedah* by providing a sacrificial replacement for Isaac).
3. Deuteronomy 13:4; Exodus 20:17— These are the false prophet passages that are grounded in the receiving of the Torah at Sinai.	A. The writing of the Torah. B. The characters of the Tablets. C. The Tablets themselves. All of these take place at Sinai.

The false-prophet trial passages are predictions made at Sinai and account for the vital role played by the Sinaitic theophany. They act as a safeguard in withstanding the test of false prophets in the future. The Torah, the characters on the Tablets, and the Tablets themselves are clearly all products of the revelation at Sinai and are substantive evidence of its mass communicative clarity.

Maimonides' resolution of the problem that the notion of trial poses for God's omniscience is implicit in the link binding the six passages where trial appears. This link is the immutable order of the universe established by God at creation, thereby excluding the possibility of any new knowledge being acquired by God. When combined with Maimonides' theory of miracles and the grouping of *Aboth* 5:5, his previous discussion on divine omniscience remains not only unchallenged but also fortified. In *GP*, III:21, the distinction between God's knowledge and human knowledge is analogous to that between knowledge the artificer has of the artifact and that which spectators have of it. God's knowledge is a priori, and man's is a posteriori: "His knowledge of things is not derived from them so there is a multiplicity and renewal of knowledge. On the contrary, the things in question follow upon His knowledge which preceded and established them as they are."[14] Any knowledge, therefore, gained from the results of any of these trials cannot possibly be for God's benefit, as all knowledge is self-contained in the origins of creation.

Ultimately, the esoteric message of the passages discussed thus far concerns the nature of prophetic knowledge, which is inextricably bound to intellectual endeavor. The prophet can tap into God and his knowledge only through intense efforts on his own part to develop his intellect and to gain an all-encompassing awareness of the workings of nature and the creation. His ability to perform miracles and render predictions is attributable to the extent he has perfected his intellect and accumulated knowledge of the creation and therefore of God. The full philosophical implications of this are obfuscated, as they place the prophetic experience outside the reach of the common man regardless of how he conducts his life. Though elsewhere Maimonides explicitly rules out mass availability of prophecy (*GP,* II:32, pp. 362–63), it is its appearance within the context of the chapter on trial that presents potentially disturbing implications for the public. My argument here advances a reading of *GP,* III:24 as a preface to the explication of the commandments. The naturalization of the prophetic process rendering its attainment virtually identical with the philosophical stance on prophecy (*GP,* p. 361) situates the prophet as a philosopher, albeit one with an active imagination (*GP,* II:36, p. 369). The prophetic mind is the only one capable of sifting out the primary from secondary perfections the Law aims at, and therefore the Law cannot be ideally fulfilled by the common man, who fails to appreciate the speculative aspect of each and every law. The faith of the common man may be placed in jeopardy at the prospect that normative perfection is just as remote as intellectual perfection.

Manna and the Natural Process of Acculturation

Once we move on to the next three passages concerning trial (and all relating to "manna" in the desert), the discussion becomes increasingly complex in that an additional meaning is assigned to the term "trial." The first meaning provides a model of religious conduct for the religious communities of the world. The particular case of manna conveys the knowledge "that those who wholly devote themselves to His service, may He be exalted, are provided by Him with food in an unthought-of way" (*GP,* p. 499). This notion is appropriate in two of the manna passages, Deuteronomy 8:2 and Exodus 16:4. It is the third passage, found in Deuteronomy 8:16, that poses a problem for Maimonides, as it suggests that God imposes suffering so that He can ultimately increase reward—an opinion already dismissed by Maimonides as conflicting with God's justice: "[W]ho fed thee in the wilderness with Manna, which thy fathers knew not, that He might afflict thee, and that He might try thee out *(nasotekha) to do thee good at thy latter end.*" The solution to this problem lies in a variant meaning of *nasotekha* as "to accustom thee." The "good," which awaits the people, is simply the contrast of rest after being accustomed to misery and weariness. It also serves to harden the people in preparation for their battle to conquer the land of Israel, "for prosperity does away with courage, whereas a hard life and fatigue necessarily produce courage, that being the 'good' that, according to the story in question, will come *at their latter end.*"[15]

Exodus 13:17–18 provides the prooftext for this last idea: "[F]or God said lest per adventure people repent when they see war and they return to Egypt. But God led the people about by way of the wilderness of the Red Sea." The supposed reason for causing the Israelites to wander the desert endlessly is to have them increasingly build up strength and courage rather than be thrown haphazardly into immediate battle and most probably "repent when they see war," that is, retreat out of fear and return to Egypt. What is crucial here, and what once again emerges out of the notion of trial, is that certain results can be achieved only via a long, arduous, and almost insurmountable process of maturity.[16]

The wilderness passage referred to provides us with the point of intersection between the world of thought and the world of action. It is this very passage that acts as the prooftext for Maimonides' rationale of animal sacrifice. That rationale is based on the psychological insight that man cannot make the transition cold turkey, so to speak, from one state to its opposite and is incapable of abandoning instantly everything to which he has become accustomed. Allowing a repugnant form of worship, while at the same time subjecting it to strict regulation and rigorous control, will eventually wean him off it: "[T]hrough this Divine ruse it came about that the memory of idolatry was effaced and that the grandest and true foundation of our belief—namely the existence and the oneness of the Deity—was firmly established—while at the same time the souls had no feeling of repugnance and were not repelled because of the abolition of modes of worship to which they were accustomed and than which no other mode of worship was known at that time."[17]

The presentation of this additional meaning of trial as "becoming accustomed to," combined with the resort-to-the-wilderness analogy here and

in *GP,* III:32, suggests that Maimonides may, in fact, be deliberately concealing a message to which only his elite readers will be attuned. That
message necessitates a painstaking process of preparation for their ultimate perfection in the realms of both thought and action. Two reasons may
account for Maimonides' choice of communicating this idea in the subtle
fashion he did:

1. The onerous requirements of training and discipline leading to intellectual perfection already prevent a large majority of the people
   from ever aspiring to reach that goal. This leaves them, at least,
   with the hope that obedience to commandments and correct action
   can still offer religious salvation and closeness to God. To impose
   the same rigor on the performance of the commandments may prove
   to be an insurmountable obstacle to the general masses, leading
   them into ultimate despair at the prospect of the challenge that
   awaits them.
2. In the world of thought, the learning process requires the comprehension of ideas and the formulation of opinions that become progressively more refined and sophisticated. The ascent to intellectual perfection entails the continuous discarding of opinions that
   have fulfilled their role in leading to the next stage of more pristine
   knowledge. To treat alike the spheres of law and action would lead
   to the conclusion that once the repetition of a certain ritual or law
   has achieved its ultimate purpose in terms of what Maimonides
   calls the "second perfection," then the external performance can
   be discarded.[18]

The further use in *GP,* III:32 of the wandering-in-the-desert analogy
renders the previous discussion of the false prophet passage and its implications with respect to miracles as nature much more pertinent. The connective thread between the trial passages becomes more evident. Within
the very same argument for the rationale behind sacrifices, the following
question is raised: What is there to prevent God from "giving us a Law in
accordance with His first intention and from procuring us the capacity to
accept this?" (*GP,* p. 528). Maimonides prefaces his response with the rhetorical remark that one may ask that same question with respect to the wan-
dering in the desert: "[W]hat was there to prevent God from making them
march by way of the land of the Philistines and procuring them the capacity
to engage in wars so that there should be no need for this roundabout way?"

(*GP*, p. 528). The response to both these questions, we are told, is identical: "God does not change at all the nature of human individuals by means of miracles . . ." (*GP*, p. 528). Even though it is within God's power "according to the foundations of the Law of the Torah, He has never willed to do it, nor shall He ever will it" (*GP*, p. 528). The wandering-in-the-desert analogy, then, points us to the proposition of the immutability of nature as a whole, including human nature, and the premise that this system will never be tampered or interfered with. The easy way out, or the quick fix, as represented by the idea of a miracle or a sudden interruption in an actual process wholly unrelated to what has preceded it and to what follows it, is not available to man. Human nature, like miracles, can be perfected only by the slow process of "acculturation."

Enduring Future Trials—The Message of Sinai

The next trial passage addressed by Maimonides is the one consisting of Moses' response to the people's plea at Sinai not to receive the divine message directly any longer, "lest we die" (Exod. 20:16). Moses admonishes them not to fear, "for God is come to try you out" (Exod. 20:17). This translates into an assurance by Moses that the personal revelation at Sinai will act as a buffer against any future pretenders who contradict what they have witnessed: "[F]or if . . . I had said to you what has been said to me without your hearing it for yourselves it would have been possible for you to fancy that what is told by another is true, even if that other had come to you with something contradicting what has been known to you."[19] In *GP*, II:33, Maimonides, basing himself on a midrash,[20] states that only the first two commandments were heard by the people *with* Moses (as opposed to *via* Moses): "[F]or these two principles, I mean the existence of the Deity and His being one, are knowable by human speculation alone" (*GP*, p. 364). These first two principles are distinguished from the other commandments, which "belong to the class of generally accepted opinions and those adopted in virtue of tradition, not to the class of the intellecta." According to Maimonides, these two principles can be the only ones heard individually by the people within the context of our chapter's discussion of Exodus 20:17. They are invincible and timeless, because they are firmly rooted in demonstration and arrived at by way of rational speculation.[21]

The excursus on trial doubles as an esoteric preface to the general discussion of the Law and its rationale. If the people at Sinai are armed with nothing more than simple human apprehension to combat alien and heretical ideas, then what hope is there for the bulk of humanity? Can they ever be sufficiently prepared to withstand the alluring persuasions of a false prophet? Can Moses' assurance of Exodus 20:17 possibly be extended to the people as a whole? Maimonides treads cautiously and covertly to convey the idea that the underpinnings of Sinai are human apprehension and speculation, which is wholly consonant with what he posits as the ultimate perfection toward which the Law aims: "to become rational in actu . . . to this ultimate perfection there do not belong either actions or moral qualities and that it consists only of opinions toward which speculation has led . . ." (*GP,* III:27, p. 511). The meaning of trial here, with its allusion to the firmly entrenched opinions received at Sinai, serves as the perfect introduction to the Law. The Law is ever looking back to Sinai, as is evidenced by the designation of animal sacrifice as a "Divine ruse" through which "the grandest and true foundation of our belief—namely the existence and oneness of the Deity—was firmly established . . ." (*GP,* p. 527). To pass a trial successfully is to travel the road back to Sinai, toward which the particular commandment points. That can be accomplished only through the long process of intellectualization that ultimate human perfection demands and to which only the elite few can aspire. Maimonides is, therefore, wary of the sense of futility the common man may have when faced with the notion that one must transcend the outer garment of the Law (i.e., physical performance) so as to arrive at its essence. That essence lies in the world of thought and intellect, a world from which the common man is, for the most part, estranged.[22]

The 'Aqedah—Abraham's Reasoned Choice

Maimonides' final illustration of trial as presented in the *'aqedah* episode imposes the theoretical construct developed thus far on the personage of a historic individual, Abraham. His trial serves as a pedagogic model for two "great notions that are fundamental principles of the Law" (*GP,* p. 500): (a) to know the limits of love and fear of God, which extend to sacrificing one's very own child; and (b) to know that prophecy does not consist of illusion but truth and that in the prophet's opinion he "has no doubts concerning anything in it and that in his opinion its status is the same as that of all existent things that are apprehended through the senses or through the intellect."

The essential component that renders this model an integral part of the trial exposition is the explanation of the time lapse between the divine command and the actual performance of the binding, which occurs days later. This demonstrates that Abraham's supreme act of sacrifice does not spring from "stupefaction and disturbance" but rather from "exhaustive reflection" (*GP*, III:24, p. 500). What the Talmud regards as an act of unconditional and immediate compliance[23] is, to Maimonides, an act of conscious, methodical, and lengthy deliberation. The three-day journey to Mount Moriah excludes the possibility that Abraham's act emerges from "a state of passion." Instead, it becomes a consequence of "thought, correct understanding, consideration of the truth of His command, love of Him and fear of Him."[24] The lesson of Abraham at the *'aqedah* is not one of blind obedience but of reasoned and studied choice. Abraham, then, provides the perfect prelude for the discussion of the rationale for the commandments. The attempt to render commandments rationally comprehensible models itself upon Abraham's coming to intellectual grips with a *mitzvah* prior to its fulfillment.

Though the limits of love and fear are specifically stated to be the moral of the *'aqedah*, Maimonides' prooftext for this notion in Genesis 22:12 deals only with fear: "for now I know that thou fearest God." The *'aqedah* is then described as a lesson so that "all the Adamites will know what the limits of *the fear of the Lord are*" (*GP*, p. 501). This notion is then corroborated with the verse that places fear as the "final end of the whole Torah, including its commandments, prohibitions, promises and narratives." This is referred to in its dictum "if thou wilt not take care to observe all the words of this Law that are written in this book, that thou mayest fear this glorious and awful name" (Deut. 2:58). Love is curiously omitted as the end goal of the *'aqedah* and Torah as a whole. Toward the end of the chapter, when summarizing the teachings of the *'aqedah*, love once again returns to the scene, and it says that Abraham's action has "made known to us the ultimate end toward which the fear and love of God may reach" (*GP*, p. 502).

I can account for this only as another deliberate attempt to confuse the issue. The masses may be prone to a sense of futility if they realize that the *'aqedah* is a tale extolling the intellect as the supreme virtue, and Maimonides wishes to prevent this from arising. It is clear that for Maimonides, Abraham is the rationalist par excellence, who arrives at knowledge of the existence of God, His unity, and His being the creator and governor of the world by way of his own keen intellectual curiosity and lengthy intensive speculation.[25] It is also clear from the comments in the Mishneh Torah that Abraham is the supreme exemplar of the *love* of God (in direct and explicit contrast to *fear* of God), who "performs the commandments and pursues the path of wisdom, not because of anything in the world, and not on account of fear of any evil and not in order to inherit the good but . . . because it is the truth . . . that is the status of Abraham. . . ."[26] The laws of repentance in his legal code conclude with the absolute dependence of love on intellectual apprehension and achievement. The caliber of love for God is directly proportional to the amount of knowledge one possesses: "[I]f a little, then a little and if a lot, then a lot."[27]

By allowing for the interplay of fear and love, Maimonides accomplishes two things. First, he leaves the masses with something to which they can cling and a religious experience for which they can strive. They can aspire to a normative life that obtains for them, if not consummate fulfillment, then at least partial fulfillment of their religious objectives (*GP,* p. 629). They can also take solace in the twofold aim of Torah depicted in *GP,* III:52: "[F]or these two ends, namely, love and fear, are achieved through two things: *love* through the opinions taught by the Law which include the apprehension of His being as He is in truth: while *fear* is achieved by means of all actions prescribed by the Law . . ." (*GP,* p. 630). If love is unattainable, then at least fear is an option. Second, the interplay, omission, and subsequent reintroduction of love at the end of the chapter are the hints planted for the other audience—the sophisticated and philosophically adept one. They will note the imaginary division of aims which, in fact, collapse into one final end—knowledge of the Creator.[28] Maimonides follows his own scholastic program[29] in which motivational devices of fear become increasingly redundant along the path toward service based on pure love: "[T]herefore when children, women and the general public are taught, they are taught only to worship out of fear and in order to obtain reward; until their knowledge is increased and they become increasingly wise, then this *secret* is revealed to them little by little and they become comfortably *accustomed* to this concept until they apprehend Him and know Him and worship Him *out of love.*"[30] Abraham himself personifies that state of pure speculation constituting love of God. He was not the source of any legislative call to the people, as was Moses. God addressed Abraham only with respect to his private affairs, and in turn "he had addressed a call to the people by means of speculation and instruction" (*GP,* I:63, p. 154).

The final verse offered as a prooftext that Abraham was the pioneer in perpetuating the belief in unity, Genesis 18:19, is itself expressive of the two divergent currents of thought that intersect in the personality of Abraham: "[F]or I have known Him, to the end that he may command his children and his household after him that they may keep the way of the

Lord, to do righteousness and judgement." This verse is quoted twice by Maimonides in his legal code, within the context of both moral action and ethical traits. The "way of the Lord" is equated with the ethical rule of the "golden mean," which is what Abraham taught his descendants.[31] One who is scrupulous in his charitable obligations becomes a member of the class known as the seed of Abraham, who "do righteousness."[32] In contradistinction to the legal code, the *Guide,* on a number of occasions, integrates this verse into the portrait of Abraham as the expositor of abstract and speculative ideas. In *GP,* II:3, Maimonides reiterates the function of Abraham as teacher, postulated in I:63, and elaborates further, basing himself on Genesis 18:19: "[T]hus Abraham taught the people and explained to them by means of speculative proof . . . attracting them by means of eloquent speeches and by means of the benefits he conferred upon them."[33]

Again in *GP,* III:51, Abraham is described as having achieved "union with God—I mean apprehension of Him and love of Him" (*GP,* p. 624). Genesis 18:19 is then referred to as indicating that "the end of all their efforts was to spread the doctrine of the unity of the Name in the world and to guide people to love Him" (*GP,* p. 624). The emphasis in both citations is on love as apprehension, and Genesis 18:19 becomes another scriptural prooftext for the Abraham trial as a speculative model rather than as a practical one. Alternatively, Maimonides' exegesis of Genesis 18:19 in the code leaves it sufficiently adaptable to accommodate the practical/ethical facet of Abraham, so that the masses can also consider themselves his disciples.

The second notion derived from the *'aqedah* is that the prophetic experience is one of reality and truth and not illusion and deception. The fact that prophecy is conveyed by way of a dream or vision does not detract from its inherent truth. The epistemological status of that "truth" is, for the prophet, the equivalent of "all existent things that are apprehended through the senses or through the intellect" (*GP,* p. 501). The proof of this is Abraham's compliance with the command to slaughter "his son, his only son, whom he loved (Gen. 22:2)," "for if a dream of prophecy had been obscure for the prophet or if they had doubts or incertitude concerning what they apprehended in a vision of prophecy they would not have hastened to do that which is repugnant to nature . . ." (*GP,* p. 502). Aside from establishing the validity of prophecy, this notion is striking when contrasted to the later characterization of certain commandments as a "Divine ruse." They were designed purposefully so that "the souls had no feelings of repugnance and were not repelled because of the abolition of modes of worship to which they were accustomed . . ." (*GP,* III:32, p. 527). The common man must be nurtured in accordance with that to which his character has become accustomed, even if it be at odds with the truth. The prophet, on the other hand, is so overwhelmed by his sense of truth to which his intellectual striving has driven him, that he will act contrary to his very nature in pursuit of that truth.

The irony of this contrast would be evident to the serious reader of the *Guide.* The vehicle of ritual sacrifice is illustrative both of the low point and the apex of human perfection. In the case of Abraham, his superlative rank of perfection is captured in a parable of human sacrifice repugnant to human nature, yet pleasing to God. In the case of the masses and mandatory animal sacrifices, there is an exact reversal of these attitudes. I would agree with those scholars who argue that Maimonides did not appreciate the *'aqedah* as an actual historical event but rather perceived it as a prophetic parable.[34] The substance of God's command is not, in itself, as significant as is its use as a stylistic tool and ironic device forming a link in a chain between thought and action. It is a parable of the limits of human perfection, where the persistent plodding of the intellect has arrived at the point of absolute truth when it can direct man to transcend his material nature. It is Abraham's "consideration of the truth of his command" that propels him to act. That truth is signified by the content of the command, which simply cannot be the literal slaughter of his son. This is further borne out by the classification of Abraham at the time of the binding as representing "the highest degree of the prophets whose states are attested to by the prophetic books, after the perfection of the rational faculties of the individual, considered as necessary by speculation has been established. . . ."[35] The eighth to eleventh degrees of prophecy listed by Maimonides in *GP,* II:45 are *visions* as opposed to lower degrees of *dreams*, and each one of those four highest degrees is exemplified by Abraham. The *visions of prophecy* are reduced by Maimonides to a common experience in which "only parables or intellectual unification are apprehended that give actual cognition of scientific matters similar to those, knowledge of which is obtained through speculation . . ." (*GP,* p. 403). Abraham's successful passage of this trial manifests itself in the world of the mind and cognition and not in the world of tangible phenomena.[36]

Omission of a Trial Passage: Bitter Waters and the Perfect Law

After having scrutinized Maimonides' explicit exegesis of the notion of trial as expressed through the six passages he accumulates, we must direct ourselves to what has been omitted. Often silence and omission are as intrinsic to the exegesis as what is overtly argued in the text. There is one instance of trial that is conspicuously absent,[37] which appears in the episode of the "bitter waters" in Exodus 15:22–26: "[T]here he made for them a statute and a judgement and there he tested them" (*GP,* II:32, p. 530). The solution to this striking omission lies in the discussion of animal sacrifice, where this very verse figures prominently in the development of his argument.

Maimonides argues that the Law aims at two intentions, the second being the prescribing of the performance of modes of worship that are not in themselves valid but are useful in the battle to efface idolatrous practices such as animal sacrifice. The first and primary intention, though, is the "apprehension of God." Maimonides supports this thesis with the introduction of Exodus 15:25 as a post-Exodus and pre-Sinaitic legislative promulgation:

> It has been made clear both in the Scriptural text and in the traditions that in the first legislation given to us there was nothing at all concerning burnt offerings and sacrifices . . . for the first command given after the Exodus from Egypt was the one given us at Marah namely . . . "there he made for them a statute and a judgement . . ." and the correct tradition says "the Sabbath and the civil laws were prescribed at Marah." Accordingly this statute referred to is the Sabbath and the judgement consists in the civil laws, that is in the abolition of mutual wrongdoing. And this is as we have explained, the first intention: I mean the belief in correct opinions, namely, the creation of the world in time . . . accordingly it is already clear to you that in the first legislation there was nothing at all concerning burnt offerings and sacrifices, for as we have mentioned these belong to the second intention. (*GP,* p. 531)

Maimonides, therefore, considered this a utopian statute that was clearly superior to Sinaitic legislation, since it addressed itself solely to matters of "primary intention." The "first" legislation, in the chronological sense, at Marah is also "first" in a qualitative sense in that it is free of secondary intentions of accommodation. Marah is both temporally prior and intrinsically superior to Sinai, as it is untainted by "second intentions," which are conditioned by the "gracious ruse" of accommodation to human nature.

In light of this bold and daring exegesis of Exodus 15:24, we can hypothesize as to its absence from the roster of trial passages in *GP,* III:24. The perfect law aims solely at the propagation of correct opinions and the prevention of mutual wrongdoing, thereby preserving the stability of the social structure. It has little use for ritual per se and is oblivious to matters of "secondary intention."[38] Maimonides' interpretation of trial serves as an ideal of the relationship between man and God, which is to be emulated and from which one can derive various teachings. The particular exegesis he has applied to this verse, rendering it as evidence of a pre-Sinaitic utopian law superior in nature to Sinai, prevents him from including it in *GP*, III:24, as it would deliver a confusing message to the common man. On the other hand, its very omission will direct the sophisticated reader of the *Guide* to it and to the realization that it is wholly consistent with the manner in which trial has been esoterically portrayed, culminating in the pre-Sinai figure of Abraham. The goal of man is to perfect his appreciation of the Law to the point where he can discern between the primary and secondary intentions. Once that is accomplished he must transcend the world of secondary intentions to reach the realm of primary intentions as Abraham did. Ultimately he must return to the "bitter waters" state of Law. Marah is the legislative equivalent to the intellectual state of Adam prior to eating the forbidden fruit. Both are utopian models toward which man must aim in the quest for human perfection. The normative ideal of Marah corresponds to the cognitive ideal of Eden.

The Quarry of Efficient Causality

Finally, we arrive full circle at the verse with which we commenced our study: "[T]he rock, his work is perfect, a God of faithfulness and without iniquity" (Deut. 32:4). The first half of the verse, coupled with the meanings assigned to the equivocal term "Rock" *(tsur)* in *GP*, I:16, is the medium through which the entire chapter coalesces. One of the figurative meanings attributed to *tsur* is "the root and principle of everything," which paves the way for Maimonides' exegesis of Isaiah 51:1–2, "look unto the Rock whence ye were hewn, look unto Abraham your father. . . ." Abraham is identified with the *tsur* in the sense that one must "tread therefore in his footsteps, adhere to his religion and acquire his character in as much as the nature of the quarry must be present in what is hewn from it" *(GP,* p. 42). That is the exoteric Rock/Abraham of the *'aqedah* representing moral stature and superlative ethics. The esoteric Abraham, though, is what is alluded to by the Rock's most sublime figurative meaning as conveyed in Deuteronomy 32:4: "He is the principle and efficient cause of all things other than Himself." The verse "and thou shalt stand erect upon the rock"

(Exod. 33:21) is then wrenched from its apparent sense of geographical location and transformed into an object of intellectual contemplation. It now means "rely upon and be firm in considering God, may He be exalted, as the first principle. This is the entryway through which you shall come to Him . . ." (*GP*, p. 42). This is the esoteric Rock/Abraham to whom the elite will turn in appreciation of the spiritual forerunner "from whence they were hewn." Ostensibly, Maimonides sets out to solve the enigma that trial poses for God's justice as indicated by the second half of Deuteronomy 32:4. The reverberating silence of the first half *(tsur)* will stimulate the elite to search elsewhere in the treatise for Maimonides' elusive teaching. In *GP*, I:16 they will discover the emergence of the following equation: Rock = Abraham = intellectual contemplation of the first principle and truth = entry to God = message of the *'aqedah*.

We have demonstrated that Maimonides' true teaching comes to the fore at a crucial juncture in *GP*, III:24 and permeates the entire treatise. The summum bonum of life consists of intellectual virtue, and Abraham is viewed, primarily, as an intellectual archetype.[39] Once all these scriptural references are understood and analyzed in terms of both their appearance and nonappearance in *GP*, III:24, and combined with references and exegesis dispersed throughout other chapters of the treatise, it can be concluded that *GP*, III:24 is a holistic endeavor crafted to equivocate regarding the summum bonum. At the same time, it lays the groundwork for the ensuing discussion on the rationale for the commandments. The primary and secondary intentions of the commandments can be seen to be the model upon which the intentions of the *Guide* itself are expressed.

CHAPTER 7

Reflections on the
Ultimate Verses of the *Guide*

The first chapter of the *Guide* is prefaced by a plea, framed in the words of Isaiah 26:2, to access a domain normally secured by gates: "Open ye the gates, that the righteous nation that keepeth faithfulness may enter in." Those who are initially locked out of that domain are Job's compatriots, morally perfected ("righteous," "faithful") but not yet wise.[1] Just as in his vision Ezekiel's chariot arrives through the "opening of the heavens" (Ezek. 1:1), so the "opening of the gates" anticipates an enlightenment of near-prophetic quality for the readers of the *Guide*.[2] Revelation is earned, not endowed, and the means to earn it is offered in Maimonides' very first exegetical exercise with biblical terminology. "Image" *(tselem)* and "likeness" *(demuth)* are scriptural expressions for that which is shared by man and God alike. Man is "like" God notionally, not tangibly, in the cultivation of his human form, intellectual apprehension. *Imitatio dei* is performed in its truest sense by the ethereal cultivation of abstract rational thought "which does not require an instrument," thereby approximating, as far as humanly possible, a divine activity.[3] Man discovers his essential form by being privy to God's mind as expressed in Genesis 1:26, "Let us make man in our image, after our likeness." Maimonides commences his treatise with the origins of man in the divine consciousness. He then constructs a hermeneutical framework throughout the corpus of the treatise within which Scripture is read so that man can conform to his prototype engendered by the design intentions uttered in Genesis 1:26.

Of course, the opening of gates in Isaiah 26:2 links up with the utopian state souls will enjoy once these gates are opened, a state envisioned at the very end of Maimonides' introduction. Upon entrance to places once restricted they "will find rest therein, the eyes will be delighted and the bodies will be eased of their toil and labour" (*GP,* p. 20). The key, though, that unlocks these gates is not, strictly speaking, knowledge of philosophy but rather is identified with the ability to penetrate Scripture and determine its import. The lexicography—the verses cited in constructing the lexicographic edifice—and all the biblical passages alluded to—provide the reader with the master key: "I shall begin to mention the terms whose true meaning, as intended in every passage according to its context, must be indicated. This, then, will be a key permitting one to enter places the gates to which were locked" (*GP,* p. 20). What I have attempted to accomplish in my book is to demonstrate how the *Guide* conforms to this stated purpose by locating its message in the ancient sources of tradition. If the Torah speaks in the language of men, then it must communicate with men of all times. Maimonides, I believe, more than anyone else in the intellectual history of Judaism, enabled the Torah to do so by liberating it of its archaisms, while at the same time allowing it to speak its core message. Reverence for Holy Writ remains undiminished.

Once the teaching of the *Guide* has been grasped, the "opening" hoped for at its inception takes the form of human enlightenment at its end. Accordingly, the penultimate verse quoted by the *Guide* says that the messianic yearnings of Isaiah will come to fruition when "the eyes of the blind will be opened [from the Hebrew root *pkh*] and the ears of the deaf shall be unstopped [from the Hebrew root *pth*]" (Isa. 35:5). The opening of gates manifests itself ultimately in the literal "opening" of ears, allowing a hearing. But that hearing follows the kind of "opening" *(pkh)* of which Maimonides tells us; it conveys only "the uncovering of mental vision and in no respect is applied to the circumstances that the sense of sight has been newly acquired" (*GP,* I:2, p. 23). Once again the reader is thrust back to the origins of man, to the Garden where, ironically, the very term for enlightenment *(pkh)* designates an intellectual deterioration of primal man: "And the eyes of them both were opened *(pkh)* and they knew that they were naked" (Gen. 3:7). The *pkh* of this verse charts the intellectual regression of man ideally occupied with truth to an inferior social, pragmatic, and political awareness resulting in a judgmental perception of "nakedness" rather than being. The pairing of *pkh* with eyes is a deliberate reference to the debacle it designates in the Garden of Eden. As a metaphor for mental awareness, the quality of that awareness must be judged by its context. To digest the message of the *Guide,* then, is to reverse the direction that the "opening of eyes" took in the Garden and retrieve that which Adam lost— his true human essence and form, his *tselem.*

The reversal of Adam's downfall is not completed with the acquisition of intellectual maturity signified by the "opening of eyes" alone. It must be combined with an unplugging of the ears. Adam failed to heed a command warranted by his intellectual capabilities.[4] His intellectual decline was preceded by a lapse in auditory function. As one of the figurative meanings of "hearing" is apprehension,[5] so Adam, in order to transgress, must not have fully appreciated the rationale for this divine commandment, something every commandment must have.[6] Within the halakhic framework as well, a deaf person *(cheresh)* is not duty bound by *mitzvot,* since he is not considered compos mentis *(bar da 'at),* and thus is incapable of fulfilling the norms dictated by the Law.[7] Maimonides' quote of Isaiah 35:5 signifies that the success of his project is dependent upon audibility as well as sight. While both senses indicate understanding, the former leads to being a proper subject of the Law. It is not sufficient to gain intellectual enlightenment that is divorced from the word of God. Maimonides has enabled the biblical texts to speak by training his disciples to hear the foreign language with which it does so. The "unstopping of ears" dictates an ongoing engagement with the text that does not cease with attaining that level of intellectual perfection symbolized by the gaining of sight. There is a midrash that captures this notion by aligning the parallelism of Isaiah 35:5 with two stages of the Sinaitic theophany in Exodus. The experience of the Israelites' present historical redemption from slavery is cast as a kind of rehearsal for the ultimate messianic redemption prophesied by Isaiah:

Even as in the Age to Come, "Then the eyes of the blind shall be opened," so now, "All the people witnessed the thunder and lighting" (Exod. 20:19).

Even as in the Age to Come, "And the ears of the deaf shall be unstopped," so now, "All that the Lord has spoken we will do and listen to" (Exod. 24:7).[8]

Just as the sight of Exodus 20:19 indicates some form of heightened mental perception, since the vision includes sounds, so it parallels the notion of sight in Isaiah. Furthermore, the "listening" of Exodus 26:7 must allude to something more than audible sound, since it follows the commitment to action "we will do," which already assumes something heard.[9] The "listening," then, that constitutes an ongoing engagement with the text[10] follows a perfunctory knowledge of a practical nature. This is precisely what I believe Isaiah's hearing in its Maimonidean context implies—that is, a perpetual commitment to listen to the text once the intellect has been properly positioned to do so.[11]

Maimonides' aspiration to cure men of their deafness and blindness is also, at one and the same time, a call for emergence out of a state of alienation from God. Succumbing to the deficiencies of matter and its appurtenant disabilities, man lives in a realm wholly dissociated from God. God is only connected to being and in no way produces privations except in an incidental and accidental manner.[12] God's critique of Moses' reluctance to be entrusted with the sacred mission of his people's liberation is what Maimonides singles out to illustrate God's absolute isolation from what man perceives as evil in his existence. Moses' momentary lapse of faith is caused by a self-appraisal that is matter oriented and therefore focuses on a deficiency of a physical nature. God immediately responds to Moses' protests of speech impediment with the rhetorical query, "Who hath set man's mouth? Or who setteth the dumb or deaf, or the seeing or the blind?" (Exod. 4:11). It is simply in the nature of matter to be prone to corruption and deterioration. Defective matter is a privation that cannot be attributed to any agent except by accident (*GP*, III:10, p. 439). Moses then can be said to have inclined toward that facet of his person wholly estranged from God (speech defect = matter) and is jolted back to the reality of positive existence by God's retort. Isaiah's messianic prophecy of verse 35:5 is transformed by Maimonides to a call to achieve messianic bliss by cultivating human form. The *Guide* supplies the means with which to pierce through the material preoccupation of the Torah so that the formal message concerning the truth of the nature of being can be heard.[13] The peace and tranquility of the messianic era is in fact heralded by another sight metaphor that signifies a universal obsession with true wisdom: "If there were knowledge, whose relation to the human form is like that of the faculty of sight to the eye, they would refrain from doing any harm to themselves and others."[14]

I think it appropriate that a study that concentrates on biblical and rabbinic citation in the *Guide* should arrive at its own conclusion with the very last verse quoted in that work, immediately following Isaiah 35:5: "The people that walked in darkness *(choshekh)* have seen a great light; they that dwelt in the land of the shadow of death *(tsalmovet),* upon them hath the light shined" (Isa. 9:1). In the introduction to the *Guide* we are told that those who "walk in darkness" are so inferior that they don't even occupy a position on the intellectual hierarchy constructed in terms of light imagery.[15] No matter how brilliant the light shines above them, they remain impervious to it: "And now men see not the light which is bright in the skies" (*GP*, introduction, pp. 7–8).[16] Although these are the sentiments expressed at the outset of his work, I will allow myself a slight liberty in offering the following conjecture.

Maimonides has adopted this closing verse to articulate an anguished longing for a messianic ideal, the very same ideal espoused at the end of the Mishneh Torah. All men share in that constituent which graces them with their humanity—the divine *tselem*. Though his pessimistic outlook for the class of people who "walk in darkness" reflects a realistic assessment of their dismal chances for ever realizing their human form, Maimonides does not succumb to utter despair. That time is yet to come when the pursuit of the truth will be so all-pervasive that the souls of even this wretched class will be stimulated to escape the darkness to which they have been consigned. The completion of the *Guide* presented an occasion for wishful optimism that the light of knowledge will eventually seep down to all mankind. This final verse is a fitting end to the present study in that the imagery of the ultimate biblical citation by the *Guide* captures the very core of the message of Jacob's ladder. Submerged in a complex web of interconnected biblical and rabbinic prooftexts, there resides the thoroughly de-anthropomorphized God with which Maimonides intended his disciples to become acquainted. Though it entailed the surrender of a traditional responsive God, it dictated a greatly enhanced role for man in establishing contact with the new, unified divine essence. God remains fixed and immutable at the top of the ladder with the sole point of intersection between man and God located in the intellect. Providential beneficence is measured in terms of human perfection that is acquired, not granted. God's scrutiny of man is portrayed in terms of a perennial shaft of reflexive light beaming from God to man and back again, all contingent on the intellect: "The being who cleaves to him and accompanies him is the intellect that overflows toward us and is the bond between us and Him, may He be exalted. *Just as we apprehend Him by means of that light which He caused to overflow to us, as it says, "In Thy light do we see light" (Ps. 36:10)[,] so does He by means of this selfsame light examine us . . .*" (*GP*, III:52, p. 629). The latter is a pictorial representation of the theory developed in *GP*, III:18 that "providence is consequent upon the intellect and attached to it" (*GP*, p. 474). The light imagery of our final verse, Isaiah 9:2, alludes to this very principle in that it precisely parallels the directional movement traced by this providential light. The first cola of the verse presents men as having "seen a great light" (= "just as we apprehended Him by means of that light"), while the second has the light shining on men (= "so does He, by means of this selfsame light examine us"). Isaiah 9:2 is a metaphorical analogue to the mechanism of providence as depicted by the reciprocal flow of light between man and God.

The ennoblement of man as a rational animal who charts his own course toward the source of all being, however, does not come without its price. The Promethean effort requisite for achieving proximity to God carries with it the loss of a Presence that can be experienced in the immediacy of existence.[17] Concealed as well in the language of Isaiah 9:2 is the austere message of a greatly diminished tangible Presence who is blocked by a nearly insurmountable barrier from ordinary men. There is only one other passage in Maimonides' writings in which a verse pairing "darkness" *(choshekh)* and "shadow of death" *(tsalmovet)* is cited. When matching the different positions of each of Job's friends with various schools of thought on the issue of providence, Elihu is identified with the message of the following verse: "For His eyes are upon the ways of men, and He seeth all goings. There is no darkness *(choshekh)* nor *shadow of death (tsalmovet)* where the workers of iniquity may hide themselves."[18] Maimonides argues that there is no analogy whatsoever between what man means by governance, based as it is on his own experience of that notion, and divine governance. Yet, despite the impossibility of ever grasping divine knowledge, purpose, acts, or governance, there is a necessary *belief* to which man must subscribe regarding the absolute omniscience of God: "[R]ather is it obligatory to stop at this point and to believe that nothing is hidden from Him" (*GP*, III:23, p. 496). The emblematic prooftext conveying this naïve "belief," Job. 34:21–22, is archetypical of the prooftext technique as formulated in this study. Articulated as it is by Elihu, the one friend who espouses the correct view on providence, it is also nuanced with the same esoteric dialect utilized throughout his speeches.

Elihu introduces a novel notion in which he is distinguished from the other friends. During the course of lengthy speeches he reiterates those other positions, lending him the appearance of being in agreement with them. This strategy is adopted "in order to hide the notion that is peculiar to the opinion of each individual, so that at first it occurs to the multitude that all the interlocutors are agreed upon the selfsame opinion; however[,] this is not so" (*GP*, p. 495). In truth, if providence is consequent upon intellect, then those who inhabit darkness do not attract God's vision. They are simply abandoned to helplessly cope with the forces of nature. Yet, at the same time, the simplistic idea that God acts in accordance with a mechanistic equation between virtue and happiness and iniquity and misfortune, as advanced by the other interlocutors, is an "obligatory belief" in the sociopolitical sense of the term. It is a belief necessary for societal welfare and individual maturity, but it is not a "true belief" in the sense of reflecting a valid account of God's governance.[19] Regardless of his wishful thinking, the verse, by its allusion to Elihu's assertion, imports a crushing dose of realism that relegates these people to the domain of necessary beliefs as distinct from true beliefs. Latent in the verse is also the hope that all men will evolve from necessary belief to truth while acknowledging that the former provides the motivational force to evolve to the latter. The reader of the *Guide*'s first verse is drawn by word association to another location in the *Guide*, Elihu's discourse on providence. He then rebounds back with its dual voicedness to the first verse, which now resonates with the necessary/ true dichotomy reflecting the protean composition of the general public to whom the text reaches out. In this way the ultimate verse is paradigmatic of the prooftext throughout the *Guide,* whose message diffracts across the spectrum of the readers with whom it comes in contact.

Text and Prooftext:

An Abrahamic/Mosaic Joint Venture toward Enlightenment

Maimonides' ongoing project to purge his tradition, both rabbinic and biblical, of what he considered to be its magical, mythical, and superstitious undercurrents was one conducted at great personal peril. Preemptive pleas addressed to readers to judge him kindly by aligning him in any way possible with long-standing and widely held beliefs (*GP,* introduction, p. 15) were destined to fall on deaf ears. The protracted controversy and divisiveness marked by his philosophic work, both prior to his death and posthumously,[1] constitute irrefutable evidence as to the futility of those pleas. Though somewhat predictable, it is unlikely that the ferocity of the ideological struggle over his legacy within the Jewish community could have been contemplated by Maimonides. His intention was never to disturb the unflinching faith of the masses but rather to offer intellectual refuge to those who could not honestly share that simple, yet philosophically unacceptable, faith. For that purpose he was willing to suffer abuse and ostracism rather than deny those truly perplexed the intellectual salvation he was so confident he could offer: "I am the man who when the concern pressed him and his way was straitened and he could find no other device by which to teach a demonstrated truth other than by giving satisfaction to a single virtuous man while displeasing ten thousand ignoramuses—I am he who prefers to address that single man by himself, and I do not heed the blame of those many creatures" (*GP,* introduction, pp. 16–17).

This passion to disseminate the truth at any cost was expressed in an age when the exchange of ideas was conducted, not as a mere pastime, but as a matter of life and death. All readers are therefore obliged to approach the text born of that sentiment with a care that aspires to match the care

159

with which it was written. Anything less would be a veritable breach of trust owed by the reader to the author, especially in light of this particular author's specific admonishment to grapple with every word in the text: "[T]he diction of this Treatise has not been chosen at haphazard, but with great exactness and exceeding precision" (*GP,* p. 5).

The present book has attempted to demonstrate that Maimonides' self-proclaimed superlatives regarding his own literary talents cannot simply be dismissed as bombast. My focus has been on the unique citation of biblical and rabbinic prooftexts, which confront the reader at virtually every turn, to substantiate Maimonides' claims of "exceeding precision." The choice of this particular feature of the text was motivated not only by its pervasiveness but also by its transformation of the text from an antiquated philosophical tract to one that fits into a uniquely Jewish exegetical tradition. The prooftext is not merely a prop on which to hang certain philosophical propositions regarding God and his relationship to the creation but rather melds with the text to form an organic continuum of thought. Scripture bears within the contours of its mythic language the "apples of gold" for which the reader must always search and to which the prooftext constantly alerts us.

According to Maimonides, idolatry is an evolutionary corruption of what was originally a universally subscribed-to pristine monotheism. Identifying the Creator with his creation, while confusing the majestic and glorious with divinity, led man down a spiral of ideological deterioration until there was virtually no trace of the authentic One remaining in the world. Abraham appears on the scene debating, convincing, and urging man to go back to a purity of Oneness pronounced "in the name of the Lord, God of the world" (Gen. 21:33).[2] With the death of Abraham, the process of conceptual deterioration toward idolatry commenced once more to the point where Abraham's descendants could no longer be distinguished from their idolatrous counterparts in Egypt. Moses was then invested by God with the mission of restoring Israel to its Abrahamic antecedents and halting its theological/philosophical decline before it became irreversible.[3] Whether or not man is inevitably destined to reenact this cycle of rise and decline, it is clear that the *Guide* is a response to another retrogressive phase in the religious history of man. The Mosaic experiment failed in the sense that the appeal of its imaginative mode of communication succeeded all too well. The majority had succumbed to the seduction of the concrete,[4] while the elite were on the verge of rejecting a sacred book that was no longer philosophically viable.

Maimonides had decided he could no longer allow this desperate state of affairs to persist. A new call "in the name of the Lord, God of the world" was imperative to meet the challenge of this new theological crisis. Guidance would surely have come by examining why his esteemed predecessors' literary and intellectual legacies in response to similar dire theological straits had in fact floundered over time. Maimonides' evolutionary account of idolatry in the Mishneh Torah formulates in the personages of Abraham and Moses two very distinct approaches to combating a pervasive corruption of humankind. Abraham confronts the enemy with an assault that is described largely in terms of artful intellectual persuasion. His own personal belief is rooted in a very arduous process of philosophical deliberation and demonstration, which is in turn exploited for gaining a consensus on monotheism over polytheism. He overwhelms his opponents with the following techniques:

1. he initially challenges firmly held assumptions *(lehashiv teshuvot)*;
2. he engages in debate *(la 'arokh din)*;
3. he informs them (presumably after convincing logical argument) that only the one God is worthy of external worship so that universal recognition of Him will be realized;
4. he is proactive in the destruction of concrete symbols so that further error does not persist;
5. he addresses each potential convert at his or her own level of intellectual sophistication *(kefi da 'ato)*;
6. he composes treatises and trains disciples to enable the ongoing struggles against paganism.

Moses, on the other hand, is far less a dialectician than a legislator. In his capacity as a recipient of superior divine communication *('asah moshe rabenu rabban shel kol hanevi 'im)* and as God's personal nominee *(veshalcho)*, he is the medium through which God is configured as a lawgiver. Israel, via Mosaic prophecy, is invested with legal obligations *(hikhtirom bamitzwot)*, instructed as to mode of worship, and exhorted with sanctions in the event of disobedience. Moses' mission is normative, while Abraham's modus operandi is cogitative. Abraham "taught the people and explained to them by means of speculative proofs . . . but he never said: God has sent me to you and has given me commandments and prohibitions."[5] Moses is the exclusive bearer of nomos.[6] This contrast between the Abrahamic and Mosaic confrontations with idolatry is carried over to the *Guide* as well. Abraham is portrayed as the master of artful persuasion, rhetoric, and cajolement, while Moses resorts to the far more aggressive measures of violence and force. These measures are effected by legislative norms such as obligating the destruction of idolatrous sancta and prohibiting the adoption of any of their cultural or social conventions (*GP,* III:29, p. 517).

Perhaps, upon reviewing these two distinct approaches and their respective failures to pass the test of endurance, Maimonides understood the desperate need for a new "call" to issue forth. The speculative call of Abraham and the prescriptive call of Moses suggested a novel hybrid medium with which to address the spiritual and intellectual languor of his time. What he devised was a radical literary form casting the two in dialogue with each other. At the same time it was necessary to construct a dialogue on which only a few could eavesdrop. As my book has hopefully demonstrated, it is the stratagem of biblical and rabbinic citation that is instrumental in sustaining this dialogue and achieving a synthesis between the Abrahamic and Mosaic ventures. The result is a sinuous weave of text and prooftext that defies disentanglement of the two. Rather than unravel the text, the reader is summoned to enter the perimeter of discourse between the two where the "golden apples" of the prophetic books are liberated from their silver confines.

Notes

Introduction

1. *Dalalat al-ha'irin,* trans. Shlomo Pines as *The Guide of the Perplexed* (Chicago: University of Chicago Press, 1963), introduction, p. 7. All references to this work will be cited hereafter as *GP.* Roman numerals refer to the section of the *Guide* and arabic numerals to the chapter in the section.

2. *GP,* p. 9. In Maimonides' introduction to the tenth chapter of *Tractate Sanhedrin (Pereq Heleq)* in his *Commentary to the Mishnah,* he announces his intention to embark upon such a work. See *Mishnah im Perush Moshe ben Maimon,* translated into Hebrew by J. Kafih (Jerusalem: Mossad Harav Kook, 1964), 4:109.

3. Maimonides, *Mishnah im Perush Moshe ben Maimon,* introduction to *Avot.*

4. See *Theological Political Treatise,* chap. 15, which assigns truth and knowledge to the sphere of reason and piety and obeisance to that of theology.

5. See the analysis of Spinoza's revolutionary biblical exegesis by Tzvetan Todorov in *Symbolism and Interpretation,* trans. C. Porter (London: Routledge & Kegan Paul, 1998), pp. 131–62.

6. Though I cannot comment on Maimonides' knowledge of the classical quarrel between the philosophers and the poets, it is instructive to examine a similar ambiguous attitude toward poetry in Plato. In spite of the *Republic*'s call for the expulsion of all poets, it allowed for their readmission if the beneficial essence of poetry could be extracted and recast by its defenders in prosaic style. See *Rep.* 10.607, where readmission depends on how well lovers of poetry plead her cause in prose, without meter, and show that she is not only delightful but also beneficial to orderly government and all the life of man. See also J. A. Elias, *Plato's Defence of Poetry* (Albany: SUNY Press, 1984). See also the discussion of this passage in Maimonides by I. Heinemann in his *Darkhei HaAggadah,* 3d ed. (Jerusalem: Magnes Press, 1970), p. 3; Heinemann is too dismissive of the *shrirut hameshororim* (poetic license). For a survey of Maimonides' attitude toward poetry, see H. Schirmann, "Maimonides and Hebrew Poetry" (in Hebrew), *Moznayim* 3 (1935): 433–36.

7. See Northrop Frye, *Anatomy of Criticism* (Princeton: Princeton University

Press, 1971), p. 89 and the comparison by Kenneth Stein between this approach and Maimonides' in "Exegesis, Maimonides, and Literary Criticism," *Modern Language Notes* 88 (May 1973): 1134–51.

8. See Steven Kepnes, "A Narrative Jewish Theology," *Judaism* 37, no. 2 (1988): 210–17, who ascribes the Jewish penchant for narrative to its ability to conceal and reveal at the same time and therefore is "the most adequate linguistic tool to lead thought to a hidden God" (p. 212).

9. See the chapter "What Is a Text?" in Paul Ricoeur, *Hermeneutics and the Human Sciences* (New York: Cambridge University Press, 1981), p. 147.

10. See Abraham Nuriel, "Dibra Torah B'lashon B'nei Adam BeMoreh Nevukhim," in *Dat VeSafah*, ed. M. Halamish and A. Kasher (Tel Aviv: Mifalim Universitiyim le-hatsaah la-or, 1981), pp. 97–103, who points out this transformation, as well as Sara Klein-Braslavy, *Perush HaRambam LeSippur Breiat HaOlam* (Jerusalem: ha-Hesra le-heker ha-Mikra be-Yisrael, 1977), pp. 24–27.

11. See for instance *GP,* I:36, p. 84.

12. See *GP,* I:33, p. 71, where the purpose of the Torah speaking the language of the common man is "to make it possible for the young, the women and all the people to begin with it and to learn it."

13. See *Sefer HaMitswot*, positive commandment no. 8 and M.T. (= Mishneh Torah), *Hilkhot Deot* 1:6.

14. See *Sefer Moreh Nevukhim* (Jerusalem: n.p., 1960), p. 3b.

15. *Yesodei Hatorah*, 2:7. See also Michael Schwarz's new Hebrew translation of part 1 of the *Guide* (Tel Aviv: Tel Aviv University, 1996), p. 4 n. 17.

16. See also B.T., *Yoma* 71a, where this term alludes to the *talmidei chachamim* or the learned class. See also the *Midrash on Proverbs*, trans. Burton Visotzky (New Haven: Yale University Press, 1992), p. 45, which may have been the very midrash Maimonides had in mind, since it clearly distinguishes between the two on this basis: "If you have [earned the] merit of upholding the words of the Torah you will be called *ishim*, as are the ministering angels. If not you are to be called *benei adam*." Note the identification of virtuous men with the "ministering angels," which could translate into the philosophical vocabulary as "active intellect."

17. *GP,* II:33, p. 364. See also *GP,* I:65, p. 159, where Maimonides makes it abundantly clear that terms conveying speech "never signify that He, may He be exalted, spoke using the sounds of letters and voice."

18. *GP,* II:33, p. 364. Even if the rabbinic tradition that the first two commandments were heard clearly by all is accepted, Maimonides stresses at p. 365 "that with regard to that *voice (qol)* too, their rank was not equal to the rank of Moses our Master." There would then still be a distinction of content depending on who the recipient of the teaching is.

19. See *GP,* I:10 on this verse, where the call to Moses is preceded by the "descent" of God, indicating "prophetic inspiration."

20. For an analogous distinction formulated between a generally accepted

opinion and the author's (Maimonides') own opinion, see his subtly nuanced discussion of providence, which moves between views ascribed to "our opinion" and those ascribed to "my opinion." See also Leo Strauss's discussion in *Persecution and the Art of Writing* (Glencoe, Ill.: The Free Press, 1952), pp. 83–84; Strauss identifies the former with the general consensus and the latter with its hidden or secret meaning.

21. See Paul Ricoeur, "The Power of Speech, Science and Poetry," *Philosophy Today* 29 (spring 1985): 66.

22. Ibid.

23. See Ricoeur's discussion in *Interpretation Theory: Discourse and the Surplus of Meaning* (Fort Worth: Texas Christian University Press, 1996), esp. the chapter entitled "Metaphor and Symbol."

Chapter 1. Midrash on Midrash

1. *Midrash Shir Hashirim Rabbah*, ed. S. Dunsky (Jerusalem: n.p., 1980), 1:8.

2. See the further interpretation of Ecclesiastes 7:24 in *GP,* I:34.

3. For a most insightful theory that what many scholars have viewed as contradictions in the *Guide* are really "divergences" and not logical contradictions, see Marvin Fox, "A New View of Maimonides' Method of Contradictions,"*Annual of Bar-Ilan University* 22–23 (1987): 19–43, special issue entitled *Moshe Schwarcz Memorial Volume.*

4. See *GP,* p. 81, where the belief in corporeality is equated with the belief "in the non-existence of the deity, in the association of other gods with Him or in the worship of other than He."

5. See M.T., *Hilkhot De'ot* 2:3–5.

6. The Aramaic translation-cum-commentary of Isaiah.

7. For a well-argued thesis calling for the application of this analysis to the commandments as well as the narrative, see Josef Stern, "Maimonides on the Covenant of Circumcision and the Unity of God," in *The Midrashic Imagination*, ed. M. Fishbane (Albany: State University of New York Press, 1993), pp. 131–54, where Maimonides' explanation of circumcision "exemplifies a mode of allegorical or parabolic interpretation that he employs not only for the narrative portions of Scripture but also the commandments" (p. 132; and see esp. the discussion at pp. 146–50).

8. See *GP,* III:27, pp. 510–12.

9. For an important and controversial study on what can ultimately be known in the Maimonidean system, see S. Pines, "The Limitations of Human Knowledge according to Al-Farabi, ibn Baja, and Maimonides," in *Studies in Medieval Jewish History and Literature,* ed. I. Twersky (Cambridge: Harvard University Press, 1979), pp. 82–109.

10. Moshe Greenberg, *Ezekiel 1–20*, Anchor Bible Series (Garden City, N.Y.: Doubleday, 1983), p. 317.

11. For Maimonides' opinion of those who view Scripture as poetry or history, see his scolding of the "learned man" who propounded a challenge to the logic of the Eden story (*GP*, I:2, p. 24).

12. Kimhi, *Commentary on Ezekiel,* 17:2.

13. See *Pesikta Rabbati*, trans. W. G. Braude (New Haven: Yale University Press, 1968), 33:11.

14. See the commentaries of Rashi and Rabbi Joseph Kara on this verse.

15. For the precise intellectual machinations involved in the prophetic process, see *GP* II:36–38, pp. 369–78, where the "true reality and quiddity of prophecy" is detailed. Alfarabi in his *Book of Letters* also sees religious laws declared by prophets as abstract philosophical truths filtered through the imagination for purposes of mass consumption. See the discussion of Miriam Galston in *Politics and Excellence: The Political Philosophy of Alfarabi* (Princeton: Princeton University Press, 1990) 136–37.

16. See David Boyarin, *Intertextuality and the Reading of Midrash* (Bloomington: Indiana University Press, 1990), p. 32, and especially the chapter on Song of Songs, pp. 105–16, where he discusses *Shir Hashirim Rabbah* 1:8.

17. Ibid., p. 107.

18. *GP*, p. 19—"whether contradictions due to the seventh cause are to be found in the books of the prophets is a matter for speculative study and investigation."

19. For a description of a worthy disciple, see *GP*, p. 3—the Epistle Dedicatory to Joseph.

20. See Gersonides' comment on this verse, which symbolizes the intellectual faculty as "king," and also Maimonides in his Mishneh Torah, *Laws of Repentance* 8:4, where "crowns on heads" are equated with "knowledge" in the imagery of the "world to come."

21. *GP*, I:54, p. 124; see also p. 453.

22. See also *GP*, II:30, pp. 353–54, where the expression *"it was good"* pronounced by God in the creation narrative has an association with external utilitarian meaning and inner hidden meaning.

23. B.T., *Yebamot* 104a.

24. See Pines's note 50 to *GP* on this point.

25. See Rashi's commentary on this expression, n. 40. See also W. Z. Harvey, "Great is the Power: On *Guide of the Perplexed* 1:46" (in Hebrew), *Daat* 37 (1996): 56–61 for an analysis of this maxim and its relationship to the *chalitsah* incident. The determination of how the latter shapes the meaning of *gadol kokhan* for Maimonides is further mandated by the fact that the Hebrew expression *gadol kokhan* and the chosen analogous Aramaic expression in *Yebamot (kamah rav guvrei),* do not necessarily equate, as Harvey points out in his article at p. 58.

26. There seems to be a second interpretation of the distinction between these second intentions offered earlier on in the chapter. According to it, the first intention is to abolish idolatry and the second intention caters toward the frailty of human nature and its resistance to sudden and abrupt changes. Ultimately, I believe the two interpretations converge, since the abolishment of idolatry leads to the inculcation of "the grandest and true foundation of our belief—namely the existence and oneness of the deity . . ." (*GP,* p. 527). The second intentions, which are sensitive to the human psyche and designed upon a model of gradual transition, in essence address the same facet of man, which needs to be regulated for the abolition of wrongdoing, i.e., the physical and material.

27. B.T., *Shabbath* 87b.

28. See *GP,* III:32, p. 531.

29. Fox, "New View of Maimonides' Method of Contradictions," p. 76.

Chapter 2. Intertextual Foils in the Guide

1. For a similar understanding of the way in which words act as signifiers by a more contemporary Jewish philosopher, see Moses Mendelssohn, *Megillat Qohelet,* as quoted by Jay Harris in *How Do We Know This?: Midrash and the Fragmentation of Modern Judaism* (Albany: SUNY Press, 1995), p. 145 and his comments thereon. At times linguistic shifts are simply attributed to aesthetics, and at others every such shift is a conscious attempt at conveying meaning.

2. Frank Kermode's general characterization of narrative as esoteric and exclusive is particularly apt for the manner in which Maimonides reads prophetic narratives as parables. They are crafted with "the property of banishing interpreters from its secret place." See his *The Genesis of Secrecy: On the Interpretation of Narrative* (Cambridge: Harvard University Press, 1979). The enigma and "radiant obscurity" that Kermode finds in narrative are what lend it its "hermeneutical potential" and are precisely what bring the prophetic narratives to life for Maimonides. See his p. 40 and p. 47 and in general the discussion at pp. 23–47.

3. *GP,* pp. 6–7. See also Kermode, *Genesis of Secrecy,* 47 for the strikingly similar way he describes narrative as proclaiming "a truth as a herald does and at the same time conceal[ing] truth like an oracle."

4. See Leo Strauss's introduction to the *GP,* xiv. He claims that the primary thrust of the *Guide* is biblical exegesis and that it is a book "written by a Jew for Jews."

5. While Maimonides, the Aristotelian, subscribed to a philosophical credo that assumed fundamental objective truths ("truth and falsehood"), I believe that in his reading and presentation of biblical and rabbinic texts he adopted the kind of modern approach implied by the term "intertextuality"; in the words of Kristeva, who coined the term, it is "an *intersection of textual surfaces* rather than a *point* [a

fixed meaning]." This would accommodate a notion of a polysemous text that defies closure and allows the kind of refashioning of its meaning undertaken by Maimonides. See Julia Kristeva, *Desire in Language: A Semiotic Approach to Literature and Art*, ed. L. S. Roudiez, trans. T. Gora et al. (New York: Columbia University Press, 1980), p. 65.

6. See Paul Ricoeur, "The Bible and the Imagination," in *The Bible as a Document of the University*, ed. Hans D. Betz (Chico, Calif.: Scholars Press, 1981), p. 67.

7. See *GP,* I:1 for the definition of the term *tselem.*

8. In the Jewish tradition the main purpose for the union of the man and woman is reproduction. See M.T., *Hilkhot Ishut* 15:2 and *Sefer Hamitswot,* positive commandment 212. For a comprehensive survey of the intellectual history regarding the commandment of Genesis 1:28 to procreate, see Jeremy Cohen, *"Be Fertile and Increase, Fill the Earth and Master It": The Ancient and Medieval Career of a Biblical Text* (Ithaca, N.Y.: Cornell University Press, 1989). The very order of the Maimonidean lexicography in the first section of the *Guide* may itself generate meaning, as in this instance. *GP,* I:6, p. 31 defines the terms "man" and "woman" in such a way that "woman" can be figuratively used "to designate any object apt for, and fashioned with a view to being in, conjunction with some other object." *GP,* I:7, 32 then deals with the term "to bear children" *(yalod),* where the figurative sense is "whoever instructs an individual in some matter and teaches them [*sic*] an opinion has . . . as it were engendered that individual." Thus the verse regarding the birth of Seth, "And Adam bore a son in his own likeness after his own image" (Gen. 5:3), is rendered as Adam endowing Seth with the intellectual perfection necessary to procure his human form. Likewise with Jacob: he is en route to union with that which is *apt* for him in order to "bear children" and thereby the human "form" is perpetuated.

9. For Maimonides' views on nonphilosophic literature see his caustic retort to the objector in *GP,* I:2, p. 24 who is accused of treating the Bible as "poetry" or "history."

10. For other solutions to this troubling condition, see for instance on this verse: (1) Nahmanides—the "if " clause is not conditional but a prediction. *Genesis Rabbah* 76:2, also quoted by Nahmanides, renders it a prayer to remain free of sin, thus relieving God of his promise; (2) Kimhi, who also quotes the *Genesis Rabbah* and adopts Maimonides' position that he is simply requesting the basic necessities for survival.

11. See *GP,* III:8, p. 434, where *Genesis Rabbah* 98 and 99 are quoted.

12. *GP,* p. 13. I disagree that the "class of individuals who possess this type of matter is limited to one, namely Moses," as I. Dobbs-Weinstein states in "Matter as Creature and Matter as the Source of Evil: Maimonides and Aquinas," in *Neoplatonism and Jewish Thought,* ed. Lenn Goodman (Albany: SUNY Press, 1992), p. 234 n. 21. See also Lenn Goodman, "Matter and Form as Attributes of

God in Maimonides' Philosophy," in *A Straight Path: Studies in Medieval Philosophy and Culture,* ed. Ruth Link-Salinger (Washington, D.C.: Catholic University of America Press, 1988), pp. 86–97.

13. *GP,* III:33, p. 533. "Similarly one of the intentions of the law is purity and sanctification; I mean by this renouncing and avoiding sexual intercourse and causing it to be as infrequent as possible." This is consistent with the attitude expressed in the Mishneh Torah. See *Hilkhot Deot* 3:2, which allows for sexual intercourse solely for medicinal purposes or to maintain the human species. See also *Deot* 4:19 and W. Z. Harvey, "Sex and Health in Maimonides," in *Moses Maimonides: Physician, Scientist, and Philosopher*, ed. F. Rosner and S. Kottek (Northvale, N.J.: Jason Aronson, 1993), pp. 33–39.

14. The conclusion of *GP,* III:8 provides the rationale for Hebrew being elevated over other languages as a "holy language" *(lashon hakodesh),* in that all terms related to the world of sex and erotica are euphemisms. One example given is copulation, which can be expressed by a number of terms; one of them is *yishkav* (lying) (p. 436). It is of note that the premier event on the journey to search for an appropriate female mate is an act of lying *(vayishkav)* (Gen. 28:11) by Jacob that is not only devoid of any sexual connotations but leads to a prophetic experience. The significance may be that Jacob's acts of *shkhiva,* while alluding to sexual activity, are directed toward activities of human perfection. Just as the figurative sense of *shakhav* from a literary perspective is abandoned, so Jacob surrenders corporeal superfluity for essential being.

15. See also remarks regarding Jacob being extremely fearful *(pachdan)* and losing his prophetic powers due to depression in the seventh chapter of the *Shemonah Peraqim*, ed. Y. Shilat (Jerusalem: Maale Adumim, 1996) as well as *GP,* II:36, p. 372, which also attributes a period of prophetic block to the personal tragedy of losing Joseph.

16. This sense is "worth nothing."

17. For the relationship of the Deity to the world as one of form to matter, see *GP,* I:69, p. 169.

18. Most of the passages where the divine epithet "Shaddai" appears in Genesis are in the context of propagation—Genesis 17:1, 28:3, 35:11, 43:14, 48:3, and 49:25. For a discussion of this name as one that designates a God with breasts or a God who suckles, see David Biale, "The God with Breasts: El Shaddai in the Bible," *History of Religions*, no. 3 (1982): 240–56 and the bibliography cited therein.

19. See M.T., *Hilkhot Deot*, I:6, *mah hu af atah.*

20. M.T., *Hilkhot Melakhim* 6:7.

21. There is a link drawn in the midrashic corpus between the divine name of Shaddai and that of circumcision. The most prominent is in the *Midrash Tanhuma,* where God is portrayed as having "put His name on Israel so that they may gain entry to the Garden of Eden. And what is the name and the seal that he put on them? It is *Shaddai.* He put *shin* on the nose, *dalet* on the hand and *yod* on the

circumcision" (*Tzav* 14). Josef Stern has cited this midrash for its importance in associating the place of circumcision particularly with the Tetragrammaton, since the letter *yod* is an abbreviation of that name, thereby signifying the notion of unity inherent in that divine name. See Stern, "Maimonides on the Covenant of Circumcision and the Unity of God," pp. 145–46. In my analysis the integrity of the midrashic association of the phallus with the particular name Shaddai is maintained and indeed is most à propos. It is precisely this divine appellation that signifies sexual restraint and, when notionally assimilated, prevents the sacred act of reproduction from becoming one of promiscuity. Josef Stern has since extensively rewritten this paper and reversed his original position in the recent volume of essays *Problems and Parables of Law: Maimonides and Nahmanides on Reasons for the Commandments* (Albany: SUNY Press, 1998). In the chapter entitled "Maimonides: The Parable of Circumcision," he now argues that, of the two reasons offered in the *Guide* for this commandment, sexual restraint constitutes the internal (gold) reason, while the second reason, which takes it as a sign of membership in a community professing the unity of God, is the external (silver). This prompted me to reflect on why Abraham is held out as the model of chastity in the excursus on circumcision in III:49. Perhaps a clue is afforded in the choice of prooftext that rabbinically establishes him as such a model. Genesis 12:11, "Behold now, I know that thou art a fair woman to look upon" (i.e., until this point in their relationship, Abraham was never conscious of Sarah's physical beauty because of his extreme modesty—cf. Talmud Bavli, *Baba Batra* 16a), occurs prior to Abraham's performance of self-circumcision. In Abraham's case, therefore, circumcision is not an instrument of his chastity; the reverse is the case. Abraham is appropriate to be the *first* bearer of this sign *because* of his chastity. In his particular instance, since sexual restraint preceded circumcision, the other symbolism attributed to circumcision, subscription to a community-held belief in the unity of God, assumes a greater prominence. Indeed, in the Mishneh Torah, Abraham is portrayed as the pioneering exponent of God's unity whose consuming mission is to convert all of humanity to this belief (M.T., *Hilkhot Avodat Kokhavim* 1:3). Circumcision as a sexual prophylactic becomes more functional with the descendants of Abraham, but this is an issue deserving further detailed exploration. For a fascinating study of this association in the kabbalistic corpus, see Elliot Wolfson, "Circumcision and the Divine Name: A Study in the Transmission of Esoteric Doctrine," *Jewish Quarterly Review* 78 (1987): 77–112. The fact that the imprinting of this divine name on the body guarantees the Jew's entry into the Garden of Eden is key to this passage, as Wolfson points out; it is also noteworthy as a possible inspiration for a rationalist such as Maimonides. The last letter of Shaddai, when branded onto the circumcised phallus, acts as a prophylactic against sexual hedonism. This in turn leads to the domination of intellect over matter and the theoretical move it entails from the world of "generally accepted things" *(mefursamot)* to that of "truth and falsehood." The latter was of course the exclusive focus of the mind in the Garden of Eden prior to Adam's sin and is what constitutes the utopian ideal of man. Admission to the Garden of Eden *(truth and falsehood)* is thereby secured. See I:2 of the *Guide.*

22. Darkness is associated with nonbeing and privation. See *GP,* III:10, p. 438—"For darkness and evil are privations." See also III:9, where various verses are cited as descriptive of God being enveloped in darkness: e.g., "He made darkness his hiding place" (Ps. 18:12) or "He manifests himself in darkness, cloud and thick darkness" (Deut. 4:11). These are all metaphors for the fact that the true essence of God is unattainable due to human limitations. "[T]he apprehension of His true reality is impossible for us because of the dark matter that encompasses us and not Him" (*GP,* III:10, p. 437). The equation is made between darkness and matter. The combination of this equation with Plato's is mentioned in I:47, wherein matter and form are designated as female and male, respectively. This yields the "Matter = Darkness = Female."

23. When presenting the "true reality and quiddity of prophecy" in *GP,* II:36, where the imaginative faculty figures prominently, its "greatest and noblest action takes place only when the senses rest and do not perform their actions" (p. 370).

24. See Abravanel's commentary on Genesis, who queries the repetition of *makom.*

25. For one example of attention being drawn to this *Leitwort* as crucial to the structures of the entire passage, see Shimon Bar-Efrat, *Narrative Art in the Bible* (Sheffield, England: The Almond Press, 1989), pp. 103–5. He notes that the parallelism of structure between the predream and postdream "acts" "emphasizes that Jacob's actions are the counterpart of the appearance of God." Though his conclusion is that "God is the initiator and man responds accordingly," my conclusion, based on the very same insight, is quite the reverse when cast in its Maimonidean mold. It is man (Jacob) who initiates by way of his perfected moral and intellectual virtues, and God who subsequently responds.

26. See *GP,* I:2, for an account of Adam's sin, which consisted of intellectual decay from the superlative concern with "truth and falsehood" to the inferior one of "good and bad." The former is the theoretical intellect that deals with absolutes, and the latter is the practical intellect whose objects of reflection are relative. For a very detailed survey tracing the roots and evolution of this theory, see S. Pines, "Truth and Falsehood versus Good and Evil: A Study of Jewish and General Philosophy in Connection with the *Guide of the Perplexed* I:2," in Twersky, *Studies in Maimonides,* pp. 95–157.

27. *GP,* III:3, p. 431. See Daniel Boyarin, *Carnal Israel: Reading Sex in Talmudic Culture* (Berkeley: University of California Press, 1993), who cites this passage as evidence of virulent misogyny on Maimonides' part; he says Maimonides' allegorization of woman as *matter* "essentializes woman into an ontological whoredom" (p. 58). To accuse him of "virulent misogyny" is insulting and does not do justice to the complete man. This allegorization of woman is at times belied

by a sensitivity to the female predicament in the practical juridical realm. See for instance the governing principles of sexual relations between husband and wife in M.T., *Hilkhot Deot* 5:4, which forbid a man from forcing himself upon his wife and mandate that it must be "in accord with the will of the two of them and in their joy." See also Maimonides' responsa as quoted and commented on by Renée Levine Melammed in "He Said She Said: A Woman Teacher in Twelfth-Century Cairo," *AJS Review* 22, no. 1 (1997): 19–35.

28. See Ibn Ezra's comments on these verses; he renders *bamakom* as *behamakom,* reading in the identificatory *hey.*

29. See *Tanhuma* on this portion, as well as *Midrash Ha Gadol,* Genesis 28:11, which renders this a prooftext for Jacob's impoverished state upon leaving his father's house to the extent that he doesn't even have proper bedding.

30. As the Aramaic Targum translates *nirveh dodim.*

31. *GP,* III:8, p. 435. Maimonides cites Hosea 2:10, *"And I multiplied into her silver and gold which they used for Baal,"* as an apt characterization of this personality. The context of this verse is a harlot who does not achieve material satisfaction from her various lovers and wishes to return to her first husband out of despair. Recognition of the link between matter and its Creator well serve to focus the mind on God as the ultimate source of all being. If the link is severed, then "matter," the "silver and gold," becomes an end in itself, thus clearing the path toward "Baal." It is interesting that the harlot of Proverbs pays no allegiance to her husband, who is the source of the "silver" that provides all her accoutrements (7:19–20). In the same manner that the Hosean harlot uses God's "gold and silver" in the service of Baal, the harlot of Proverbs exploits her husband's cash for her infidelities.

32. For Maimonides, the all-consuming, obsessive love that a man may have for a woman constitutes the optimum model for the love of God. It is a love that allows no space for anything else in life and occupies every moment of daily existence—a love so obsessive that it can be clinically diagnosed as a malady. See M.T., *Helkhot Teshuvah* 10:3. At first this may seem quite a daring analogy, but in effect what Maimonides is calling for is a neutralization of an extreme emotional experience whereby it is rerouted from the sensual to the intellectual. The "benefit granted" man of such a romantic ideal is only for the purpose of affording a model for the love of God. If it is not quickly drained of any romance and continues to be indulged, then the benefit is transformed into "committing an act of disobedience with regard to Him who has granted the benefit." The ultimate intention of this formulation in the M.T. is to sublimate *eros,* thus enhancing *sophos.* For the same reasons, Maimonides may have chosen the Arabic term *ishq* (passionate love) precisely to designate the highest intellectual love of God (*GP* III:51, p. 627). Whereas his predecessors such as Saadia, Bahya ibn Paqudah, and Ha-Levi eschewed the use of this term to denote the love of God because of its erotic connotations, Maimonides may have purposefully adopted it so that its sexual denotation is exchanged for a purely intellectual one. See Steven Harvey's study of this term in

"The Meaning of Terms Designating Love in Judaeo-Arabic Thought and Some Remarks on the Judaeo-Arabic Interpretation of Maimonides," in *Studies in Muslim Jewish Relations*, ed. Norman Gold (Chur, Switzerland: Harwood Academic Publishers, 1997), 3:175–96. At p.181 Harvey credits Maimonides with first introducing this term for love of God into Judeo-Arabic thought. For a different perspective on this passage that maintains a more positive role for erotic love, see Harvey, "Sex and Health in Maimonides," pp. 38–39.

33. I adopt here the translation of R. B. Y. Scott in the Anchor Bible series, as I believe it is the most appropriately nuanced for our context (at p. 65). There is a school of thought influenced by G. Bostrom that takes *shlm* in a modal sense of "to produce": "I must provide a sacrificial meal, today I am to fulfil my vows." According to this, Bostrom claimed that the foreign woman was a devotee of an Aphroditic cult who had pledged to have sexual relations with a stranger during an orgiastic feast. See *Proverbiastudien: Die Weisheit und das fremde Weib in Spr. 1–9* (Lund: Gleerup, 1935), pp. 103–4, and also see the more recent article by Karel Van der Toorn, "Female Prostitution in Payment of Vows in Ancient Israel," *JBL* 108, no. 2 (1989): 193–205, who raises the interesting possibility that women may have had to resort to prostitution to fulfill legitimate sacred vows.

34. See Leviticus 7:11–21 and the Mishnah in 5:7.

35. See Leviticus 19:8, which declares that the meat of the *shelamim* retains its holiness up until the time it is disposed of. Anyone who eats of it after the three-day limitation period is considered a defiler of the sanctum inherent in the meat.

36. *GP*, III:35, p. 537. In the Mishneh Torah as well, the laws concerning sexual relations, forbidden foods, and vows are grouped together. Book 4 is Women; book 5 is Sanctity, which covers sexual relations and forbidden foods; and book 6 is Expression, dealing with vows. In L. Berman's configuration of the commandments in the Mishneh Torah he locates those books in the division dealing with man-God relations. I agree with his rationale for their inclusion in this section as opposed to man-man sections, as these regulations are aimed at "helping man control his appetites." See L. Berman, "The Structure of the Commandments of the Torah in the Thought of Maimonides," in *Studies in Jewish Religious and Intellectual History*, ed. S. Stein and R. Loewe (University: University of Alabama Press, 1975), p. 55. The virtue of naziritism is that it promotes an ascetic tendency in its avoidance of wine and so inspires the attitude "that people should content themselves with no more of it than necessary." This corresponds to the self-sufficiency Jacob represents, as developed in this chapter.

37. It is probably no coincidence that the thirteenth class of commandments, which includes the laws of forbidden foods and vows, is followed by the fourteenth and final class comprising the laws dealing with sexual relations (*GP*, III:49). Gluttony and sexual permissiveness seem to always go hand in hand, and the "totality of the purposes of the perfect law" is to subdue those desires as much as possible, since "most of the lusts and licentiousness of the multitude consists in an

appetite for eating, drinking and sexual intercourse" (III:33). My view on the dietary laws is consistent with that asserted by Hannah Kasher in "Well-Being of the Body or Welfare of the Soul: The Maimonidean Explanation of the Dietary Laws," in Rosner and Kottek, *Moses Maimonides: Physician, Scientist, and Philosopher*, p. 131.

38. See *GP,* I:34, pp. 74–75. In the imagery of the palace parable in III:51, those whose opinions are derived solely from traditional authority "have come up to the habitation and walk around it" searching for its gate. Jacob presumably is the recipient of this kind of truth as a result of his upbringing but must move beyond this by "plung[ing] into speculation concerning the fundamental principles of religion" in order to gain admission to the king's antechambers. The process of intellectual inquiry is symbolized by Jacob's departure from his father's house, and its success is determined by the discovery of the *house of Elohim* consequent to his dream.

39. See Frank Talmage, "Apples of Gold: The Inner Meaning of Sacred Texts in Medieval Judaism," in *Jewish Spirituality: From the Bible through the Middle Ages*, ed. Arthur Green (New York: Crossroad, 1986), pp. 313–55 for an excellent survey of the technique and uses of allegoresis that this gave rise to in medieval Jewish literature. Particularly interesting is the all-pervasive nature of allegory to which the medieval mentality was exposed, expressed not only in literature but in art and architecture as well. See his eloquent description of how the architecture of Moorish Spain, exemplified by the Alhambra, mirrors the search for hidden meaning that allegoresis uncovers (p. 317).

40. See Ricoeur, "The Bible and the Imagination," pp. 67, 71.

Chapter 3. *"The Lord hath forsaken the earth"*

1. See M.T., *Hilkhot Yesodei Hatorah.*

2. See *GP,* I:58, pp. 134–37.

3. *GP,* p. 145. Man "has an apprehension of Him that is different from what He really is, but I shall say that he has abolished his belief in the existence of the deity without being aware of it."

4. See Zvi Disendruck, "Samuel and Moses ibn Tibbon on Maimonides' Theory of Providence," *HUCA* 2 (1936): 341–56, who identifies Job's final enlightened view of providence with Aristotle despite Maimonides' identification of Job's initial primitive view with Aristotle in *GP,* III:23, p. 294.

5. See Barry Mesch, *Studies in Joseph ibn Caspi* (Leiden: Brill, 1975), pp.103–4.

6. *Moreh Nevukhim*, Hebrew translation by Samuel ibn Tibbon, with commentaries by Efodi, Shem Tov, Crescas, Abravanel and Narboni in part 3, p. 27b.

7. See his introduction to the *GP,* 1xvi–1xvii. See also Alvin Reines, "Maimon-

ides' Concepts of Providence and Theodicy," *HUCA* 43 (1972): 169–205; and Norbert Samuelson, "The Problem of Free Will in Maimonides, Gersonides, and Aquinas," *CCAR Journal* 17 (1970): 4–9.

8. See, for example, the study by Charles Raffel, "Providence as Consequent upon Intellect: Maimonides' Theory of Providence," *AJS Review* 12 (1987): 25–71. Raffel deftly distinguishes between an "our account" and an "I account" of providence.

9. For the account of Maimonides' own belief, see *GP,* III:17, pp. 471–74.

10. *GP,* p. 494. See also Raffel, "Providence as Consequent upon Intellect," p. 53.

11. *GP,* II:29, p. 345. See also Maimonides' commentary on the Mishnah in *Aboth* 5:5

12. *GP,* p. 465. See also Reines's description of this theory as one of "incidental specific providence" ("Maimonides' Concepts of Providence and Theodicy," pp.180–81); and Samuelson, "The Problem of Free Will in Maimonides, Gersonides, and Aquinas," p. 5, where he queries any substantive difference between Maimonides' and Aristotle's version of providential extension.

Chapter 4. Divine Immutability and Providence

1. See Sara Klein-Braslavy, "Perushe HaRambam LeHalom Hasulam Shel Yaakov," *Bar Ilan Annual* 22 and 23 (1988): 329–49, special edition entitled *Sefer Moshe Shwarcz*. In note 1 of her article she offers five arguments against the authenticity of this letter and says that it doesn't reflect Maimonides' true belief.

2. See Pines's note on this term in I:15 of the *GP*.

3. For Maimonides' attraction to the number seven in structuring the *Guide,* see Leo Strauss's schema in his introduction to Pines's edition of the *Guide,* pp. xi–xiii, and his comments on p. xiii immediately following the schema.

4. Ibid., p. 472. See also M.T., *Hilkhot Yesodei Hatorah* 2:2, where the same verse is quoted as an expression of absolute insignificance arousing "fear" of God.

5. In *GP,* III:17 a lengthy discussion ensues, distinguishing animals from man in that they are not subject to providence. "For this reason killing them and employing them usefully, as we wish, has been permitted and even enjoined" (p. 473). Almost the identical judgment is applied to ignorant men, who are analogous to animals and therefore "For this reason it is a light thing to kill them and has been even enjoined because of its utility" (p. 475).

6. "[T]he Law also makes a call to adopt certain beliefs, belief in which is necessary for the sake of political welfare. Such for instance is our belief that He is violently angry with those who disobey Him" (*GP,* p. 512, and again at p. 514, where anger is "belief necessary for the abolition of reciprocal wrongdoing" in contradistinction to a "correct belief").

7. *GP,* pp. 37–38. One cannot necessarily derive from this statement that there is in fact some "relation" between God and what is other than He. There is a "relation" between Him and what is external to Him, i.e., a nonexistent one. See *GP,* I:56, p. 130: "in view of the fact that the relation between us and Him is considered as non-existent—I mean the relation between Him and that which is other than He. . . ."

8. *GP,* p. 491. The problematic nature of this is highlighted by the struggle of the classic medieval commentators on the *Guide* to come to terms with this statement. For instance, Efodi identifies "relationship" with "knowledge" and simply takes it for granted that individuals of the human species are being singled out, "Divine knowledge extends to the species of existents and not to their individuals except for the human species." Abravanel vehemently disagrees and offers a resolution of the dilemma that is based on the distinction between knowledge that is the subject of *GP,* III:17 and relationship that is the subject of I:11. Shem Tov closes his comments to this chapter with cautionary advice: "It is fitting to truly comprehend this chapter since matters of *sitrei Torah* are hinted in it for which open discussion is not appropriate."

9. Embedded within the contexts of all three verses in (1) and (2) there are clues that direct the reader to Maimonides' hidden agenda:

(1) Isaiah 33:10—The "rising" of this verse is prefaced by a pessimistic account of man that includes the remark in 33:8 that "man is of no account." Isaiah 33:10 also continues with God "exalting" and "lifting" himself. Both these terms are dealt with in *GP,* I:20 as conveying the sense of "elevation in degree, exalted station and great worth" (p. 42). The fact that one term can yield a number of different meanings is indicative, says Maimonides, of the premise that all attributes "refer to one and the same notion. That notion is His essence and nothing outside his essence" (p. 42). This is of course fundamental to the understanding of a Being that is incapable of change.

(2) Psalm 12:6, which is a duplicate version of Isaiah 33:10, is followed by verse 7, which describes God's words as "pure words, silver, refined, exposed to the earth seven times purified." This contextually refers to the words of God in the previous verse—"Now will I rise"—and for those familiar with the "apples of gold" metaphor should act as a prescription to subject these words to a "refinement" process revealing esoteric intent.

(3) Psalm 102:14—this verse is preceded by one referred to in the previous chapter (*GP,* I:11) on "sitting": "[And] Thou O Lord sittest for all eternity," which figuratively translates into "The stable One who undergoes no manner of change." The "rising" God must therefore be the God defined as changeless and static.

10. A few verses later the identical expression is again used when berating Ahimelech for feeding and arming David "to rise up against me as one who lies in wait as of this day" (v. 13). The last phrase dovetails with the conclusion of verse 8 and certainly means that this support allows David to continue with his rebellion.

11. See *GP,* I:56–60.

12. Some commentators see this as solid testimony to divine providence. See, for instance, David Kimhi's comments; Kimhi sees this punishment as confirmation of the words conveyed through the prophets and therefore as a vindication of God's knowledge and awareness of the deeds of man.

13. One can appreciate the extent to which Maimonides was forced to deconstruct rabbinic sources in order to accord with his views, since a perusal of the sources clearly corroborates an anthropomorphic understanding of God. See Alon Goshen Gottstein, "The Body as Image of God in Rabbinic Literature," *HTR* 87, no. 2 (1994): 172–95, who concludes, after examining the rabbinic sources concerning the image of God, that "The physical and bodily understanding of the image of God is nowhere refuted and emerges as the only rabbinic understanding of the image of God" (p. 195).

14. Babylonian Talmud, *Hagigah* 15a.

15. This is the text Maimonides had quoted in his commentary on the Mishnah in the third principle of faith as developed in the tenth chapter of *Sanhedrin (Perek Heleq),* Heb. trans. Joseph Kafih, vol. 2 (Jerusalem: Mossad Harav Kook, 1963), p. 211. Also see M.T., *Hilkhot Yesodei Hatorah* 1:11. There are discrepancies between variant texts as to how this reads. For instance, Rashi deletes the word "standing." Many of the standard versions of the Talmud have *tacharut* (competition) in place of *amidah* (standing) as Maimonides has it.

16. In his study of the "four who entered Pardes," of which this text forms a part, Yehuda Liebes has already noted this incongruity but draws an entirely different conclusion: "[T]his is testimony to the fact that the Rambam could not find any rabbinic sayings which conformed to his purpose—the negation of physicality from God." See *Heto shel Elisha Arbaah she-nikhnesu le-Pardes ve-tivah shel ha-Mistikah ha-Talmudit* (Jerusalem: Academon, 1990), p. 31 n. 5. I disagree for the reasons mentioned, and disagree with the assumption that Maimonides would have foreseen that this "discrepancy" would not have escaped his more sophisticated readers. My preference is for the conclusions of Sarah Stroumsa in attributing the inconsistencies between the Maimonidean portrait of Elisha and that of the Talmud to conscious design rather than error, as "such an error is not at all characteristic of Maimonides and seems particularly unlikely in light of the numerous times that Maimonides alludes to the second chapter of *Hagigah* in the *Guide*." She therefore opts for an analysis similar to my own, where blatant "error" is seen as a "pointer" arousing the attention of the reader to the fact that Maimonides' remarks here are not intended to be understood literally. See Sarah Stroumsa, "Elisha ben Abuyah and Muslim Heretics in Maimonides' Writings," *Maimonidean Studies* 3 (1992–93): 182–83. For various reasons Sara Klein-Braslavy disagrees with the "creative" approach suggested by Stroumsa and inclines toward the possibility that Maimonides was operating with a version that differs from all the manuscripts presently extant. See S. Klein-Braslavy, *King Solomon and Philosophical*

Esotericism in the Thought of Maimonides (Jerusalem: Magnes Press, 1994), pp. 139–40, 139n.

17. *GP,* II:6, p. 262; see also II:10, p. 269. "It is known and generally recognized in the books of the philosophers speaking of governance that governance of this lower world . . . is said to be brought about through the forces overflowing from the spheres." It would therefore seem that there is an identity of belief between the Law and the philosophers on the issue of governance.

18. *GP,* p. 262, where angels can connote messengers, causes of animal motion, elements, men, prophets, and separate intellects.

19. M.T., *Hilkhot Yesodei Hatorah* 2:7.

20. *GP,* pp. 471–72, also at p. 474: "[P]rovidence is consequent upon the intellect and attached to it. . . . " Accordingly, everyone with whom something of this overflow is united will be reached by providence to the extent to which he is reached by the intellect, and at *GP,* III:51, p. 624, it says, "[P]rovidence watches over everyone endowed with intellect proportionately to the measure of his intellect. . . ."

21. For a detailed study tracing differing Jewish interpretations of Metatron, see Daniel Abrams, "The Boundaries of Divine Ontology: The Inclusion and Exclusion of Metatron in the Godhead," *HTR* 87, no. 3 (1994): 291–321, and esp. 293–98.

22. Or the tenth level of angels known as *ishim*. See M.T., *Hilkhot Yesodei Hatorah* 2:7.

23. B.T., *Sanhedrin* 38b. See also Nahmanides in his biblical commentary on Exodus 12:12, where Metatron is identified as the primary agent of God for all His activities on earth, and Exod. 24:2, which refers to *Sanhedrin* 38b. See also Rashi on Exodus 23:2, who points out the equivalence of the numerical value of the name Metatron with the divine appellation "Shaddai."

24. See also *GP,* II:18, p. 300 for an explanation of the misperception that the Active Intellect acts like matter passing from potentiality to actuality. This is not so, "For if the Active Intellect necessarily acts at a certain time and does not act at another time this does not result from a certain cause subsisting in its essence, but from the disposition of the portions of matter. For its action is perpetual with regard to all things properly disposed. Hence if there is an obstacle to this action this results from a material disposition and not from the Intellect itself." This is supportive of the contention that what we perceive as initiated from above is, in reality, a factor of the preparedness of man to receive what is a perpetual reflex of the Active Intellect.

25. See *GP,* introduction, p. 6 and M.T., *Hilkhot Yesodei Hatorah,* where the Pardes of the "four who entered" recounted in *Hagigah* is explicitly identified with the subject matter of the first four chapters of M.T., i.e., *maaseh bereshit* and *maaseh merkavah.*

26. *GP,* I:32. I differ from Stroumsa, "Elisha ben Abuyah and Muslim Heretics," as to the object of Elisha's aspirations. For her it is the Account of the Cre-

ation that led Elisha to the belief in the eternity of the universe. For me it is the mechanics of divine providence.

27. *GP*, II:6, p. 265. See the very lucid discussion of Maimonides' theory of the Intellect in Herbert Davidson's *Alfarabi, Avicenna, and Averroes on Intellect* (New York: Oxford University Press, 1992), pp. 197–207, and his conclusion at p. 206 that "Maimonides transforms the deism of the Arabic Aristotelians into a rationalistic theism. . . . " This is accomplished by refuting the emanation scheme of Alfarabi and Avicenna in favor of an emanation from a First Cause by an act of will.

28. See Jerome Gellman, "Radical Responsibility in Maimonides' Thought," in *The Thought of Moses Maimonides: Philosophical and Legal Studies*, ed. I. Robinson et al. (New York: Edwin Mellen Press, 1990), 249–65, where he states: "[A] new understanding emerges from chapters 5–9 of Teshuvah, an understanding of oneself as responsible, in total freedom, for one's fate in a world where God's intervention is minimized or does not exist" (p. 254).

29. Here I adopt Liebes's interpretation of the talmudic legend "A heavenly voice went forth and said: 'Return, backsliding children' (Jer. 3:14)—except Aher" to an exegetical move by Aher himself and not to the *bat qol*. The *bat qol*'s declaration is simply the verse in Jeremiah 3:14 advocating the turn to repentance, whereas Aher, impelled by his extreme hubris, applies a midrashic technique to the verse's general rubric. See Yehuda Liebes, *Heto shel Elisha Arbaah she-nikhnesu le-Pardes ve-tivah shel ha-Mistikah ha-Talmudit,* pp. 44–45. Liebes raises the psychodramatic possibility of Aher being so self-absorbed that he instantly formulated the "midrash" in his mind "and was entirely unaware that this was his own gloss to the words of the bat qol" (p. 45). The fact that the imagination plays such a central role in the reception of any heavenly communication, along with the fact that we are dealing here with a communication of inferior quality *(bat qol),* tends to substantiate this as a viable Maimonidean reading.

30. "Foot" is the subject term of *GP*, I:28.

31. See A. Ravitzky, "'To the Utmost Human Capacity': Maimonides on the Days of the Messiah," in *Perspectives on Maimonides*, ed. Joel Kraemer (Oxford and New York: Oxford University Press, 1991), pp. 221–56. Ravitzky sees this aspect of communal salvation as the distinctive mark of Maimonides' messianism: ". . . Torah, which is today confused within the personal domain, is meant to burst forth into the public domain; intellectual apprehension, which in the beginning of Mishneh Torah were defined as exclusive and esoteric . . . are destined[,] as he stated at the end of his work, to become the inheritance of the community . . . " (p. 248).

32. *GP*, p. 624. The naturalistic view of providence subscribed to in this book seems to be contradicted by a kind of personal providence implied in the statements that a person of this rank is always protected by God and "no evil at all will befall him" (*GP*, p. 626), to the point that in the midst of a blood soaked battlefield

he will remain impervious to its dangers (p. 627). Moses Narboni offers a tantalizing solution by referencing the "him" of "no evil will befall him" to the true form of man, the intellect. Since that is what constitutes man's humanity, it is that which is protected and impenetrable, as opposed to the material body, which indeed can be harmed. *Perush le Moreh Nebukhim,* ed. J. Goldenthal (Vienna, 1852), pp. 64–65.

33. See also Lawrence Kaplan, "'I Sleep, but My Heart Waketh': Maimonides' Conception of Human Perfection," in Robinson et al., *Thought of Moses Maimonides,* pp. 131–66 and his explanation of why this speculative rank is restricted to Moses and the Patriarchs at pp. 146–47. I respectfully disagree with his conclusion that in the case of the rare individual who has achieved the acme of human perfection, the contemplative life and the active life are equal partners that "blend in a consummate unity, as both contemplation and action join together in the pure worship of God" (p. 148). The fact that the active political life is characterized as being carried out "with their limbs only" and is only "outwardly involved with people" indicates to me that, though a necessary by-product of intellectual perfection, the active life is held in much lower esteem. I incline more toward the parallel drawn by H. Kreisel between the activity of those perfect men and of the separate intellects, where the constant overflow that governs the sublunar world does not entail any deficiency, since "their intellection is permanently fixed on the One. . . . The prophets' intellects thus are similar to the divine intellects. In attaining final perfection, the prophets at the same time complete the chain of divine governance of man." Kreisel, "Maimonides' View of Prophecy," *Daat* 13 (1984): xxiv–xxv.

34. For an interesting argument (contra Pines) that *GP,* III:51 is intended as the real conclusion to the *Guide* rather than III:54, but that the reverse order is instrumental in concealing Maimonides' real positions, see David Shatz, "Worship, Corporeality, and Human Perfection: A Reading of *Guide of the Perplexed,* III:51–54," in Robinson et al., *Thought of Moses Maimonides,* pp. 77–129.

35. See, for instance, Abravanel's comments that attempt to make sense out of its curious positioning since, logically, it should have followed or preceded the chapter dedicated to the terms "man" *(ish)* and "woman" *(ishah).*

36. See Abravanel's comment on this and the appendix to W. Z. Harvey's unpublished Ph.D. dissertation, "Hasdai Crescas' Critique of the Acquired Intellect" (Columbia University, 1973).

37. Prophecy represents "the highest degree of man and the ultimate term of perfection that can exist for his species. . . . This is something that cannot by any means exist in every man" (*GP,* II:36, p. 369).

38. This reading is supported by a comment made in one of Maimonides' responsa as to the common practice in Hebrew of omitting prepositions such as which/since *(asher),* citing this perplexing word *beshegam* as an example. See *Teshuvot HaRambam,* ed. J. Blau (Jerusalem: Mekize Nirdamim, 1989), 2:378, responsa #214. See also Nahmanides in his *Commentary on the Torah,* Genesis

6:3, who also considers the flesh and man's inclination to it an impediment to the reception of God's *ruach*.

39. See, for instance, Saadya Gaon's comments on this verse in his *Commentary on Psalms* and his *Book of Beliefs and Doctrines,* 2:83, for a different interpretation.

40. See *GP,* p. 374 for the difference between "prophets" and "those who govern cities."

41. The same phrase, *benei elohim* (sons of Elohim), can bear the equivocal meaning of angels in a different context. See Job 1:6 and its interpretation in *GP,* III:22.

42. This is the rationale for the highly imaginative framework by which the Torah is rendered communicable to the masses. They are incapable of digesting anything else. See *GP,* I:26: "[T]he Torah speaks in the language of the sons of man."

43. I concur here with Jacob Levinger's perceptive remark that "without an explanation of the term 'sons of the Most High' in the former verse the meaning given by Maimonides to the term 'men' *(adam)* in the latter verse could not be understood," though not necessarily with the conclusions he derives. Jacob Levinger, "Maimonides' Exegesis of Job," in *Creative Biblical Exegesis: Christian and Jewish Hermeneutics through the Centuries,* ed. B. Uffenheimer and H. Reventlow, USOT Supplement Series 59 (Sheffield, England: JSOT Press, 1988), p. 87.

44. *GP,* I:42, p. 93. See also I:40: one of the meanings of *ruach* (air) is "the thing that remains of man after his death and that does not undergo passing-away," and I:41, for "soul" *(nephesh),* "it is a term denoting the thing that remains of man after death."

45. See W. Z. Harvey, "Perush HaRambam LeBereshit 3:22," *Daat* 12 (19): 15–22, which surveys a host of medieval exegetes who interpreted the word "lest" *(pen)* in the verse "Lest he send forth his hand and take also of the tree of life" in a positive vein, i.e., Adam now has the possibility or opportunity to send forth his hand. Among those he lists are Samuel ibn Tibbon, Moses ben Samuel ibn Tibbon, Emmanuel HaRomi, Joseph ibn Kaspi, Gersonides, and Narboni (pp. 18–21). See also his conclusion as to Maimonides' interpretation of this verse, with which I am in complete agreement: "Adam, in his rebellion, abandoned the life of the intellect (Tree of Life) and sunk into the life of generally accepted things (Tree of Knowledge). In this imperfect state man is like other animals. However, he is distinct from them in that he has the capability,—and since he has he can even achieve this at present!—to choose to partake of the Tree of Life and live forever" (p. 22).

46. For a cryptic treatment of the fall of Adam, see *GP,* II:30 and the references to various fantastic midrashim, which he refuses to explicate, "For I will not be one who divulges a secret" (p. 355).

47. *GP,* p. 358. They are *bar'o* (create), *'assoh* (make), *qanoh* (to acquire), and *'El* (God).

48. *GP,* p. 358. Pines, in a note, surmises that the ambiguous pronoun "them" "probably refers to the heaven and the earth." Though this may be correct in the context, the statement lends itself to a generalization about the overall usage of the term *assoh* even in respect of other creations.

49. *GP,* p. 23. I am in full agreement with Sara Klein-Braslavy that I:14 hints at viewing Adam in the creation story in a historical sense; for Maimonides, "the stories about Adam are not an anthropogony but a philosophical anthropology." Klein-Braslavy, "The Creation of the World and Maimonides' Interpretation of Gen. I–IV," in *Maimonides and Philosophy,* ed. S. Pines and Y. Yovel (Dordrecht: Martinus Nijhoff, 1986), p. 72. Her emphasis, though, is how this fits in with Maimonides' view on creation, while mine is on the issue of providence.

50. See *GP,* II:36 for the "true reality and quiddity of prophecy."

51. Though the third verse of Psalm 2:2, "The kings of the earth stood erect," does not refer to Moses, it does share the theme of the other two in which the characters who are "standing erect" lack some informative data. The remedy for the arrogance of these kings in Psalm 2:2 is the admonition of 2:10, "Now you kings be wise" (*haskilu,* from the root for the mind, *sekel*).

52. See *GP,* I:54.

53. This is evidenced by the distinction between the request for God's "glory" (essence), to which a favorable reply is denied, and God's "ways" ("attributes of action"), which is favored.

54. Various forms of this root appear repeatedly in the Mishneh Torah, especially in *Hilkhot Yesodei Hatorah.* David Blumenthal distinguishes five principal meanings in Maimonides' use of the root in "Maimonides on Mind and Metaphoric Language," in *Approaches to Judaism in Medieval Times,* ed. D. R. Blumenthal (Chico, Calif.: Scholars Press, 1985), 2:123–32, no. 2 in his commentary. Of particular interest to our study is the third principal meaning, which he identifies as "a purposeful double entendre intended to convey both of the previous meanings, 'intellectual capacity' to the philosophically untrained and 'intellect' to the philosophically trained" (p. 126).

55. See also *GP,* II:30, p. 352, where "because of this equivocality of terms, the true heaven is likewise called firmament just as the true firmament is called heaven." The "true heaven" is not the heaven that is visible to man or part of nature, but something else.

Chapter 5. The Seven Units of Jacob's Ladder and Their Message

1. See the index of rabbinic passages at the end of Kafih's *MN,* where the listing under *Genesis Rabbah* exceeds any other with a total of forty-five references.

2. See *GP,* p. 573, "For these [namely, the midrashic] have in their opinion

the status of poetical conceits; they are not meant to bring out the meaning of the text in question." Maimonides felt no compunction about rejecting one sage in favor of another in the realm of Aggadah. See for instance his rejection of the opinion in *Mishneh Berakhot* regarding the law of sending away the mother from her nest (*GP,* p. 600).

3. Some variants have the exact same expression for the SLM-SML equation as for the Sulam-Sinai one: "*'otiyot deden hu 'otiyot deden.*" See Chanoch Albeck, *Midrash Bereshit Rabbah* (Jerusalem: Sefrei Waharman, 1965).

4. There are only three appearances: Deuteronomy 4:16, Ezekiel 8:3, and 2 Chronicles 33:7. The Aramaic Targum in Ezekiel 8:3 renders *semel* as *tselem,* and therefore the Aramaic *tselem* of Daniel 2:31 can be translated into Hebrew as *semel*.

5. *Hilkhot Yesodei Hatorah* 4:1.

6. See *Hilkhot Yesodei Hatorah* 3:11 and 4:2.

7. See M.T., *Hilkhot Yesodei Hatorah,* 3:10, where the term for uninformed matter is *golem.* In *Pirkei Avot, golem* is a character type the antithesis of which is the wise *(chakham)* person (5:7). In his commentary on this mishnah, Maimonides characterizes the *golem* as one who possesses both moral qualities and intellectual acumen but is prone to confused and erroneous intellections that are lacking in form and incomplete. The prooftext cited for this sense of *golem* is Psalm 139:16: "Your eyes saw my *informed body* [*golem*], that is, my basic matter before it achieved human form." This is most probably a reference to the initial fetal stage in the womb. The verse continues, "and on Your book they were all written," which appropriately conveys the sense of predestined and predetermined. Providence for *golem* is merely the unfolding of what has always been there.

8. See, for instance, his discussion in *GP,* II:29 on miracles and how they fit into the scheme of creation, which basically reduces them to another feature of nature. He relies on midrashim, indicating that "miracles too are something that is, in a certain respect, in nature. They say that when God created that which exists and stamped upon it the existing natures, He put it into these natures that all the miracles that occurred would be produced in them at the time when they occurred" (p. 345). Note that when Maimonides distinguishes himself from Aristotle on this issue he confines the distinction at p. 346 to a belief in creation as opposed to eternity *a parte ante* and not his view of nature subsequent to creation.

9. Or in ibn Tibbon *r'ishon* and *hathala.* See also Kafih's translation of the *Guide* in Hebrew (Jerusalem: Mossad Harav Kook, 1972) and his objection to ibn Tibbon's choice of words at p. 379 n. 1 of vol. 2 of that work.

10. I adopt here the translation of ibn Tibbon, which is at odds with that of Munk, Friedlander, and Pines, all of whom translate this phrase in the sense of the head's anatomical position with respect to the body. It cannot be the location of the head that underlies the "principal" meaning, since the implication here is the head's role in sustaining life or as the foundation and source of life for "living beings."

11. See Rashi.

12. Deuteronomy 1:17 for "approach" and Genesis 18:23 for "come near."

13. See the JPS translation, which renders the verse "For her *punishment* reaches to heaven."

14. See *GP,* III:20, p. 480, and A. Ivry, "Providence, Divine Omniscience, and Possibility: The Case of Maimonides," in *Divine Omniscience and Omnipotence in Medieval Philosophy,* ed. T. Rudavsky (Dordrecht and Boston: D. Reidel Publishing Co., 1985), p. 154: "God knows all of them through the formal principles with which he endows them: and he knows the future and the present, since for God there is neither past, future or present, just an eternal now." This notion of the "eternal present" is formulated artfully by Aquinas, ". . . His knowledge is measured by eternity, as is also His being and eternity, being simultaneously whole comprises all time. . . . Hence all things that are in time are present to God from eternity . . . because His glance is carried from eternity over all things as they are in their presentiality." *Summa Theologica,* Ia, q.14, art. 13, in *Basic Writings of St. Thomas Aquinas,* trans. and ed. A. C. Pegis (New York: Random House, 1945), 1:155.

15. See also Mishneh Torah.

16. In *GP,* II:48 Maimonides asserts that prophetic attributions of things "produced in time" directly to God must be taken only in the sense that He is the "First Cause of all things." One must read in all the intermediary proximate causes that were "omitted in the dicta of the prophets." As an example of one of these "omissions," which falls under human free choice, he cites an introductory verse to Jeremiah 51: "And I will send unto Babylon scatterers who shall scatter her" (51:2). This is perfectly consistent with the point being made here that nature is merely taking its course with no direct involvement by God except in the remotest causal sense.

17. The first half of the verse, "We tried to cure Babylon but she was incurable . . . ," can now be understood as a direct consequence of the theory of divine knowledge espoused by the second half. It is an expression of the utter futility of attempting to change the course of history since, from the divine vantage point, all of history is already contained in the divine self-reflecting mind. Man has no control over the divine intellectual blueprint that mapped out everything for all time.

18. See for instance Abravanel in his comment on the chapter. For a modern commentator see Yehuda Even Shmuel's edition of the *Guide,* vol. 2, part 1 (Jerusalem: Mossad Harav Kook), p. 92, who comments that Maimonides is singling out two exceptions to the alternatives of physical contact or intellectual union. These two verses represent a third alternative of retribution.

19. Genesis 2:17; 2 Kings 15:15; Job 1:11, 19:22; Psalm 104:32; 2 Chronicles 26:20.

20. See Marvin Fox, *Interpreting Maimonides* (Chicago: University of Chicago Press, 1990), chap. 11, "Prayer and the Religious Life," which is a revised translation of "Ha-Tefilla be-Machshavto shel ha-Rambam," in *Prayer in Judaism:*

Continuity and Change, ed. G. H. Cohen (Ramat Gan: Kedem, 1978). Fox argues for the inconsistency of two conceptions of prayer, both of which Maimonides adhered to: "[Maimonides'] theory of providence seems to have the effect of making all petitionary prayer superfluous and useless. Prayer cannot be legitimately understood as having a direct causal connection with the way in which God governs us and determines our destiny" (p. 306). See also Alvin Reines, "Maimonides' True Belief Concerning God: A Systematization," in Pines and Yovel, *Maimonides and Philosophy,* pp. 24–35, who argues that Maimonides' doctrine of absolute transcendence is totally incompatible with prayer. A very thoughtful and eloquent response to these positions that seeks to maintain the validity of prayer within the Maimonidean system is offered by Ehud Benor in *Worship of the Heart: A Study of Maimonides' Philosophy of Religion* (Albany: SUNY Press, 1995), especially chap. 3, "Prayer and God's Knowledge."

21. See *GP,* II:10, p. 272, where natural governance of all species is identified as a "divine decree."

22. See Maimonides' approval of the rabbinic dictum that Satan, the evil inclination, and the angel of death are all one and the same (*GP,* III:22, p. 489). For a summary of various theories regarding the identification of Satan in Maimonides' thought, see A. Nuriel, "The Concept of Satan in the *Guide of the Perplexed*" (in Hebrew), *Jerusalem Studies in Jewish Thought* 5 (1986): 83–91. After rejecting positions equating Satan variously with absolute privation, acquired privation matter, and imagination, Nuriel distinguishes between Satan #1, who represents change tied to human choice, and Satan #2, as particular privation that characterizes nature.

23. *GP,* p. 487. See Job 1:1, 1:8, and 2:3, all of which describe Job as "sincere and upright, God-fearing and shunning evil."

24. I agree with Kasher, who demonstrates that Maimonides' account of Job, replete with contradiction, is in essence a vindication of Aristotle's position on providence and a rejection of the fifth opinion on providence outlined in III:17 as "that believed by the multitude of our scholars." See H. Kasher, "Job's Image and Opinion in the *Guide of the Perplexed*" (in Hebrew), *Daat* 15 (1985): 81–87.

25. See *GP,* I:41, p. 91.

26. See L. Kravitz, "Maimonides and Job: An Inquiry as to the Method of the *Moreh*," *HUCA* 38 (1967): 149–58, who like Kasher ("Job's Image and Opinion in the *Guide of the Perplexed*") views Job as the vehicle for an esoteric position on providence. The key to this position is found in Elihu's discourse, through which Job is educated to move from a Satan/imagination *Weltanschauung* to one that is angel/Active Intellect oriented. The former is a world devoid of providence, and the latter is the only means to acquire it.

27. See *GP,* III:10 where Maimonides considers all evil to be "privation," and therefore "[I]t may in no way be said of God . . . that He produces evil in an essential act. . . . Rather all His acts are an absolute good; for He only produces being and all being is good." He concludes *GP,* III:10 with a rabbinic dictum that

substantiates this thesis—"Nothing that is evil descends from above" (*Genesis Rabbah* 51).

28. See M.T., *Yesodei Hatorah* 1:1: "The foundation of all foundations and the pillar of wisdom is to know that there is a prime existent. . . ." See also *GP,* I:58, generally and at p. 135: "[W]e are only able to apprehend the fact that He is and cannot appreciate His quiddity."

29. See. M.T., *Yesodei Hatorah* 3:1, where the spheres are divided into *shamayim, raki'a, zebul,* and *araboth.* See also *GP,* II:30, where his equivocality results in the *rakia* being called "heaven" and I:70, where *araboth* is the highest heaven. See also III:4, which attributes the designation of heaven as *galgallim* to their sphericity.

30. *GP,* I:71, p. 175 (a). See also II:18, p. 302, "[T]here is no proof indicating to us the existence of the Maker, according to our opinion, like the indication deriving from the heaven," and II:19, p. 310, "[T]here is no proof of purpose stronger than the one founded upon the differences between the motions of the spheres and upon the fact that the stars are fixed in the spheres. For this reason you will find that all the prophets used the stars and the spheres as proofs for the deity's existing necessarily."

31. See M.T., *Abodath Zarah* 1:9 for a description of how the patriarch Abraham arrived at a clear demonstration of the existence of the Deity. The primary proof was the observance of the perpetual motion of the spheres. His conclusions were based on pure reason without the assistance of tradition or instructive upbringing. This, of course, is the surest method of gaining true knowledge. Abraham essentially follows the first proof offered in *GP,* II:11 for the existence of a Prime Mover who is the "First Cause which moves the sphere."

32. Exodus 17:16. Jewish exegesis, both classical and medieval, has understood this phrase to be an oath formula reading *kisse* (throne) for the unusual *kes.* See *Tanhuma, kiTeze* 11, and the comments of Rashi, Nahmanides, and ibn Ezra on the verse.

It is interesting, simply as an observation, that the Septuagint renders this word *kruphaia* or "secret" which, according to Nahum Sarna, is based on understanding the Hebrew root *k-s-h,* "to cover up." See *JPS Torah Commentary—Exodus,* p. 250 n. 18. The following analysis assumes that the verse does indeed cover up an inner secret—divine providence.

33. Thus the most perfect nonderivative name for God, "I am that I am" (Exod. 33:14), is a tautologous declaration in which the second word predicated of the first is identical with it. "Accordingly Scripture makes[,] as it were, a clear statement that the subject is identical with the predicate" (*GP,* I:63, p. 155). Language is unequipped to deal with this unique existence in any other way.

34. God's existence is identical with his essence and vice versa, and so it is with attributes such as life, power, and knowledge, "for all these attributes refer back to the notion in which there is no idea of multiplicity."

35. Since God is not subject to time, to say that He is eternal is simply to convey the notion that "He is not subject to change and that no notion is produced in Him anew." Eternal indicates "that He has not come into being in time," and therefore even this predicate has serious consequences for the issue of divine providence, since the very word, in its philosophical equivocal sense, divorces God from history and from time-bound events. See *GP,* I:57, p. 133 and I:13, p. 281, which rules out even statements that God existed *prior* to the creation, since they are based on "an imagining of time and not due to the true reality of time." See also T. M. Rudavsky, "The Theory of Time in Maimonides and Crescas," *Maimonidean Studies* 1 (1990): 150.

36. The political expediency of this imagery may be to teach that if God Himself does battle with evil, then a fortiori man should shoulder that responsibility as well.

37. For a good summary of the dominant positions in the scholarly debate concerning Maimonides' true stance on creation—as represented by Davidson (Platonic), Kaplan and Harvey (Aristotelian), and Fox (traditional/scriptural)—and a critique of each, see Norbert Samuelson, "Maimonides' Doctrine of Creation," *HTR* 84, no. 3 (1991): 249–71 and the citations for the various articles on the subject therein.

38. Abravanel disagrees with Efodi and does not consider this an instance of contradiction, "since the Master does not shy away from allowing one verse numerous interpretations and here [I:9] he interpreted this verse in one fashion and there [II:26] in another." This, in my opinion, is not a very convincing rebuttal to Efodi, since *GP,* I:9 offers the verse as irrefutable authority for the unity of throne and divine essence, "*For it states explicitly . . . whereby it indicates that the throne is a thing inseparable from Him.*" If the verse admits of an alternative meaning offered by I:26, where "throne" and God are disengaged, then this proof is nothing short of puerile.

39. B.T., *Nedarim* 39b and *Gen. Rab.* I:5. The third source is found in B.T., *Pesahim* 54a, which bases itself on Jeremiah 17:12, "A throne of glory set on high from the first is the place of our sanctuary," which is also the prooftext for the preexistence of the sanctuary.

40. Alfred Ivry claims that, in his discussion of this midrash, Maimonides treats the "snow" and the "throne of glory" as representing the same thing—sublunar prime matter. This is true in the manner upon which the discussion proceeds, as they seem to be interchangeable. My disagreement lies in viewing this as an esoteric strategy planned to motivate the reader to mine the text for the true message. See Ivry's article "Maimonides on Creation" (in Hebrew), *Mehkerei Yerushalyim B'Mahshevet Yisrael* 9, pt. II (1990): 115–37, 135–36 nn. 54–58.

41. See *GP,* II:28, p. 335: "The works of the Deity are most perfect—accordingly they are of necessity permanently established as they are, for there is no possibility of something calling for a change in them."

42. See W. Z. Harvey, "A Third Approach to Maimonides' Cosmogony-Prophetology Puzzle," *HTR* 74, no. 3 (1981): 287–305 for his very detailed and convincing arguments in support of Maimonides having advocated the Aristotelian theory of eternity, and especially Harvey's remarks on p. 297: "... Maimonides' teaching that God's will, wisdom and essence are one and inscrutable effectively strips the concept of God's will of any cognitive meaning."

43. See *GP,* I:59, p. 138, "[Y]ou come nearer to the apprehension of Him with every increase in the negations regarding Him ... ," and at p. 139, "[I]n every case in which the demonstration that a certain thing should be negated with reference to Him becomes clear to you, you become more perfect. ... " For a full discussion of the medieval debate surrounding the theology of negative attributes, see David Burrell, *Knowing the Unknowable God* (Notre Dame, Ind.: University of Notre Dame Press, 1986). For a stimulating argument that the epistemic thesis that restricts any knowledge of God to negation does not rule out the semantic thesis that allows for a rich symbolic God-talk, see Ehud Benor, "Meaning and Reference in Maimonides' Negative Theology," *HTR* 88, no. 3 (1995): 339–10. His claim is that the establishment of a reference to God through an austere theology of negation allowed Maimonides "to resort instead to symbolic ideas of God that provide context for religious thought as they point beyond themselves and deny their literal or metaphorical truth" (p. 352).

44. There is a confusing passage whose correct translation is subject to much scholarly debate, since it directly contradicts the statements that the heavens provide the greatest proofs for the existence of God: "[F]or it is impossible for us to accede to the points starting from which conclusions may be drawn about the heavens; for the latter are too far away from us and too high in place and in rank. And even the general conclusion that may be drawn from them, namely, that they prove the existence of their Mover, is a matter the knowledge of which cannot be reached by human intellects" (*GP,* II:24, p. 327). This constituted such a glaring inconsistency that it actually gave rise to an emendation by Samuel ibn Tibbon (printed in the edition of the *Moreh Nevukhim,* revised and vocalized by Even Shmuel [Jerusalem: Mossad Harav Kook, 1960–87], pt. 2, vol. 1, p. 316) to resolve it. For a summary of the various attempts to grapple with this problem and the text's correct translation by Joel Kraemer, Joseph Kafih, and Herbert Davidson and reasons for their rejection, see Warren Z. Harvey, "Maimonides' First Commandment, Physics, and Doubt," in *Hazon Nahum, Studies in Jewish Law Thought and History,* ed. Y. Elman and J. Gurnock (New York: Yeshiva University Press, 1997), pp. 149–62. Harvey concludes at p. 161 that this proof is at the most a "possible" one that is preparatory to the Avicennian proof from contingent existence to necessary existence. Doubt and perplexity, therefore, are built into the whole process of obtaining knowledge of God, and his conclusion is consistent with my thesis that ultimately the one certain theological inference to be drawn from the heavens is "the remoteness of the apprehension of the Deity" (*GP,* III:14, p. 456).

45. Marvin Fox considers this remark as evidence that, when faced with opposing propositions regarding God such as here, where God is both entirely separate from the world and yet present in it as its cause, we are really faced with "divergences" rather than logical contradictions. The result is that both can be adhered to in a kind of dialectical tension. See Fox, "Maimonides' Method of Contradiction," in *Interpreting Maimonides,* pp. 82–83.

46. *GP,* I:69, p. 168. See also II:1. See Marvin Fox, "Maimonides' Account of Divine Causality," in *Interpreting Maimonides,* pp. 229–50, in which he identifies three different and irreconcilable accounts in the *Guide:* physical, metaphysical, and religious. Instead of determining the real account, Fox opts for a combination of all three, which live in a deliberate dialectical tension between the philosophic and religious view.

47. See Kenneth Seeskin's recent discussion of the purpose this popular notion of God serves if it is not simply taken at face value, at which point it remains idolatrous, in *Searching for a Distant God: The Legacy of Maimonides* (New York: Oxford University Press, 2000). Chapter 7 is a sensitive account of popular religion as providing "a systematic way to get to higher levels" at p. 167.

48. *Genesis Rabbah* 68:9.

49. See *GP,* II:28, p. 334, for the different nuances of the word *olam.* In the ensuing discussion various prooftexts are cited to support the view that the world will last forever *a parte post,* the consequence of which is that things which "are made are permanently established according to their nature forever"; and again, all the works of the Deity "are permanently established as they are, for there is no possibility of something calling for a change in them."

50. Even when outlining the fifth opinion on providence, which is attributed to the followers of "our Law," in *GP,* III:17, p. 469, human freedom of choice and animal motor functions are ultimately rooted in "His eternal volition in the eternity a parte ante." This latter "eternity" is of course one that is wholly segregated from the world as presented to us, since it precedes time, so to speak. Time-bound eternity (eternity *a parte post*) associated with the created world is not a continuation of pre-time eternity *(a parte ante).* Since there is no common ground between the two, it is difficult to conceive of the relevance anything in *a parte ante* has on *a parte post.* God endures in that time we call eternity *a parte ante* even after the creation, since time is a created thing that is only conceived of through a human and material perspective. Time entails change, which excludes the changeless God, and thus the world and God seem to end up as two solitudes. For an interesting discussion of the philosophical quandary in attempting to comprehend the notion of God's knowledge in eternity, see David Burrell, "Maimonides, Aquinas, and Gersonides on Providence and Evil," *Religious Studies* 20 (1984): 335–51 and especially Peter Geach's formulations of the problem on pp. 345–46.

51. B.T., *Abodah Zarah* 54b.

52. B.T., *Hagigah* 12b.

53. This is how Maimonides describes the allegorical method utilized by midrash, which often employs audacious imagery (*GP,* I:70, p. 174).

54. For a discussion as to how the socioethical and metaphysical/religious aspect of these terms as developed in the *Guide* in essence complement each other, see Yona Ben Sasson, *Hagut Yehudit Iyun VeHeker* (Jerusalem: Misrad ha-hinukh veha-tarhut, 1987), pp. 279–88.

55. See *GP,* I:54, p. 125. "Accordingly wherever one of His actions is apprehended, the attribute from which this action proceeds is predicated of Him, may He be exalted, and the name deriving from that action is applied to Him."

56. See Norbert Samuelson, "Divine Attributes as Moral Ideals in Maimonides' Theology," in Robinson et al., *Thought of Moses Maimonides:* "[O]n final analysis statements about God do not inform us about God; rather they instruct us in human ethics. In other words, Maimonides' theory of negative attributes is an explanation of the principle of *imitatio dei*" (p. 71).

57. See M.T., *Hilkhot Deot* 1:6–7, which refers to the *Sifre, Ekev* 1:22 of *mah hu af attah* (as He is so shall you be), calling on man to emulate those traits perceived as divine. See also B.T., *Sabbath* 133b; *Mechilta,* Exod. 14:2; and *Sefer Hamitzvot* (positive, no. 8). Note that Maimonides is careful to point out that all these guidelines are merely metaphorical expressions: "Similarly the prophets referred to God by various 'epithets' [*kinuim*—this is the same term used to classify all corporeal references to God in *Hilkhot Yesodei Hatorah* 1:6, which implies pure metaphor], such as 'long suffering,' 'abundant in kindness,' 'righteous,' 'just'" (*Hilkhot Deot;* 1:6). Again in *GP,* I:7 Maimonides explains that these are referred to as the "way of God" only by virtue of the fact that the "Creator is called by these terms," that is, it is only a construct of human language and not of ontic reality.

58. This is, in essence, what was accomplished by Moses in his request to *know God* (Exod. 33:13). He sought the guidance required, in his capacity as a political leader, to "perform actions that I must seek to make similar to Thy actions in governing them" (*GP,* I:54, p. 125).

59. I disagree with Pines's divergence from the original biblical context of "God of Eternity" to "God of the World." It is precisely the connotations of immutability that eternity conveys that render it appropriate in capturing rank of perfection rather than governance. "God of the World" implies relationship, whereas "God of Eternity" removes God from that context and results in an ontic appellative. See Pines's note 87 on p. 358 of the *Guide* as to why he prefers "God of the World" to "God of Eternity," the latter being its original biblical meaning.

60. See M.T., *Hilkhot Avodat Zarah* 1:7 and *GP,* II:13, p. 282, III:29, p. 516.

61. Virtually every one of Maimonides' written works is captioned by this verse. See Saul Lieberman, *Hilkhot HaYerushalmi LeRabbenu Moshe ben Maimon* (New York: Jewish Theological Seminary, 1995), who on p. 5 n. 7 lists the works that commence with this verse.

62. These same verses are quoted as proof of the same identity between angels and prophets at *GP,* II:6, p. 262 and II:42, p. 389.

63. See, for instance, Kafih's remarks in his Hebrew edition of the *GP*, vol. 1, p. 44 n. 11.

64. See letter of Rav Hasdai (as dealt with by Sara Klein-Braslavy, cited in note 1 of chapter 4), who actually addresses this problem to Maimonides himself. The response therein must be treated with some skepticism for the reasons given by Klein-Braslavy and by Kafih in his Hebrew edition, *Letters of Maimonides* (Jerusalem: Mossad Harav Kook, 1972).

65. Many of the medieval commentators agree that the four angels described in *GP,* II:20 as ascending and descending the ladder represent the basic four elements of the world, based upon an accepted postulate of Aristotelian physics. See for instance Efodi, Shem Tov, and Crescas. See also S. Klein-Braslavy, "Perushe HaRambam LeHalom Hasulam Shel Yaakov," p. 336 n. 1, who agrees.

66. See *GP,* II:32, p. 361 and II:36, p. 372.

67. The route that leads to prophecy follows the following path: Active Intellect—Rational Faculty—Imaginative Faculty (*GP,* II:36, p. 369). The first phase of the overflow to the rational faculty is sufficient for the self-awareness of the prophet, while the second phase is required to translate the first phase into some more popular form so that the general population can be addressed. See also *GP,* II:38, p. 377 and M.T., *Hilkhot Yesodei Hatorah* 7:1, which requires the prophet's primary focus to be directed toward matters that transcend political/social affairs.

68. M.T., *Hilkhot Yesodei Hatorah* 7:1.

69. The "holy forms" *(tsurot)* are clearly the separate intellects as evidenced by this term's usage in M.T., *Yesodei Hatorah* 2:3, 5, 7, 8. There are ten, the highest being the *chayot* and the lowest the *'ishim*. The point of divine contact with the prophet is only through the medium of the *'ishim* (2:7, 7:1).

70. The fifth contradiction is one that Maimonides resorts to for pedagogical reasons in his own treatise and is presented in the *Guide*. It is not a contradiction in Scripture or the prophetic books.

71. See also *GP,* I:2, p. 23.

72. The term designates any causal force in the universe. Since every movement in the world can be figuratively considered to have obeyed God's command, they therefore qualify as God's messengers. See *GP,* p. 263, "For all forces are angels," and II:7, p. 266, where *angel* "includes the intellects, the sphere and the element inasmuch as all of them carry out orders." Also at II:6, p. 264 they can symbolize all "individual natural and psychic forces," including sexual desire and orgasm. The term "angels" is thereby thoroughly demythologized, and an obvious biblical and rabbinic belief in supernatural beings and members of the divine retinue is converted into an overarching naturalism. See also H. Blumberg, "The Separate Intelligences in Maimonides' Philosophy," *Tarbiz* 40 (1971): 216–25 for

Maimonides' conception of these intellects and how he differs from Aristotle on this issue. Essentially they agree on the overall structural scheme of existence, with the crucial bone of contention centering on the origin of all being. For Aristotle the links of the chain of being are all forged by necessary causation, whereas for Maimonides, of course, they can be linked back to an originating act of divine will.

73. See also M.T., *Hilkhot Yesodei Hatorah* 2:3, where this tripartite division is duplicated and where the separate intellects are identified as *angels,* as opposed to the world of generation and corruption and the sphere and stars. Only the names of the separate intellects are designated as angels and not the spheres or the elements. See 2:7, 3:1, and 4:1.

74. See M.T., ibid. 2:11 where the subject matter of the first two chapters of *Yesodei Hatorah*, which includes the separate intellects, is identified as *maaseh merkavah* or metaphysics.

75. For example, in *GP,* I:13 "rise against" as an expression of anger is transformed to "denote the execution of God's decree."

76. See *GP,* I:10, p. 36, "[M]an is too insignificant to have his actions visited and to be punished for them were it not for the pre-eternal will."

77. See Herbert Davidson, "Averroes on the Active Intellect," *Viator* 18 (1987): 191–225, whose comments regarding Avicenna's concept of the Active Intellect would equally apply to Maimonides. Davidson says, "The Active Intellect, which owes its origin to Aristotle's few enigmatic remarks, reached its acme in Avicenna, for whom it is virtually the vicar of God on earth" (p. 191).

78. See *GP,* I:36, where adherence to beliefs that entail God being subject to affectability is considered more heinous a crime than worshiping idols: "Such a man is indubitably more blameworthy than a worshipper of idols who regards the latter as intermediaries . . ." (p. 84).

79. See M.T., *Yesodei Hatorah* 3:1, which lists nine, as well as *GP,* II:4, p. 257, which counts the all-encompassing sphere, the sphere of the fixed stars, and the spheres of the seven planets for a total of nine.

80. Though the numbers 9, 8, and 18 appear variously when enumerating different types of spheres, the number 4 does not. See M.T., *Yesodei Hatorah* 3:1, 2, 5 and *GP,* I:72, p. 185 for the number 18, which is the absolute minimum for spheres encompassing the world, though there is the possibility that they may exceed this number.

81. See M.T., *Yesodei Hatorah* 2:5.

82. See ibid.

83. See *GP,* I:1, p. 23.

84. Maimonides was heavily indebted to Avicenna for this hierarchy of being. For an excellent summary of Avicenna's emanationist scheme of the cosmos, see S. H. Nasr, *An Introduction to Islamic Cosmological Doctrines* (Cambridge: Belknap Press of Harvard University Press, 1964), esp. his chapter entitled "The Anatomy of Being."

85. "For the overflow coming from Him, may He be exalted, for the bringing into being of separate intellects[,] overflows likewise from these intellects so that one of them brings another one into being and this continues up to the Active Intellect . . . a certain other act of bringing into being overflows from every separate intellect until the spheres come to an end . . . " (*GP,* II:11, p. 275). See Arthur Hyman, "Maimonides on Creation and Emanation," in *Studies in Philosophy and the History of Philosophy*, vol. 17: *Studies in Medieval Philosophy*, ed. J. Wippel (Washington, D.C.: Catholic University of America Press, 1987), pp. 45–61, who very succinctly summarizes Maimonides' attitude toward emanation as follows: "While Maimonides rejects emanation as an explanation of creation, he finds it useful for explaining one kind of causality operative in the world" (p. 60).

86. *GP,* I:72, p. 187. On this see Arthur Hyman, "From What Is One and Simple, Only What Is One and Simple Can Come to Be," in *Neoplatonism and Jewish Thought*, ed. L. Goodman (Albany: SUNY Press, 1992), chapter 2, p. 131 n. 20.

87. See Davidson's masterful work *Alfarabi, Avicenna, and Averroes on Intellect,* p. 124, and especially his account of Maimonides' theory of the Active Intellect at pp. 197–207. According to Davidson, Avicenna is the source for much of his emanationist scheme, such as the designation of the Active Intellect as the *giver of form* and conjunction with the Active Intellect, with some variation attributable to ibn Bajja and Alfarabi.

88. See the third degree of prophecy, *GP,* II:45, p. 400, which classifies most of Zechariah's parables as this type.

89. See the analysis of the term "sons" in *GP,* I:7, pp. 32–33.

90. See M.T., *Hilkhot Yesodei Hatorah* 2:7. The *benei elohim* do appear in a verse cited from Job 38:7 in *GP,* II:5, p. 260, whose context is clearly of spheres and not of intellects. There are two existents, though, referred to in this verse as praising God: the "morning stars" and the *benei elohim* (sons of God). I believe the verse is cited for the former, who are the spheres. The talmudic source in B.T., *Hullin* 91b, cites this verse as proof of the chronological order of the *benei elohim* breaking out in song *after* the "morning stars"; this identifies the former with the "ministering angels" of Isaiah 6:3, who praise God as thrice *Holy*. Though the authors of this praise in Isaiah are not the *benei elohim*, they are the seraphim, who also occupy a level of separate intellects in the list compiled at M.T., *Hilkhot Yesadei Hatorah* 2:7. Though the morning stars represent Israel in the talmudic source, it seems more probable that the verse is incorporated by Maimonides in *GP,* II:5 to indicate the capacity for intellecting the Deity by the two main divisions of the upper domain: the spheres and stars, and the separate intellects. Their precise idea conveyed in II:5 is encapsulated in *Hilkhot Yesodei Hatorah* 3:9, where once again the "angels" are distinguished from the stars and spheres by their superior caliber of praise for the Creator.

91. *GP,* pp. 262–63. This passage is reminiscent of that in the *Timaeus,* which has the Demiurge contemplating the forms when he creates the world. For an argu-

ment that actually identifies the Demiurge with the forms and responds to opposing prevalent views of their separate identities, see Eric Perl, "The Demiurge and the Forms: A Return to the Ancient Interpretation of Plato's *Timaeus*," *Ancient Philosophy* 18 (1998): 81–92.

92. See *GP,* I:1.

93. See Maimonides' *Treatise on the Art of Logic*, trans. Charles Butterworth, in *Ethical Writings of Maimonides*, ed. R. L. Weiss and C. E. Butterworth (New York: New York University Press, 1975), pp. 158–61. There, one of the meanings of *mantiq* (*logos*, speech or logic) is "the expression in language of the notions impressed upon the soul. They call this meaning external reason."

94. See M.T., *Hilkhot Yesodei Hatorah* 4:8, which interprets Genesis 1:26 as instilling in man the capacity to apprehend those intelligibles that have no body— such as the angels who are pure form with no matter—to the point where he resembles them.

95. The corruption of language is the inconsistency between internal and external reason. Logic is the science that maintains harmony between the two in that it "gives rules which are common to all languages, by which external reason is shown the way to what is correct and is guarded from error. In this way what is expressed by the tongue conforms to what is in the mind and is identical with it." See *Ethical Writings of Maimonides,* p. 158. For a detailed analysis of chapter 14 of the *Treatise* or *Logic,* see Joel Kraemer, "Maimonides on the Philosophical Sciences in His *Treatise on the Art of Logic,*" in Kraemer, *Perspectives on Maimonides*, pp. 76–104, and esp. 80–82.

96. See *GP,* II:7 and *GP,* II:36, p. 369.

97. See the Anchor Bible, where modern critics take note that the four airs are the four directions, i.e., all of existence.

98. The spare imagery of Jacob's vision in comparison with Ezekiel's indicates its superiority. See *GP,* III:6, where Isaiah's truncated version of Ezekiel's vision is considered a more intimate account, since "the apprehension that amazed Ezekiel and was regarded by him as terrible was known by Isaiah through a knowledge, the exposition of which did not require extraordinary language, the subject being well known to those who are perfect" (p. 427). The more inundated the vision is with anthropomorphic detail, the more inferior it is. As Josef Stern has astutely pointed out to me, the *ma'aseh merkavah* of Ezekiel turns out to be a parabolic interpretation of Jacob's ladder, a type of philosophical inner biblical interpretation. This merits further exploration as a study itself.

99. I disagree with Sara Klein-Braslavy, who claims that Maimonides wishes us to dismiss the detail of a third of the world as irrelevant to the esoteric subtext of the dream. It is not in itself significant except to account for all the angels ending up on one level. She finds support in the statement that the breadth of the angels is seen *in the vision of prophecy*. This, for her, indicates that it is only relevant for the visual coherency but not for any esoteric allusions. But all the details transpire

within a prophetic vision—the number of angels; the number of steps; the ascending and descending; and so on. How does one determine what is discounted and what is not? Furthermore, the idea of a third of the world seems to hold a special appeal for Maimonides, for he emphasizes and dwells on its significance more than on the other details. Her reference to the segment under discussion at *GP,* II:6, where those who believe this deem themselves to be Sages of Israel and are not sages in reality, is of course exactly the point. They are not truly wise, since they understand it literally. This does not mean that it is devoid of any esoteric meaning; see Klein-Braslavy, "Perushe HaRambam LeHalom Hasulam Shel Yaakov," p. 335 n. 14.

100. See *GP,* I:27, 28, 36, 37, 48, 66, II:33, 41. For deference to the exegetical acumen of the Targum Onkelos in a halakhic setting, see M.T., *Issurei Biah* 12:13 and *Abel* 5:19.

101. For a detailed challenge to the generally accepted view endorsing Maimonides' antianthropomorphic characterizations of the Targum Onkelos, see Michael L. Klein, *Anthropomorphisms and Anthropopathisms in the Targumim of the Pentateuch* (in Hebrew) (Jerusalem: Makor, 1982) and the review thereof by Moshe Bernstein in *JQR* 77, no. 1 (1986): 65–70. See also the study by Dov Raffel, "The Theology of Targum Onkelos" (in Hebrew), *Bet Mikra* 26 (1980): 28–60, and his discussion of *yekara* (glory) at pp. 38–39; and Yehudah Komlosh, "Distinguishing Features in Targum Onkelos" (in Hebrew), *Bar Ilan Annual* 6 (1968): 181–90.

102. I adopt here Pines's categorization, who agrees that the two conceptualizations present contradictory beliefs and that the true belief to which Maimonides subscribes is that of absolute transcendence. See Reines, "Maimonides' True Belief Concerning God," pp. 24–35, and especially the list of individual remarks expressing qualified transcendence on pp. 26–28.

103. The third alternative of an actual created light can be discounted for the interpretation of Jacob's dream, since it is confined to extrinsic geographical locations such as the tabernacle and Mount Sinai. A dream or vision that takes place in the mind would be an inappropriate locale for a tangible phenomenon such as a "created light."

104. See references to "created light" in *GP,* I:5 (the presence in the burning bush), p. 29; I:11 (revelation to Moses on Mount Sinai), p. 37; I:22 (God "passing by" before Moses' face), p. 51; I:25 (description of God "dwelling" in particular locations), p. 55; and I:28 (Onkelos's translation of "throne of glory"), p. 60. See also I:18, pp. 44–45.

105. Maimonides is simply advancing an exegetical process already undertaken by the rabbis to broaden the scope of sacred space that the Bible had localized to places such as the Temple and Jerusalem. In order to fill the void left by the destruction of the Temple, the rabbis developed a theology that asserted that God could be experienced everywhere. See Baruch Bokser, "Approaching Sacred Space,"

HTR 78, nos. 3–4 (1985): 279–99, who concludes, "While the Bible may assume that holiness inherently exists, or the divine Potent presence dwells, in such fixed places as a tabernacle or Temple[,] the early rabbinic system, recognizing the potential for sacredness in the whole world, taught that extra Temple sacredness needs to be activated" (p. 299). See also Arthur Green, "Sabbath as Temple," in *Go and Study: Essays and Studies in Honour of Alfred Jospe,* ed. Raphael Jospe and Z. Fishman (Washington, D.C.: Bnai Brith Hillel Foundations, 1980), 287–305 for an example of how the rabbis transformed sacred space into one of sacred time replacing Temple-based worship.

106. The Aramaic translation of *nitzov* is *meated* which conveys a sense of preparation or readiness, rather than the root *kam* for standing. See, for instance, the targum to Exodus 18:14. The only other instance of *nitzov* as descriptive of God is Exodus 34:5, which is also translated by a form of *ated,* but no attempt is made by the Targum to distance God from direct action. Inconsistencies in Maimonides' theory of the Targum's methodology are variously ascribed to: (a) the referent being either an angel or in a dream, as with Genesis 46:4 (*GP,* I:27, pp. 58–59); (b) conveyance of some superior theological distinction, such as the case with "seeing" (*GP,* I:48, p. 107); and (c) scribal errors (I:48, p. 108). Or they are simply left incomprehensible, as in Genesis 31:18 (*GP,* I:66, pp. 160–61). See also Nahmanides' relentless critique of Maimonides on this issue in lengthy comments to Genesis 46:1 and particularly with respect to rationale (a) above. If it were the case that visions in a dream can be translated literally (since they do not refer to reality), then what is one to do with a verse such as that about Jacob's ladder, where God "standing" occurs in a dream and yet the Targum applies its antianthropomorphic method?

107. See *Pesikta De Rav Kahana* 23:12; *Vayikra Rabbah* 29:12; *Tanhuma: Vayetze; Shemot Rabbah* 32:7 *Pirke de Rabbi Eliezer* 35.

108. Klein-Braslavy, "Perushe HaRambam LeHalom Hasulam Shel Yaakov," p. 331 and note 9 on that page.

109. From the translation of W. Braude and I. J. Kapstein (Philadelphia: JPS, 1975).

110. For a complete analysis of chapter 23 of *Pesiqta DeRav Kahana* and how all the strands are woven into one thematic theological statement, see Lou Silberman, "A Theological Treatise on Forgiveness: Chapter 23 of *Pesiqta DeRav Kahana,*" in *Studies in Aggadah, Targum, and Jewish Literacy in Memory of Joseph Heinemann,* ed. J. Petuchovski and E. Fleischer (Jerusalem: Magnes Press, 1981), pp. 95–107.

111. I do not intend to enter the debates as to whether ethical perfection is the ultimate end or simply a means to a higher intellectual perfection. For a comprehensive study of this issue, see Menahem Kellner, *Maimonides on Human Perfection* (Atlanta: Scholars Press, 1990), and the bibliography therein. See also H. Kreisel's attempt to resolve the apparent contradictions between ethics as necessary for individual perfection and ethics as necessary for communal welfare in

"Individual Perfection vs. Communal Welfare and the Problem of Contradiction in Maimonides' Approach to Ethics," *PAAJR* 58 (1992): 107–41.

112. For an analysis of this archetype of human perfection, see Kaplan, "I Sleep, but My Heart Waketh," pp. 130–66, who claims that intellectual contemplation and political governance are not unrelated but rather "blend together in a perfect harmony; they are two sides of the same coin" (p. 145). See also David Shatz's claim ("Worship, Corporeality and Human Perfection: A Reading of *Guide of the Perplexed*, III:51–54," in Robinson et al., *Thought of Moses Maimonides*) that chapter III:51 is the real end of the *Guide*, as opposed to III:54. The reason for the inversion is that Maimonides would rather end on the simplistic note contained in *GP*, III:54 than that of III:51, which reflects his true opinion but is "fraught with complexities, tension, ambiguities and uncertainties." For a mystical characterization of Maimonides' typology of "worship" where the highest level is "completely post-intellectual, post-ratiocinative," see David Blumenthal, "Maimonides, Prayer, Worship, and Mysticism," in *Prière, mystique, et judaïsme*, ed. R. Goetschel (Strasbourg: Presses Universitaires de France, 1984), p. 95. See also on this passage Eliezer Goldman, "The Worship Peculiar to Those Who Have Apprehended True Reality" (in Hebrew), *Bar-Ilan Annual* 6 (1968): 287–313.

113. I base myself here on Narboni's resolution of the apparent contradiction in the views on providence at *GP*, II:17 and III:51. The "person" referred to in III:51 as insulated from any evil whatsoever is the true person, that is, the intellect. Therefore, even though the natural body is still subject to all the affectabilities of nature, the "true self" remains unaffected when it is actualized. See his *Perush Le-Morch Nevukhim*, ed. J. Goldenthal (Vienna, 1852), chap. 51. See also Samuel ibn Tibbon's communication to Maimonides regarding this glaring inconsistency, in Z. Diesendruck, "Samuel and Moses ibn Tibbon on Maimonides' Theory of Providence," *HUCA* 2 (1936): 353–62.

114. *GP*, p. 624. Pines notes an alternative meaning to this Arabic phrase, which is that he cannot aspire to *guide others* in achieving this rank.

115. See Shatz, "Worship, Corporeality and Human Perfection," p. 104, who classifies the inability of Maimonides to explain how this phenomenon can logically evolve within his own system by what is known in contemporary philosophical jargon as a "monological dangler."

116. See Blumenthal, "Maimonides, Prayer, Worship, and Mysticism," p. 95.

117. I believe that Maimonides would consider the manna an allegory of some sort rather than a substantive physical phenomenon. When discussing the use of prophetic hyperbole and exaggeration that cannot be taken literally, one of the verses cited illustrative of this figurative language is Psalm 78:23–24, "And opened the doors of heaven and caused manna to rain down on them." If the source of manna is to be taken figuratively, then the manna itself must be viewed on the same plane of interpretation. Also, Maimonides draws our attention to the verse introducing Ezekiel's vision, "The heavens were opened," which is prefatory to a parable. He

advises us to consider this phrase and its figurative sense and lists four other biblical instances of heavenly gates and doors being opened, one of which is again
Psalm 78:23–24. All these verses operate on a figurative level where the objects
disclosed by the opening of doors are intangible.

118. This verse is the standard of justice that God is incapable, by nature, of
violating. See *GP,* III:17, p. 469: "All the calamities that befall men . . . are all of
them determined according to the deserts of the men concerned through equitable
judgement in which there is no injustice whatever." Also, at p. 471: "[T]he good
and evil that befall them are consequent upon the deserts. . . . " Even the firmly
entrenched rabbinic notion of "sufferings of love" is ruled out on this basis, since
one "should not ascribe injustice to God, may He be exalted above this, so that he
believes that Zayd is innocent of sin and is perfect and does not deserve what
befell him" (*GP,* III:24, p. 498).

119. *GP,* II:36, p. 372. It is of special relevance to our exposition of this midrash
that the discussion of negative impacts on prophecy proceeds to focus on exile as
an unfriendly environment for prophecy. Exile entails foreign domination by inferior intellects (as with the four empires, which are emblematic of Israel's entire
exilic destiny), "for what languor or sadness can befall a man in any state that
would be stronger than that due to his being a thrall slave in bondage to the ignorant who commit great sins and in whom privation of true reason in united to the
perfection of the lusts of beasts" (p. 373). See also *GP,* I:71, p. 175, where the loss
of philosophic and scientific knowledge among the Jews is attributed to "our being
dominated by the pagan nations." As Isadore Twersky has pointed out, it is not
Israel's precedence and exclusive supremacy that determines the vibrancy of prophecy, but rather political and social stability. "The focal point is not geography but
rather the oppressive, adverse consequence of the Exile." See his "Maimonides
and Eretz Yisrael," in Kraemer, *Perspectives on Maimonides,* pp. 279–81.

120. Howard Kreisel, "Maimonides' View of Prophecy as the Overflowing Perfection of Man," *Daat* 13 (1984): xxiv.

Chapter 6. Chapter III:24 of the Guide

1. For various studies dealing with Maimonides' brand of scriptural exegesis, see W. Bacher, *Die Bibelexegese Moses Maimunis* (1896; reprint, Farnborough:
Gregg, 1972), which essentially collects much of the material in which Maimonides
comments on scriptural verses; it does not make any attempt to analyze those exegetical references. In the same vein see S. Weisblatt, "Pesuke Tanak u'Maamare
Hazal be Asmaktaot le Deot Philosophiyot," *Bet Mikra* 38 (1969): 59–79, who
organizes scriptural references in Maimonides according to subject matter.

For studies that deal more analytically with the issue of Maimonides' exegesis
of Scripture, see L. S. Kravitz, "Maimonides and Job—An Inquiry as to the Method

of the Moreh," *HUCA* 38 (1967): 149–58, which deals with Maimonides' commentary on the Book of Job as evidenced in the *Guide;* and S. Rosenberg, "Hearot Le Parshanut HaMikra VehaAkeda Bemoreh Nebukhim," in *Memorial Volume to Jacob Friedman*, ed. S. Pines (Jerusalem: Hamakhon Leradae ha-yahudut, 1974), pp. 215–21, which provides important insights into Maimonides' exegetical methodology in regard to Scripture. See also his more extensive article, "On Biblical Exegesis in the *Guide*" (in Hebrew), *Mehqerei Yerushalayim be-Mahshevet Yisrael* 1, no. 1 (1981): 116.

Finally, for the most exhaustive studies to date of Maimonides' exegesis focusing on one particular topic, see Sara Klein-Braslavy, *Maimonides' Interpretation of the Story of Creation* (in Hebrew) (Jerusalem: Achva Press, 1978); idem, *Maimonides' Interpretation of the Adam Stories in Genesis* (in Hebrew) (Jerusalem: Hahevra le-heker ha-Mikra be-Yisrael, 1986); and idem, *King Solomon and Philosophical Esotericism in the Thought of Maimonides*.

For a study of Maimonides' exegesis in his legal writings, see H. Rabinovitz, "Parshanut Hamikra be Mishneh Torah La Ha Rambam" (in Hebrew), *Shanah be Shanah*, 1967, 223–33; and the comprehensive study by Moshe Greenberg identifying fifteen different hermeneutical procedures for all the prooftexts in *Sefer Hamadda* in "The Use of Scripture in Classical Medieval Judaism: Prooftexts in Maimonides' Code," in *The Return to Scripture in Judaism and Christianity*, ed. P. Ochs (New York: Paulist Press), pp. 197–232.

2. S. Pines, "How to Begin to Study the *Guide of the Perplexed*," introductory essay to *Guide of the Perplexed*, ed. Pines, xiii.

3. See H. Kasher, "Sufferings without Sin—Meaning of Trial in the *Moreh*," *Daat* 26 (1991): 35–41; S. Feldman, "The Binding of Isaac: A Test Case of Divine Foreknowledge," in *Divine Omniscience and Omnipotence*, ed. T. Rudavsky (Dordrecht and Boston: D. Reidel Publishing Co., 1985), pp. 109–12; the response in the same volume by J. Cohen, "Philosophical Exegesis in Historical Perspective: The Case of the Binding of Jacob," pp. 135–42; and A. Nuriel, "Maimonides on Parables Not Explicitly Defined as Such" (in Hebrew), *Daat* 25 (1990): 85–91. For a comparative analysis, see A. Van der Heide, "Maimonides and Nahamanides on the Concept of Trial," in *Sobra la vida y obra de Maimonides*, ed. Jesus Pelalez Dal Rosal (Cordoba: Edicion El Almendro, 1991), pp. 305–14.

4. I agree with Strauss's conclusions, though with some reservation, when he says, "[T[he Guide is devoted to the explanation of an esoteric doctrine. But this explanation is itself of an esoteric character. The Guide is, then, devoted to the esoteric explanation of an esoteric doctrine. Consequently it is a book with seven seals." Leo Strauss, "The Literary Character of the *Guide of the Perplexed*," in *Persecution and the Art of Writing*, p. 55.

5. See *The Book of Beliefs and Opinions*, trans. S. Rosenblatt (New Haven: Yale University Press, 1948), p. 213

6. *GP,* p. 42. The original Arabic reads: *Idh huwa al-mabda'u wa al-sababu*

al-fā'ilu li kulli mā siwāhu. I believe that "efficient" *(fā'ilu)* cause here must be taken in a remote sense, that is, God can be considered the efficient cause of all else, since He is the origin of the chain of causation and all events, actions, and existents can ultimately be traced back to a divine source. In *GP,* I:69, Maimonides discusses at length the sense in which "efficient" cause can be ascribed to God in a way that is consonant with His role as a first mover. For all generated things there is a continuous chain of efficient causes ultimately ending in the first mover "who is in true reality the efficient cause of all these intermediaries" (p. 168). The following characterization must therefore inhere in the usage of the term "efficient cause" in *GP,* I:16: "In this way every action that occurs in Being is referred to God, as we shall make clear, even if it is worked by one of the proximate efficient causes: *God, considered as efficient cause is then the remotest one*" (p. 168, emphasis is mine).

For a practical application of this concept to prophetic texts see *GP,* II:48, where Maimonides asserts that all prophetic dicta that ascribe acts produced in time directly to God must be read in the above sense—that is, the prophet has skipped all the intermediary causes and gone straight to the "First Cause of all things" (pp. 409–10). By way of contrast, and possible similarities, see Marmura's engaging treatment of the usage of this term in the writings of an influential Islamic predecessor. Michael Marmura, "The Metaphysics of Efficient Causality in Avicenna (Ibn Sina)," in *Islamic Theology and Philosophy,* ed. Michael E. Marmura (Albany: SUNY Press, 1984), pp. 172–88.

As is often the case, the language of the *Guide* is susceptible to differing interpretations, and this instance is no exception. The phrase "principle and efficient cause of all else" may also be taken in a rhetorical sense as the first and last cause of all that is, expressing more of a religious sentiment than a scientific postulate. The phrase accommodates both the traditional religious sensibility of an omnipresent God as well as the abstract philosophical notion expressed above without surrendering an inch to the Kalam.

7. *GP,* III:12, p. 442. On the issues of providence and theodicy, see Reines, "Maimonides' Concept of Providence and Theodicy," pp. 169–206. Particularly pertinent to our discussion is the comment at p. 172 that for Maimonides, Scripture, the Talmud, and the Midrash are "works intended primarily for religious education of the philosophically uneducated masses, whereas truth comes through a knowledge of metaphysics and science. . . . As such they contain two entirely different sets of meanings: an external mythological sense appropriate to the masses' deficient understanding and a secret true sense intended for the qualified intellectual elite." In our study this very principle is operative for the understanding of the *Guide* as well.

8. *GP,* I:38, p. 87. For the debate on what man can know in Maimonides' philosophical system, see Pines, "The Limitations of Human Knowledge according to Al Farabi, Ibn Bajja, and Maimonides"; Herbert Davidson's detailed critique

of Pines's position in "Maimonides on Metaphysical Knowledge," *Maimonidean Studies,* vol. 3: *1992–93,* ed. A. Hyman (New York: Yeshiva University Press, 1995), pp. 49–103; N. Roth, "Knowledge of God and God's Knowledge: Two Epistemological Problems in Maimonides," in *Maimonides: Essays and Texts, 850th Anniversary* (Madison, Wis.: Hispanic Seminary of Medieval Studies, 1985), pp. 69–87; and Schubert Spero, "Is the God of Maimonides Truly Unknowable?" *Judaism* 22 (1973): 66–78. I agree with the position that man can attain some knowledge of God, as demonstrated by Norbert Samuelson in "On Knowing God; Maimonides, Gersonides, and the Philosophy of Religion," *Judaism* 18 (1969): 64–77. What is crucial for our present study, though, is the centrality of striving to attain whatever knowledge is available of God. See also A. Altmann, "Maimonides on the Intellect and the Scope of Metaphysics," in *Von der mitteralterlichen zur modernen Aufklärung* (Tübingen: Mohr, Siebeck, 1987) pp. 60–129.

9. *GP,* 1:5, p. 29. For the unique position Moses has on the scale of prophetic knowledge, see M. Kellner, "Maimonides and Gersonides on Mosaic Prophecy," *Speculum* 52 (1977): 62–79.

10. Maimonides follows the lead of Saadia Gaon, who transforms the standard translation of *Yadati* as *'araftu* (For now I know) in Genesis 22:12 to *'arraftu alnas*. (I have made known to mankind). Feldman correctly points out that the difference centers on their understanding of the verb *nisa* (to test). In verse 1 Saadia understands it as connoting "afflict," and Maimonides suggests that it should be construed as connoting "making a paradigm." Feldman's construction of verse 1 is "And God decided to make Abraham a paradigm of what it is to fear and love God." Feldman, "The Binding of Isaac," p. 110. It seems to me that the source for Maimonides' interpretation can be traced back to a midrash that reads "For now I know" as "For now I shall make known to all that you are my lover." *Bereshit Rabbah* 56:12, ed. Theodor Albeck.

11. Though Maimonides seems to argue for creation ex nihilo, he leaves open the possibility of the eternity of the world *a parte post.* See *GP,* II:27, p. 332. On the issue of eternity, see J. W. Malino, "Aristotle on Eternity—Does Maimonides Have a Reply?" in Pines and Yovel, *Maimonides and Philosophy,* pp. 52–64. On the issue of Maimonides' stand on eternity *a parte post,* see Seymour Feldman, "The End of the Universe in Medieval Jewish Philosophy," *AJS Review* 2 (1986): 53–57; and for an opposing view, see Roslyn Weiss, "Maimonides on the End of the World," in Hyman, *Maimonidean Studies,* 3:195–218.

12. For a number of studies on Maimonides' theory of miracles, see J. E. Heller, "Maimonides' Theory of Miracles," in *Between East and West,* ed. A. Altmann (London: East & West Library, 1958), pp. 112–27; and A. J. Reines, "Maimonides' Concept of Miracles," *HUCA* 45 (1974): 243–85. For a particularly thought-provoking article that argues for the philosophic possibility of miracles within his system, see M. Z. Nehorai, "Maimonides on Miracles" (in Hebrew), *Jerusalem Studies in Jewish Thought* 9, pt. 2 (1990): 1–18.

13. Some editions of the Mishnah have inserted the words *erev shabbat,* but it seems that Maimonides did not have that variant reading. See *Mishnah im Perush Rabbenu Moshe Ben Maimon,* trans. J. Kafah (Jerusalem: Mossad Harav Kook, 1964).

14. *GP,* p. 484. See also Feldman, "The Binding of Isaac," p. 111: "Whereas man acquires his knowledge primarily from sensation, God simply *has* His knowledge; in this sense God's cognition is original or non-acquired. . . . Our knowledge is always derivative; that of God is never derivative."

15. *GP,* p. 500. Maimonides was strongly of the conviction that historical/political challenges such as war and battle must be overcome by a natural process of maturation. This conviction comes to the fore in one of the reasons he gives for renouncing belief in astrology. In his "Letter on Astrology" he attributes the downfall of the Jewish republic to this belief in astrological ideas: "Our forefathers spent their time in following such teachings out of which they expected great benefits instead of concentrating their efforts upon learning the art of war and conquering of neighbouring countries." "Letter on Astrology" (in Hebrew), ed. Alexander Marx, *HUCA* 3 (1926): 320.

16. For a similar idea with respect to the world of ideology and opinions, see Maimonides' "Letter on Resurrection" in *Iggerot,* ed. J. Kafih (Jerusalem: Mossad Harav Kook, 1972), p. 96, where it is argued that in order to entrench the idea of resurrection in the people's minds a long, gradual process of development and adaptation is required. A very emotional controversy arose in the twelfth and thirteenth centuries as to whether Maimonides espoused the doctrine of corporeal resurrection. For an analysis of the "Maamar Tehiyat Hametim" that parallels our approach to the *Guide,* see R. S. Kirschner, "Maimonides' Fiction of Resurrection," *HUCA* 51 (1981): 163–93, who argues that "Maimonides creates a kind of legal fiction by which he virtually eviscerates the doctrine he claims to profess. Thus he sustains the multitude's necessary belief in corporeal reward while signalling his true belief to the enlightened."

17. *GP,* III:32, p. 527. This account is totally absent from the Mishneh Torah's presentation of the complex laws of sacrifice. Twersky explains this "divergence" on the basis of the "two distinct kinds of intelligibility and purposiveness" aimed at by the two works. The method of the religious philosopher in the *Guide* is to look for continuity in history between prior and subsequent events so that arbitrariness is eliminated and an intelligible whole is fashioned. "This, however, all its rationality withstanding, has no spiritual-ethical consequences. The Mishneh Torah is primarily concerned with bringing to the surface those underlying motives and overarching goals which discipline the human faculties . . . and advance the individual toward ethical-intellectual perfection." Twersky, *Introduction to the Code of Maimonides* (New Haven: Yale University Press, 1980), pp. 430–33. The thrust of my chapter is respectfully at odds with this position, as ethical-intellectual perfection is indeed the goal of the *Guide* as well, and this historical account of sacrifice must be viewed in that light.

18. See *GP,* III:27, p. 511. The "good" of Deuteronomy 8:16 should be compared with the *tov* of Deuteronomy 6:24, which states, "And God commanded us to perform all His statutes, to fear the Lord our God so that it will be good for us. . . ." The links between law and our chapter are once again more apparent. *Tov* is defined at *GP,* III:13, p. 453 as "an expression applied by us to what conforms to our purpose." On different levels there is conformity with a multipurpose law.

19. *GP,* p. 500. See also *Iggeret Teman,* ed. Kafih, for an exposition of all the various trials the Jews have withstood throughout history on account of the Sinai event.

20. B.T., *Makoth* 24a.

21. For an examination of Maimonides' view on collective revelation at Mount Sinai and its interpretations by various medieval commentators, see S. Regev, "Collective Revelation and Mount Sinai: Maimonides and His Commentators" (in Hebrew), *Jerusalem Studies in Jewish Thought* 9, pt. 2 (1990): 251–67.

22. The kind of intellectual acumen and training required to overcome the various impediments to true intellectual perfection as outlined in *GP,* I:34 virtually excludes from attaining that goal all but those "few solitary individuals that 'are the remnant whom the Lord calls' (Joel 3:14)." Maimonides concludes the chapter by reserving matters that constitute human excellence for "a few solitary individuals of a very special sort, not for the multitude." *GP,* p.79.

23. B.T., *Pesahim* 4a. See also Rashi's comments on Genesis 22:3.

24. *GP,* p. 501. This would be in stark contrast to the later characterization by Kierkegaard of Abraham as a "knight of faith" who separates the religious and the rational/ethical, allowing for a teleological suspension of the ethical. See his *Fear and Trembling,* trans. Walter Lowrie (Garden City, N.Y.: Doubleday, 1954).

25. See M.T., *Hilkhot Abodah Zarah* 1:9–10 and *GP,* III:29, pp. 514–16 for an account of Abraham's intellectual journey from his pagan roots to monotheism.

26. M.T., *Hilkhot Teshuvah* 10:3–4.

27. M.T., *Hilkhot Teshuvah* 10:10–11.

28. See the explication of what gives rise to love and fear in M.T., *Hilkhot Yesodei Hatorah* 2:1–2. For a small sampling of articles on the love of God in Maimonides, see M. Gellman, "The Love of God in Maimonides' Religious Philosophy," in Dal Rosal, *Sobra la vida y obra de Maimonides,* pp. 219–28; and N. Lamm, "Maimonides on the Love of God," in Hyman, *Maimonidean Studies,* 3:131–42.

29. See Maimonides, *Introduction to Perek Heleq* (the tenth chapter in the *Tractate Sanhedrin*) in the *Commentary on the Mishnah,* ed. Kafih (Jerusalem: Mossad Harav Kook, 1963–68), for a detailed outline of this program, which becomes increasingly sophisticated with the age and maturity of the student. For a detailed look at Maimonides the teacher, see S. M. Blumenfeld, "Toward a Study of Maimonides the Educator," *HUCA* 23 (1950–51).

30. M.T., *Hilkhot Teshuvah* 10:9.

31. M.T., *Hilkhot Deot* 1:7.

32. M.T., *Hilkhot Matnot Aniim* 10:1; for further studies on the ethical "golden mean" rule, see S. Schwarzschild, "Moral Radicalism and Middlingness in the Ethics of Maimonides," *Studies in Medieval Culture* 2 (1977): 65–94; and M. Fox, "The Doctrine of the Mean in Aristotle and Maimonides," in *Interpreting Maimonides,* pp. 93–123. Fox argues that unlike Aristotle, Maimonides preferred, as the guiding principle of the good life, a "single controlling ideal: The good is that which leads to true knowledge and continuing contemplation of the divine being" (p. 122). See also the recently published study by L. Berman, "The Ethical Views of Maimonides within the Context of Islamicate Civilization," in Kraemer, *Perspectives on Maimonides*, pp. 13–32, for a detailed study of this ethics in light of Aristotle's *Nicomachean Ethics.*

33. *GP,* p. 379. It is of interest to note that Abraham himself is a follower of Maimonides' pedagogic advice to attract people to the truth by way of a "Pavlovian" method.

34. See for example Nuriel, "Maimonides on Parables Not Explicitly Defined as Such," pp. 88–91, who argues that according to Maimonides, the entire *aqedah* was a prophetic experience and not an actual historical event for three reasons: (1) any lesson of faith it is meant to teach can just as easily be conveyed by parable or actual event; (2) there is no question that God's directive and the two angelic appearances occurred in a prophetic vision; (3) it is impossible that God would mandate the death of any human being for no reason. See also O. Leaman, "Maimonides, Imagination, and the Objectivity of Prophecy," *Religion* 18 (1988): 69–89, who makes the case that the objectivity of prophecy lies in "the relationship between how we think of a state of affairs and the state of affairs which as a consequence is made comprehensible to us. . . . We can defuse much of the literalist critique and regard the question 'but did it really happen?' as beside the point" (p. 79).

35. *GP,* II:45, p. 402. Listed as the eleventh degree of prophecy.

36. This would explain why Maimonides would not opt for a solution to the trial enigma such as that offered by Nahmanides: "[O]n the part of the One, blessed be He, who tries the person it is a command that the one being tested should bring forth the matter from the potential into actuality so that he may be rewarded for a good deed, not for a good thought alone." Ramban, *Commentary on Torah, Genesis,* trans. C. Chavel (New York: Shilo Publishing House, 1971), p. 275.

37. Aside from Deuteronomy 33:8, which is a poetic reference to the tribulations of the Levite tribe and does not relate to a particular event within that verse except by reference.

38. For the role of law in the religious model, see L. Goodman, "Maimonides' Philosophy of Law," *Jewish Law Annual* 1 (1978): 72–107; and K. Bland, "Moses and the Law according to Maimonides," in *Mystics, Philosophers, and Politicians: Essays in Jewish Intellectual History in Honour of A. Altmann,* ed. Jehuda Reinharz and Swetschinski (Durham, N.C.: Duke University Press, 1981), pp. 49–66.

39. The debate as to what constitutes the summum bonum for man in Maimonides rages on. For the two polar extremes of the debate, see Pines in his introduction to the *Guide:* "[The view] that Maimonides at the end adopted the quasi Kantian idea that the ordinary moral virtues and moral actions are of greater importance and value than intellectual virtues and the theoretical way of life . . . is completely false" (p. cxxii); and Schwarzschild, "Moral Radicalism and Middlingness in the Ethics of Maimonides," p. 70: "Maimonides' exegesis is clear: man's purpose is to 'know' God, but the God who is to be known is knowable only insofar as He practices grace, justice and righteousness in the world and to know him is synonymous with imitating these practices of His in the world." Altmann tries to steer a middle course between the two: "*Imitatio dei* is, therefore, but the practical consequence of the intellectual love of God and is part and parcel of human perfection." Altmann, "Maimonides' Four Perfections," in *Essays on Jewish Intellectual History* (Hanover, N.H.: University Press of New England, 1981), p. 73. See also D. Frank, "The End of the *Guide:* Maimonides on the Best Life for Man," *Judaism* 34 (1985): 485–95. For a host of treatments of human perfection in Maimonides, see the essays in Robinson et al., *Thought of Moses Maimonides,* pp. 1–166.

Chapter 7. Reflections on the Ultimate Verses of the Guide

1. See *GP,* III:22, where the "most marvelous and extraordinary thing about the story" is that Job is ascribed moral virtue but no intelligence. This deficiency is the source of all his problems.

2. The "opening" of Isaiah 26:2 is cited in *GP,* III:7 as bearing the same figurative meaning as that of Ezekiel 1:1.

3. *GP,* I:2, p. 23. See also I:68, p. 165, where the process of intellecting is identical in God and man, which yields a "numerical unity of the intellect, the intellectually cognizing subject and the intellectually cognized object." For a discussion of the apparent contradiction this poses to Maimonides' negative theology, see Pines's introduction to the *GP,* pp. xcvii–xcviii.

4. *GP,* p. 23: "It was likewise on account of it [i.e., the image of God] that he was addressed by God and given commandments. . . ."

5. See *GP,* I:45, p. 96.

6. See *GP,* III:31 and especially p. 524.

7. See M.T., *Hilkhot Edut* 9:11 and *Hilkhot Melakhim* 10:12.

8. *Pesikta Kahana,* ed. Mandelbaum, 105.

9. The fact that the Israelites committed themselves to act prior to an act of obeisance based on hearing has been considered an extremely noble gesture in Jewish exegetical tradition. See, for instance, B.T., *Sabbath* 88a. See also *GP,* II:33 for an account of what was "heard" at Mount Sinai.

10. In Exodus 24:7 it is the *sefer habrit,* the "book of the covenant." It is

interesting that one of the qualities necessary to be a recipient of esoteric teachings is to be "wise in crafts" *(chakhaum charashim)*. Of such a person B.T., *Hagigah* 14a declares, "When he speaks, they all become deaf." This of course is a pun evoking the similarity between the word "crafts" *(charashim)* and "deaf" *(chereshim)*. Maimonides finds this an apt description of the qualified disciple who has, among other things, "the gift of finely expressing himself in communicating notions in flashes" *(GP,* I:34, p. 78). For our purposes the one who has "unplugged ears" must have the ability to express ideas that will unplug some ears while at the same time letting others remain plugged.

11. Judah Goldin's characterization of the methodology operative in this midrash can be applied to Maimonides as well: "[F]or according to the Rabbis, the biblical vocabulary addressed past generations, but present and future ones no less, each according to its requirements. . . . " Goldin, *Studies in Midrash and Related Literature*, ed. Barry Eichler and Jeffrey Tigay (New York: JPS, 1988), pp. 359–60.

12. See *GP,* III:10.

13. See *GP,* I:3, where Adam's change in direction is charted from intellect to matter and therefore ultimately ends up where Moses starts, with a "speech impediment." "Adam, unable to dwell in dignity, is like the beasts that speak not" (Psalm 49:13).

14. *GP,* III:11, p. 441. See also the very end of the M.T., *Hilkhot Melakhim,* which concludes with the same sentiments and the exact same verse from Isaiah 11:9: "For the earth shall be full of the knowledge of the Lord as the waters cover the sea." This links up neatly with the opening of the Mishneh Torah that frames the very first commandment in rationalist terms so as to gain demonstrable knowledge of a primary existent. Ultimately messianic redemption entails all mankind being engaged in this rational exercise.

15. See *GP,* introduction, pp. 7–8: "those who never ever once see a light but grope about in their night, of them it is said, *'They walk about in darkness'* (Ps. 82:5). . . . They are the vulgar among the people. There is then no occasion to mention them here in this Treatise."

16. The quote is from Job 37:21.

17. I am adopting here contemporary religious existentialist terminology. For one eloquent example of an understanding of biblical anthropomorphic language as a record of authentic God-man meetings, see Franz Rosenzweig's suggestion in *God, Man, and the World,* trans. B. Galli (Syracuse, N.Y.: Syracuse University Press, 1998), p. 144 for revising an encyclopedic entry under "anthropomorphism." Biblical anthropomorphism "stems from the unspoiled knowledge of the way in which God meets man: namely that he enters into his, the creature's concrete, that is, momentary bodily and spiritual reality with equally concrete momentary corporeal and ensouled meeting." What for Maimonides must be transcended and

ultimately discarded as imaginative language is, for Rosenzweig, a genuine record of the manner in which man encounters God face to face.

18. The quote is from Job 34:21–22.

19. For a particularly insightful analysis of one specific "necessary belief," divine anger, which also highlights the distinction between beliefs that are necessary *(hechrechiyot)* and those that are true *(amitiyot),* see H. Kasher, "The Myth of the 'Angry God' in the *Guide of the Perplexed*" (in Hebrew), in *Myth in Judaism,* ed. H. Pedaya, Eshel Ber-Sheva: Occasional Publications in Jewish Studies, vol. 4 (Jerusalem: Mossad Bialik, 1996), pp. 95–111.

Conclusion

1. For a history of the controversy in its initial stages, see Daniel J. Silver, *Maimonidean Criticism and the Maimonidean Controversy* (Leiden: E. J. Brill, 1965). The controversy raged to such an extent as to lead to actual denunciations of the Inquisition, excommunications, and book burnings. See the last chapter of Silver's book.

2. M.T., *Hilkhot Avodat Kochavim,* chap. 2.

3. M.T., *Hilkhot Avodat Kochavim,* 2:3.

4. See *GP,* I:1, p. 21. It was considered heretical for the common man to deny God a body by taking biblical language at face value.

5. See *GP,* II:39, p. 379.

6. *GP,* II:39, p. 379: "Hence, according to our opinion there never has been a Law and there never will be a Law except the one that is the Law of Moses our Master."

Bibliography

PRIMARY SOURCES

Maimonides

The Authorized Version of the Code of Maimonides: The Book of Knowledge and the Book of Love (in Hebrew). Edited by S. Z. Havlin. Jerusalem: Ofeq, 1997.

Crisis and Leadership: Epistles of Maimonides. Translated by Abraham Halkin; discussions by David Hartman. Philadelphia: Jewish Publication Society of America, 1985. Includes Epistle on Martyrdom, Epistle to Yemen, Essay on Resurrection.

Ethical Writings of Maimonides. Edited by Raymond Weiss with Charles Butterworth. New York: New York University Press, 1975.

The Guide of the Perplexed. Abridged with introduction and commentary by Julius Guttman. Translated from Arabic by Chaim Rabin. New introduction by Daniel Frank. Indianapolis, Ind.: Hackett Publishing, 1995.

The Guide of the Perplexed. Translated with introduction and notes by Shlomo Pines. Chicago: University of Chicago Press, 1963.

Guide of the Perplexed —Part One (in Hebrew). Edited and translated with notes by Michael Schwarz. Tel Aviv: Tel Aviv University Press, 1997.

Hilkhoth Ha-Yerushalmi (The Laws of the Palestinian Talmud) of Rabbi Moses ben Maimon (in Hebrew). Edited by Saul Lieberman. New York and Jerusalem: Jewish Theological Seminary Press, 1947.

Iggerot ha-Rambam (Letters of Maimonides). Edited and translated by I. Shailat. 2 vols. Maale, Israel: Adumim, 1988.

Iggerot ha-Rambam (Letters of Maimonides). Hebrew texts, edited by Mordecai D. Rabinowitz. Jerusalem: Mossad Harav Kook, 1968.

Iggerot ha-Rambam (Letters of Maimonides). Edited by David H. Baneth. Jerusalem: Mekize Nirdamim, 1946.

Iggerot, Rabbi Moshe Ben Maimon (Letters of Maimonides). Arabic original with new Hebrew translation and commentary by Joseph Kafih. Jerusalem: Mossad Harav Kook, 1972.

Iggeret Teman (Epistle to Yemen). Arabic text with three Hebrew versions, edited with introduction (in Hebrew) by Abraham S. Halkin. New York: AAJR, 1952.

The Introductions of Rambam to the Mishnah (in Hebrew). Translation and commentary by I. Shailat. Jerusalem: Hotsaat Shilat-Maaleh Adumim, 1996.

"Letter on Astrology." Hebrew text edited by Alexander Marx. *HUCA* 3 (1926): 349–58 and 4 (1927): 493–94.

"Letter of Astrology." Translated by Ralph Lerner. In *Medieval Political Philosophy: A Sourcebook*, edited by Ralph Lerner and Muhsin Mahdi, pp. 227–36. Glencoe, Ill.: Free Press, 1963.

Letters of Maimonides. Translated and edited with introduction and notes by Leon D. Stitskin. New York: Yeshiva University Press, 1977.

Ma'amar Tehiyyat ha-Metim (Treatise on resurrection). Edited with notes by Joshua Finkel. *AAJR Proceedings* 9 (1939): 57–105, 1–42 (Hebrew section).

Mishneh Torah (Code). Hebrew text, edited by S. T. Rubenstein et al. Jerusalem: Mossad Harav Kook, 1967–73.

Moreh ha-Nebukhim—Dalalat al-Ha'rin (Guide of the perplexed). Arabic original and Hebrew translation by Joseph Kafih. 3 vols. Jerusalem: Mossad Harav Kook, 1972.

Moreh ha-Nevukhim (Guide). Hebrew translation by Judah al-Harizi. Tel Aviv: Mahbarut Lesifrut, 1952.

Moreh Nevukhim (Guide). Hebrew translation by Samuel ibn Tibbon with commentaries by Efodi, Shem Tov, Crescas, and Abravanel. 1904. Reprint, Jerusalem, 1960.

Moreh Nevukhim (Guide). Hebrew translation by ibn Tibbon, revised and vocalized by Yehuda ibn Shmuel. Jerusalem: Mossad Harav Kook, 1987.

Perush ha-Mishnah (Commentary to Mishnah). Hebrew translation by Joseph Kafih. 7 vols. Jerusalem: Mossad Harav Kook, 1963–69.

Sefer ha-Mitzvot (Book of commandments). Arabic original and Hebrew translation, edited by Joseph Kafih. Jerusalem: Mossad Harav Kook, 1971.

Sefer ha-Mitzvot (Book of commandments). Hebrew translation by Moses ibn Tibbon. Edited with notes by Hayyim Heller. Jerusalem: Mossad Harav Kook, 1946.

Teshubot Ha Rambam (Responsa). Hebrew and Arabic texts, edited by Jehoshua Blau. 4 vols. Jerusalem: Mekize Nirdamim, 1989.

Treatise on Logic: "Maimonides' Treatise on Logic," edited by Israel Efros. *PAAJR* 34 (1966): 1–42. English translation by Efros, *PAAJR* 8 (1938): 34–65.

Rabbinic Texts

Babylonian Talmud (in Hebrew). Vilna: Romm, 1880–86. Most extant editions of the Babylonian Talmud are photocopies of this edition.

Bereshit Rabba (in Hebrew). Edited by J. Theodor and Ch. Albeck. 3 vols. Berlin: H. Itzkowski, 1912.

Bereshit Rabba (in Hebrew). Edited by J. Theodor and Ch. Albeck. 2d ed. 2 vols. Jerusalem: Wahrmann Books, 1965.

Jerusalem Talmud (in Hebrew). Jerusalem: Krotozhin, n.d.

Midrash D'varim Raba (in Hebrew). Edited by S. Lieberman. 3d ed. Jerusalem: Wahrmann Books, 1974.

Midrash Vayikra Raba (in Hebrew). Edited by Mordechai Margulies. 5 vols. 1953–60. Reprint in 3 vols., Jerusalem: Wahrmann Books, 1972.

Midrash Raba (in Hebrew). Edited by Aryeh Mirkin. 11 vols. Tel Aviv: Yavneh, 1958–67.

Midrash Tanhuma (in Hebrew). 2 vols. Jerusalem: Eshkol, 1972.

Pirkei D'Rabbi Eliezer (in Hebrew). Commentary by R. David Luria. Warsaw: Bamber, 1852. Photocopy, Jerusalem, 1963.

Shisha Sidrei Mishnah (in Hebrew). Edited by Ch. Albeck. Punctuated by Ch. Yalon. 6 vols. Jerusalem: Mossad Bialik; Tel Aviv: Dvir, 1952–58.

Torah Shelemah: Talmudic Midrashic Encyclopedia on the Pentateuch (in Hebrew). Edited by Menahem M. Kasher. 12 vols. Jerusalem: Beth Torah Shelemah, 1992.

SECONDARY SOURCES

Abrams, Daniel. "The Boundaries of Divine Ontology: The Inclusion and Exclusion of Metatron in the Godhead." *HTR* 87, no. 3 (1994): 291–321.

Alter, Robert. *The Art of Biblical Narrative.* New York: Basic Books, 1981.

———. *The Art of Biblical Poetry.* New York: Basic Books, 1985.

———. *The World of Biblical Literature.* New York: Basic Books, 1992.

Altmann, Alexander. "The Ladder of Ascension." In *Studies in Religious Philosophy and Mysticism,* 41–72. Ithaca, N.Y.: Cornell University Press, 1969.

Bacher, Wilhelm. *Die Bibelexegese Moses Maimuni's.* Budapest, 1896. Translated into Hebrew by A.Z. Rabinowitz (Tel Aviv, 1932). Also see review by I. Drenstag in *Sinai* 55 (1964): 45–72.

Baron, S. W. "The Historical Outlook of Maimonides." *PAAJR* 6 (1935): 5-113. Reprinted in his *History and Jewish Historians* (Philadelphia, 1960).

Braude, William G. "Maimonides' Attitude to Midrash." In *Studies in Jewish Bibliography, History, and Literature in Honor of E. Kiev,* ed. Charles Berlin, 75–83. New York: Ktav Publishing House, 1971.

Benor, Ehud. "Meaning and Reference in Maimonides' Negative Theology." *HTR* 88, no. 3 (1995): 339.

———. *Worship of the Heart: A Study of Maimonides' Philosophy of Religion.* Albany: State University of New York Press, 1995.

Berman, L. "Maimonides on the Fall of Man." *AJS Review* 5 (1980): 1–17.

———. "The Structure of the Commandments of the Torah in the Thought of Maimonides." In *Studies in Jewish Religious Intellectual History*, edited by S. Stein and R. Loewe, 51–66. University: University of Alabama Press, 1975.

Bernfeld, Shimon. "The Allegorical Method of the Rambam" (in Hebrew). In his *Daat Elohim.* 1897. Reprint, Jerusalem: Hotsaat Makor, 1970–71.

Bland, Kalman. "Moses and the Law According to Maimonides." In *Mystics, Philosophers*, and Politicians: Essays in Jewish Intellectual History in Honour of A. Altmann, edited by Jehuda Reinharz and Daniel Swetschinski, 49–66. Durham, N.C.: Duke University Press, 1981.

Blumberg, H. "The Separate Intelligences in Maimonides' Philosophy." *Tarbiz* 40 (1971): 216–25.

Blumenthal, David. "'Lovejoy's Great Chain of Being and Medieval Jewish Tradition." In *Jacob's Ladder and the Tree of Life: Concepts of Hierarchy and the Great Chain of Being*, edited by M. Kuntz, 179-190. New York: Peter Lang, 1986.

———. "Maimonides on Mind and Metaphoric Language." In *Approaches to Judaism in Medieval Times*, edited by David Blumenthal, 2:123–32. Chico, Calif.: Scholars Press, 1985,

———. "Maimonides, Prayer, Worship, and Mysticism." In *Prière, mystique, et judaïsme*, edited by R. Goetschel, 89-106. Strasbourg: Presses Universitaires de France, 1984

Bokser, Baruch. "Approaching Sacred Space." *HTR* 78, nos. 3–4 (1985): 279–99.

Boyarin, Daniel. *Intertextuality and the Reading of Midrash.* Bloomington: Indiana University Press, 1990.

Burrell, David. *Knowing the Unknowable God.* Notre Dame, Ind.: Notre Dame University Press, 1986.

———. "Maimonides, Aquinas, and Gersonides on Providence and Evil." *Religious Studies* 20 (1984): 335–51.

Davidson, Herbert. *Alfarabi, Avicenna, and Averroes on Intellect.* New York: Oxford University Press, 1992.

————. "Averroes on the Active Intellect." *Viator* 18 (1987): 191–225.

————. "Maimonides on Metaphysical Knowledge." *Maimonidean Studies* 3 (1992–93): 49–103.

————. "Maimonides' Secret Position on Creation." In *Studies in Medieval Jewish History and Literature*, edited by I. Twersky, 1:16-40. Cambridge: Harvard University Press, 1979.

————. "The Middle Way in Maimonides' Ethics." *PAAJR* 55 (1987): 31–72.

Dienstag, I. "Bibliography on Rambam as a Biblical Exegete." In vol. 1 of *Gevaryuhu Jubilee Volume*, edited by B. Luria and S. Abramsky, 346–66. Jerusalem: Kiryat Sefer, 1989.

Diesendruch, Z. "Samuel and Moses ibn Tibbon on Maimonides' Theory of Providence." *HUCA* 2 (1936): 353–62.

Dobbs-Weinstein, Idit. "Matter as Creature and Matter as the Source of Evil: Maimonides and Aquinas." In *Neoplatonism and Jewish Thought*, edited by Lenn Goodman. Albany: State University of New York Press, 1992.

Efros, I. *Philosophical Terms in the Moreh Nebukhim*. New York: Columbia University Press, 1924.

Elbaum, Yaakov. "From Sermon to Story: The Transformation of the Akedah." *Prooftexts* 6 (1986): 97–116.

Federbush, S., ed. *Ha Rambam: Torato Ve Ishiyato*. New York: Mahleket ha-tarbut shel ha-Kongres ha-yehud, ha-olari be-Nyu-York, 1956.

Feldman, Seymour. "The Binding of Isaac: A Test Case of Divine Foreknowledge." In *Divine Omniscience and Omnipotence in Medieval Philosophy*, edited by T. Rudavsky, 109–12. Dordrecht and Boston: D. Reidel Publishing Co., 1985.

Finkelstein, L. "Maimonides and the Tannaitic Midrashim." *JQR* 25 (1935): 469–517.

Fishbane, Michael. *Biblical Interpretation of Ancient Israel*. Oxford: Clarendon Press, 1985.

Fox, Marvin. *Interpreting Maimonides*. Chicago: University of Chicago Press, 1990. See particularly chap. 3, "The Esoteric Method"; chap. 4, "Maimonides' Method of Contradiction"; and chap. 11, "Prayer and the Religious Life."

Fraade, Steven D. "Interpreting Midrash 1: Midrash and the History of Judaism." *Prooftexts* 7 (1987): 179–94.

————. "Interpreting Midrash 2: Midrash and Its Literary Contexts." *Prooftexts* 7, no. 2 (1987): 284–300 (with corrigenda in 7, no. 3 [1988]: 179–84).

Fraenkel, Jonas. "Bible Verses Quoted in Tales of the Sages." *Scripta Hierosolymitana* 22 (1971): 80–99.

————. *Exploration of the Spiritual World of the Aggadic Story* (in Hebew). Tel Aviv: Kibbutz HaMeuchad, 1981.

———. "Paranomasia in Aggadic Narratives." *Scripta Hierosolymitana* 27 (1978): 27–66.

———. "Time and Its Shape in the Aggadic Story" (in Hebrew). In *The Methods of the Aggadah,* edited by I. Heinemann, 133–62. 3d ed. Jerusalem: Magnes Press, 1970.

Frye, Northrop. *Anatomy of Criticism.* Princeton: Princeton University Press, 1971.

———. *The Great Code: The Bible and Literature.* New York: HBJ, 1982.

Galston, Miriam. "The Purpose of the Law According to Maimonides." *Jewish Quarterly Review* 69 (1978): 27–51.

Gellman, Jerome. "Maimonides' Ravings." *Review of Metaphysics* 45, no. 2 (1991): 309–28.

———. "Radical Responsibility in Maimonides' Thought." In *Thought of Moses Maimonides: Philosophical and Legal Studies*, edited by Ira Robinson et al., 249–65. New York: Edwin Mellen Press, 1990.

Ginzberg, Asher. "The Supremacy of Reason." In *Maimonides Octocentennial Series*, ed. J. Agus, 3–52. 1935. Reprint, New York: Arno Press, 1973.

Goldman, Eliezer. "The Worship Peculiar to Those Who Have Apprehended True Reality" (in Hebrew). *Bar Ilan Annual* 6 (1968): 287–313.

Goodman, Lenn. "Maimonides' Philosophy of Law." *Jewish Law Annual* 1 (1978): 72–107.

———. "Matter and Form as Attributes of God in Maimonides' Philosophy." In *A Straight Path: Studies in Medieval Philosophy and Culture*, edited by Ruth Link Salinger, 86–97. Washington, D.C.: Catholic University of America Press, 1988.

Goshen-Gottstein, Alon. "The Body as Image of God in Rabbinic Literature." *HTR* 87, no. 2 (1994): 172–95.

Green, Arthur. "Sabbath as Temple." In *Go and Study: Essays and Studies in Honour of Alfred Jospe*, edited by R. Jospe and S. Z. Fishman, 287–305. Washington, D.C.: B'nai B'rith Hillel Foundations, 1980.

Green, Kenneth H. *Jew and Philosopher: The Return to Maimonides in the Jewish Thought of Leo Strauss.* Albany: State University of New York Press, 1993.

Greenberg, Moshe. *Ezekiel 1–20.* Anchor Bible Series. Garden City, N.Y.: Doubleday, 1983.

———. "The Use of Scripture in Classical Medieval Judaism: Prooftexts in Maimonides' Code." In *The Return to Scripture in Judaism and Christianity,* edited by P. Ochs, 197–232. New York: Paulist Press.

Guttman, Julius. *Philosophy of Judaism.* Translated by D. Silverman. Northvale, N.J.: Aronson, 1988.

Halbertal, Moshe, and Avishai Margalit. *Idolatry.* Cambridge: Harvard University Press, 1992.

Halevi, J. *Kuzari*. Translated by H. Hirschfield. New York: Pardes Publishing Co., 1946.

Handelman, S. *The Slayers of Moses: The Emergence of Rabbinic Interpretation in Modern Literary Theory*. Albany: State University of New York Press, 1982.

Harris, Jay. *How Do We Know This?: Midrash and the Fragmentation of Modern Judaism*. Albany: State University of New York Press, 1995.

Hartman, David. *Maimonides, Torah, and Philosophic Quest*. Philadelphia: Jewish Publication Society, 1976.

Harvey, W. Z. "Great is the Power: On *Guide of the Perplexed* I:41" (in Hebrew). *Daat* 37 (1996): 53–61.

———. "How to Begin to Study the *Guide of the Perplexed*, I, 1" (in Hebrew). *Daat* 21 (1988): 5–23.

———. "Maimonides' First Commandment, Physics, and Doubt." In *Hazon Nahum: Studies in Jewish Law, Thought, and History*, edited by Y. Elman and J. Gurock, 149–62. New York: Yeshiva University Press, 1997.

———. "Perush Ha Rambam Le Bereshit 3:22" (in Hebrew). *Daat* 12 (1984): 15–22.

———. "A Third Approach to Maimonides' Cosmogony-Prophetology Puzzle." *HTR* 74, no. 3 (1981): 287–305.

Heinemann, I. *The Methods of the Aggadah* (in Hebrew). 3d ed. Jerusalem: Magnes Press, 1970.

Henshke, David. "On the Question of Unity in Maimonides' Thought" (in Hebrew). *Daat* 37 (1996): 37–51.

Heschel, A. J. "Ha Heemin Ha Rambam she Zakha Le Nevuah." In *Louis Ginzberg Jubilee Volume*, ed. A. Marx, 159–88 (Hebrew section). New York: American Academy for Jewish Research, 1946.

Husik, Isaac. *A History of Medieval Jewish Philosophy*. Philadelphia: JPS, 1941.

Hyman, Arthur. "From What Is One and Simple, Only What Is One and Simple Can Come to Be." Chapter 2 in *Neoplatonism and Jewish Thought*, edited by Lenn Goodman. Albany: State University of New York Press, 1992.

———. "Maimonides on Creation and Emanation." In *Studies in Philosophy and the History of Philosophy*, vol. 17, *Studies in Medieval Philosophy*, edited by J. Wippel, 45–61. Washington, D.C.: Catholic University of America, 1987.

Idel, Moshe. "The Ladder of Ascension—The Reverberations of a Medieval Motif in the Renaissance." In *Studies in Medieval Jewish History and Literature*, edited by I. Twersky, 2:83–93. Cambridge: Harvard University Press, 1984.

Ivry, Alfred. "Providence, Divine Omniscience, and Possibility: The Case of Maimonides." In *Divine Omniscience and Omnipotence in Medieval Philosophy*, edited by T. Rudavsky, 143–59. Dordrecht and Boston: D. Reidel Publishing Co., 1985.

————. "Strategies of Interpretation in Maimonides' *Guide of the Perplexed.*" *Jewish History* 6, nos. 1–2 (1992): 113–30.

Kafih, Joseph. *Ha Mikra baRambam.* Jerusalem: Mossad Harav Kook, 1972.

Kaplan, Lawrence. "I Sleep but My Heart Waketh: Maimonides' Conception of Human Perfection." In *Thought of Moses Maimonides: Philosophical and Legal Studies,* edited by Ira Robinson et al., 131–66. Lewiston, N.Y.: Edwin Mellen Press, 1990.

Karl, Z. "Ha Rambam Ke Parshan Ha Torah." *Tarbiz* 6 (1935): 99–138.

Kasher, Hanna. "Job's Image and Opinion in the *Guide of the Perplexed*" (in Hebrew). *Daat* 15 (1985): 81-87.

————. "Suffering Without Sin—Meaning of Trial in the Moreh." *Daat* 26 (1991): 35–41.

Kellner, Menachem. *Maimonides on Judaism and the Jewish People.* Albany: State University of New York Press, 1991.

Kepnes, Steven. "A Narrative Jewish Theology." *Judaism* 37 (1988): 210–17.

Kermode, Frank. *The Genesis of Secrecy: On the Interpretation of Narrative.* Cambridge: Harvard University Press, 1979.

Kirschner, R. S. "Maimonides' Fiction of Resurrection." *HUCA* 51 (1981): 163–93.

Klein, Michael. *Anthropomorphism and Anthropopathisms in the Targumim of the Pentateuch* (in Hebrew). Jerusalem: Makor, 1982.

Klein-Braslavy, Sara. "King Solomon and Metaphysical Esotericism According to Maimonides." *Maimonidean Studies* 1 (1990): 57–86.

————. *King Solomon and Philosophical Esotericism in the Thought of Maimonides.* Jerusalem: Magnes Press, 1996.

————. "Maimonides' Interpretation of the Dream of Jacob's Ladder" (in Hebrew). *Bar Ilan* 22–23 (1989): 329–49.

————. *Maimonides' Interpretation of the Story of Creation* (in Hebrew). 2d ed. Jerusalem: ha-Hevra le-heker ha-Mikra ha-Yisrael, 1987.

Kook, Abraham Isaac. "On the Unity of the Rambam" (in Hebrew). In *Maamarei ha-Reyiah,* 105–12. Jerusalem: Mossad Harav Kook, 1984.

Kraemer, Joel. "Maimonides on the Philosophical Sciences in His Treatise on the Art of Logic." In *Perspectives on Maimonides,* edited by Joel Kraemer, 76–104. New York: Oxford University Press, 1991.

Kravitz, Leonard. "Maimonides and Job: An Inquiry as to the Method of the *Moreh.*" *HUCA* 38 (1967): 149–58.

————. "The Revealed and the Concealed—Providence, Prophecy, Miracles, and Creation in the *Guide.*" *CCAR Year Book* 16 (1969): 2–30 and 18 (1971): 59–62.

Kreisel, Howard. "Imitatio Dei in Maimonides' *Guide of the Perplexed*." *AJS Review* 19, no. 2 (1994): 169–211.

———. "Individual Perfection vs. Communal Welfare and the Problem of Contradiction in Maimonides' Approach to Ethics." *PAAJR* 58 (1992): 107–41.

———. "Maimonides' View of Prophecy." *Daat* 13 (1984): xxi–xxvi.

Kugel, James L. *The Idea of Biblical Poetry: Parallelism and Its History*. New Haven: Yale University Press, 1981.

———. "Two Introductions to Midrash." In *Midrash and Literature*, edited by G. Hartman and S. Budick, 77–103. New Haven: Yale University Press, 1986.

Leaman, Oliver. "Maimonides, Imagination, and the Objectivity of Prophecy." *Religion* 18 (1988): 69–89.

———. *Moses Maimonides*. London: Routledge, 1990.

Leibowitz, Yeshayahu. *The Faith of Maimonides* (in Hebrew). Tel Aviv: Israel Defence Ministry, 1980.

Levinger, Jacob. "Maimonides' Exegesis of Job." In *Creative Biblical Exegesis: Christian and Jewish Hermeneutics through the Centuries*, edited by B. Uffenheimer and H. Reventlow, 81–88. Journal for the Study of the Old Testament Supplement Series 59. Sheffield, England: JSOT Press, 1988.

Liebes, Yehuda. *Heto Shel Elisha: Arbaah she-Nikhnesu Le Pardes ve-Tivah shel ha-Mistikah ha-Talmudit*. Jerusalem: Academon, 1990.

Loewe, Raphael. "The 'Plain' Meaning of Scripture in Early Jewish Exegesis." *Papers of the Institute of Jewish Studies, London* 1 (1964): 140–85.

Marmura, Michael. "The Metaphysics of Efficient Causality in Avicenna (ibn Sina)." In *Islamic Theology and Philosophy*, edited by Michael Marmura, 172–88. New York: State University of New York Press, 1984.

Nasr, S. H. *An Introduction to Islamic Cosmological Doctrines*. Cambridge: Belknap Press of Harvard University Press, 1964.

Nahmanides. *Perush ha-RaMBaN 'al ha-Torah (Commentary on the Torah)* (in Hebrew). Edited by C. Chavel. 3 vols. Jerusalem: Mossad Harav Kook, 1959–63.

Nehorai, M. Z. "Maimonides on Miracles" (in Hebrew). *Jerusalem Studies in Jewish Thought* 9, pt. 2 (1990): 1–18.

Novak, David. "Maimonides and the Science of the Law." In *Jewish Law Association Studies 4*, edited by B. S. Jackson, 99–134. Atlanta: Scholars Press, 1990.

———. *The Theology of Nahmanides Systematically Presented*. Atlanta: Scholars Press, 1992.

Nuriel, A. "The Concept of Satan in the *Guide of the Perplexed*" (in Hebrew). *Jerusalem Studies in Jewish Thought* 5 (1986): 83–91.

———. "Maimonides on Parables Not Explicitly Defined as Such" (in Hebrew). *Daat* 25 (1990): 85–91.

————. "The Torah Speaks in the Language of the Sons of Man in the *Guide of the Perplexed*" (in Hebrew). In *Dat Ve Safah*, edited by M. Halamish and A. Kasher, 97–103. Tel Aviv: Mifalim universitiyim le-hotsaah la-or, 1981.

Pines, Shlomo. "The Limitations of Human Knowledge According to al-Farabi, ibn Bajja, and Maimonides." In *Studies in Medieval Jewish History and Literature*, edited by I. Twersky, 1:82–109. Cambridge: Harvard University Press, 1979.

————. "The Philosophical Purport of Maimonides' Halachic Works and the Purport of the *Guide of the Perplexed*." In *Maimonides and Philosophy*, edited by S. Pines and Y. Yovel, 1–14. Dordrecht: Martinus Nijhoff, 1986.

————. "Truth and Falsehood versus Good and Evil: A Study of Jewish and General Philosophy in Connection with the *Guide of the Perplexed* I:2." In *Studies on Maimonides*, edited by I. Twersky, 95–157. Cambridge: Harvard University Press, 1990.

Puig, Josep. "Maimonides and Averroes on the First Mover." In *Maimonides and Philosophy*, edited by S. Pines and Y. Yovel, 213–23. Dordrecht: Martinus Nijhoff, 1986.

Rabinovitz, H. "Parshanut Ha Mikra be Mishneh Torah Le HaRambam." *Shanah be Shanah,* 1967, 223–33.

Raffel, Dov. "The Theology of Targum Onkelos" (in Hebrew). *Bet Mikra* 26 (1980): 28–60.

Ravitzky, Aviezer. "The Esoteric Doctrine of the *Guide of the Perplexed*" (in Hebrew). *Mehqerei Yerushalayim be-Mahshevet Yisra'el* 5 (1986): 59–66.

————. "Samuel ibn Tibbon and the Esoteric Character of the *Guide of the Perplexed*." *AJS Review* 6 (1981): 231–72.

————. "The Secrets of the *Guide to the Perplexed:* Between the Thirteenth and Twentieth Centuries." In *Studies in Maimonides,* edited by I. Twersky, 159–207. Cambridge: Harvard University Press, 1990.

————. "'To the Utmost Human Capacity': Maimonides on the Days of the Messiah." In *Perspectives on Maimonides*, edited by Joel Kraemer, 221–56. New York: Oxford University Press, 1991.

Regev. S. "Collective Revelation and Mount Sinai: Maimonides and His Commentators" (in Hebrew). *Jerusalem Studies in Jewish Thought* 9, pt. 2 (1990): 251–67.

Reines, Alvin. "Maimonides' Concept of Providence and Theodicy." *HUCA* 43 (1972): 169–206.

————. "Maimonides' True Belief Concerning God: A Systematization." In *Maimonides and Philosophy*, edited by S. Pines and Y. Yovel, 24–35. Dordrecht: Martinus Nijhoff, 1986.

Ricoeur, Paul. "The Bible and the Imagination." In *The Bible as a Document of the University*, edited by Hans D. Betz, 49–75. Chico, Calif.: Scholars Press, 1981.

———. *Hermeneutics and the Human Sciences*. New York: Cambridge University Press, 1981.

———. *Interpretation Theory: Discourse and the Surplus of Meaning*. Fort Worth: Texas Christian University Press, 1996.

———. "The Power of Speech, Science, and Poetry." *Philosophy Today* 29 (Spring 1985): 59–70.

Rosen, I. "Ha-RaMBaM ve-yakhaso la-Midrashot." *Shma'tin* 6, no. 23 (1969): 48–59.

Rosenberg, Shalom, "On Biblical Exegesis in the *Guide*" (in Hebrew). *Mehqerei Yerushalayim be-Mahshevet Yisrael* 1, no. 1 (1981): 85–157.

———. "Remarks on Biblical Exegesis and the Akedah in the *Guide*" (in Hebrew). In *Memorial Volume to Jacob Friedman*, edited by S. Pines, 215–21. Jerusalem: Hamakhan Lemadoc ha-yahadut, 1974.

Roth, Norman. "Knowledge of God and God's Knowledge: Two Epistemological Problems in Maimonides." In *Maimonides: Essays and Texts, 850th Anniversary,* 69–87. Madison, Wis.: Hispanic Seminary of Medieval Studies, 1985.

Rudavsky, Tamar. "The Theory of Time in Maimonides and Crescas." *Maimonidean Studies* 1 (1990): 145–62.

Saadia, Gaon. *The Book of Beliefs and Opinions*. Translated by S. Rosenblatt. New Haven: Yale University Press, 1948.

Samuelson, Norbert. "Divine Attributes as Moral Ideals." In *Thought of Moses Maimonides: Philosophical and Legal Studies*, edited by Ira Robinson et al., 69–76. New York: Edwin Mellen Press, 1990.

———. "Maimonides' Doctrine of Creation." *HTR* 84, no. 3 (1991): 249–71. Includes a summary of all recent scholarship on the issue of creation.

———. "On Knowing God: Maimonides, Gersonides, and the Philosophy of Religion." *Judaism* 18 (1969): 64–77.

Schweid, Eliezer. *Iyunim be Shemonah Perakim Le Rambam*. Jerusalem: Academon, 1989.

Seeskin, Kenneth. *Jewish Philosophy in a Secular Age*. Albany: State University of New York Press, 1990.

———. *Maimonides: A Guide for Today's Perplexed*. West Orange, N.J.: Behrman House, 1991.

———. *Searching for a Distant God: The Legacy of Maimonides*. New York: Oxford University Press, 2000.

Shatz, David. "Worship, Corporeality, and Human Perfection: A Reading of *Guide of the Perplexed* III 51:54.." "In *Thought of Moses Maimonides: Philosophical and Legal Studies*, edited by Ira Robinson et al., 77–129. New York: Edwin Mellen Press, 1990.

Silberman, Lou. "A Theological Treatise on Forgiveness: Chapter 23 Pesikta De Rav Kahana." In *Studies in Aggadah, Targum, and Jewish Literacy in Honour of J. Heinemann*, edited by J. Petuchovski and E. Fleischer, 95–107. Jerusalem: Magnes, 1981.

Sirat, Colette. *A History of Jewish Philosophy in the Middle Ages.* Cambridge: Cambridge University Press, 1985.

Smalley, Beryl. *The Study of the Bible in the Middle Ages.* Notre Dame, Ind.: Notre Dame University Press, 1978.

Soloveitchik, Haim. "Maimonides' *Iggeret Ha Shemad:* Law and Rhetoric." In *Joseph Lookstein Jubilee Volume*, edited by Leo Landman, 1–39. New York: KTAV, 1979.

Spero, Schubert. "Is the God of Maimonides Truly Unknowable?" *Judaism* 22 (1973): 66–78.

Spinoza, B. *A Theological-Political Treatise.* Translated by R. H. M. Elwes. 1883. Reprint, New York: Dover, 1951.

Stein, Kenneth. "Exegesis, Maimonides, and Literary Criticism." *Modern Language Notes* 88 (1973): 1134–54.

Stern, David. "Midrash and Indeterminacy." *Critical Inquiry* 15 (1988): 132–61.

Stern, Josef. "Maimonides on the Covenant of Circumcision and the Unity of God." In *The Midrashic Imagination*, edited by M. Fishbane, 131–54. Albany: State University of New York Press, 1993.

———. "Nahmanides' Conception of the *Taa'mei Mitzvot* and Its Maimonidean Background." In *Community and Covenant: New Essays in Jewish Political and Legal Philosophy*, edited by Daniel Frank. Albany: State University of New York Press, 1995.

———. "On an Alleged Contradiction between Maimonides' *Mishneh Torah* and the *Guide of the Perplexed*" (in Hebrew). *Shenaton Ha-Mishpat Ha-Ivri* 14–15 (1989): 283–98.

———. *Problems and Parables of Law: Maimonides and Nahmanides on Reasons for the Commandments.* Albany: State University of New York Press, 1998.

Sternberg, Meir. *The Poetics of Biblical Narrative: Ideological Literature and the Drama of Reading.* Bloomington: Indiana University Press, 1985.

Strauss, Leo "How to Begin to Study *The Guide of the Perplexed*." In *The Guide of the Perplexed*, by Moses Maimonides, translated by Shlomo Pines, xi–lvi. Chicago: University of Chicago Press, 1963.

———. "The Literary Character of the *Guide of the Perplexed*." In *Persecution and the Art of Writing*. Glencoe. Ill.: Free Press, 1952.

———. "Notes on Maimonides' Book of Knowledge." In *Studies in Mysticism and Religion Presented to Gershom G. Scholem on his Seventieth Birthday by Pupils, Colleagues, and Friends,* edited by E. E. Urbach, R. J. Zwi Werblowsky, and C. Wirszubski, 269–83. Jerusalem: Magnes Press and Hebrew University Press, 1967.

———. "On the Plan of *The Guide of the Perplexed.*" In *Harry A. Wolfson Jubilee Volume,* edited by Saul Lieberman, 775–92 (English section). Jerusalem: American Academy for Jewish Research, 1965.

———. *Philosophy and Law: Essays Towards the Understanding of Maimonides and His Predecessors.* Translated by Eve Adler. Albany: State University of New York Press, 1995.

Stroumsa, Sarah. "Elisha ben Abuyah and Muslim Heretics in Maimonides' Writings." *Maimonidean Studies* 3 (1992–93): 182.

Talmage, Frank. "Apples of Gold: The Inner Meaning of Sacred Texts in Medieval Judaism." In *Jewish Spirituality from the Bible through the Middle Ages,* edited by Arthur Green, 319–21. New York: Crossroad, 1986.

Todorov, Tzvetan. *Symbolism and Interpretation.* Translated by C. Porter. London: Routledge, 1998.

Twersky, Isadore. "Concerning Maimonides' Rationalization of the Commandments: An Explication of *Hilkhot Me'ilah* viii, 8" (in Hebrew). In *Studies in the History of Jewish Society in the Middle Ages and in the Modern Period,* edited by E. Etkes and Y. Salmon, 24–32. Jerusalem: Magnes Press, 1980.

———. *Introduction to the Code of Maimonides (Mishneh Torah).* New Haven: Yale University Press, 1980

———. "Maimonides and Eretz-Israel: Halachic, Philosophical, and Historical Aspects." In *Culture and Society in Medieval Jewry,* edited by M. Ben-Sasson, Robert Bonfil, and Joseph R. Hacker, 353–81. Jerusalem: The Historical Society of Israel, 1989.

———. "Some Non-Halakhic Aspects of the *Mishneh Torah.*" In *Jewish Medieval and Renaissance Studies,* edited by Alexander Altmann, 95–118. Cambridge: Harvard University Press, 1967.

Urbach, Ephraim E. *The Sages: Their Concepts and Beliefs* (in Hebrew). 2d ed. Jerusalem: Magnes Press, 1971.

Van de Hede, A. "Maimonides and Nahmanides on the Concept of Trial." In *Sobra la vida e obra de Maimonides,* edited by Jesus Pelalez dal Rosal, 305–14. Cordoba: Edicion El Almendro, 1991.

Weingreen. J. "The Torah Speaks in the Language of Man" (title and quotations in Hebrew). In *Interpreting the Hebrew Bible: Essays in Honor of E. I. J. Rosenthal,* edited by J. A. Emerton and Stephan C. Reif, 267–75. Cambridge: Cambridge University Press, 1982.

Weisblatt, S. "Pesuke Tanakh u Maamare Hazel ke Asmahtaot leDeot Philosophyot." *Bet Mikra* 37 (1969): 59–79.

Weiss, Raymond L. *Maimonides' Ethics.* Chicago: University of Chicago Press, 1991.

Weiss, Roslyn. "Maimonides on *Shilluah Ha-Qen.*" *Jewish Quarterly Review* 79, no. 4 (1989): 345–66.

———. "Maimonides on the End of the World." *Maimonidean Studies* 3 (1992–93): 195–218.

Weiss-Halivni, David. *Peshat and Derash.* New York: Oxford University Press, 1991.

Wolfson, Elliot, "By Way of Truth: Aspects of Nahmanides' Kabbalistic Hermeneutic." *AJS Review* 14, no. 2 (1989): 103–79.

———. "Circumcision and the Divine Name: A Study on the Transmission of Esoteric Doctrine." *Jewish Quarterly Review* 78 (1987): 77–112.

Wolfson, Harry A. "Maimonides on Negative Attributes." In *Louis Ginzberg Jubilee Volume on the Occasion of His Seventieth Birthday*, edited by A. Marx, 411–46. New York: AAJR, 1945.

———. "Maimonides on the Unity and Incorporeality of God." *Jewish Quarterly Review* 55 (1965): 112–36.

———. "The Veracity of Scripture in Philo, Halevi, Maimonides, and Spinoza." In *Alexander Marx Jubilee Volume*, edited by Saul Lieberman, 603–30. New York: Jewish Theological Seminary of America, 1950.

Index